Emile Durkheim: Selected Writings

EMILE DURKHEIM: SELECTED WRITINGS

Edited, translated, and with an introduction by

ANTHONY GIDDENS

Fellow of King's College, and University Lecturer in
Sociology, Cambridge

CAMBRIDGE

at the University Press 1972

Published by the Syndics of the Cambridge University Press
Bentley House, 200 Euston Road, London NW1 2DB
American Branch: 32 East 57th Street, New York, N.Y.10022

ISBNs: 0 521 08504 7 hard covers
       0 521 09712 6 paperback

Printed in Great Britain
by Western Printing Services Ltd,
Bristol

Contents

Preface   vii

Abbreviations   ix

INTRODUCTION

Durkheim's writings in sociology and social philosophy   1

SELECTED TEXTS

1   The field of sociology   51

2   Methods of explanation and analysis   69

3   The science of morality   89

4   Moral obligation, duty and freedom   108

5   Forms of social solidarity   123

6   The division of labour and social differentiation   141

7   Analysis of socialist doctrines   155

8   Anomie and the moral structure of industry   173

9   Political sociology   189

10   The social bases of education   203

11   Religion and ritual   219

12   Secularisation and rationality   239

13   Sociology of knowledge   250

INDEX   269

Preface

The reception of Durkheim's work has been considerably affected by the uneven manner in which his writings have appeared in published form. In his lifetime, he published four major books – *De la division du travail social, Les règles de la méthode sociologique, Le suicide,* and *Les formes élémentaires de la vie religieuse* – as well as various shorter monographs and numerous articles and reviews. But no fewer than five additional works, consisting of lectures which he prepared for the various courses which he taught at different points in his career, have appeared posthumously: *L'éducation morale* (1925), *Le socialisme* (1928), *L'évolution pédagogique en France* (1938), *Leçons de sociologie* (1950) and *Pragmatisme et sociologie* (1955). Only one of the first four books (*Les formes élémentaires*) was translated into English while he was alive: the others followed at long intervals. None of the latter group of works appeared in English until very recently, and two still await translation. Thus although his ideas have exerted a very extensive influence in the English-speaking world, they have been subject to frequent misrepresentations and distortions.

The present book is the first to provide a comprehensive set of selections from the whole corpus of Durkheim's writings. All of the selections are newly translated, regardless of whether or not they have previously appeared in English. When planning the book initially, I intended to include sections from existing translations, where available. But in comparing these with the originals it became apparent that they contained numerous dubious or erroneous renderings, and consequently I decided to offer a fresh set of translations. However I have, of course, referred to previous translations, and have followed most of the established conventions with regard to key terms in Durkheim's writings. The phrase *conscience collective* I have left untranslated since this has now become quite familiar to English readers of Durkheim: in one or two instances, I have in fact substituted this for the expression *conscience commune*, which occasionally appears in the original texts. I have attempted to resist the temptation to 'modernise' Durkheim's language, even where the resultant rendering has a distinctly archaic ring. All footnotes have been excluded, except where they contain material of substantial importance: in that case they have been incorporated into the text. I have sometimes inserted notes into the text – indicated by the use of square brackets – to clarify the context in which a particular statement is made. Ordinary rounded parentheses are Durkheim's own. The Introduction is wholly devoted to a discussion of some of the leading themes in Durkheim's writings. I have considered it unnecessary to give a survey of Durkheim's life and academic career; various biographical accounts can be found in other readily accessible sources.

A number of people have helped in the preparation of this book: I should like to thank, in particular, Sam Hollick and Claudine Fisher.

ANTHONY GIDDENS

22 July 1971

Abbreviations used in the text

DTS *De la division du travail social* (Seventh ed.) 1960.
EM *L'éducation morale.* 1925.
EPF *L'évolution pédagogique en France* (Second ed.) 1969.
ES *Éducation et sociologie.* 1922.
FE *Les formes élémentaires de la vie réligieuse* (Fourth ed.) 1960.
LS *Leçons de sociologie.* 1950.
MR *Montesquieu et Rousseau.* 1953.
PS *Pragmatisme et sociologie.* 1955.
RMS *Les règles de la méthode sociologique* (Eleventh ed.) 1950.
Soc. *Le socialisme.* 1928.
SP *Sociologie et philosophie.* 1924.
Su *Le suicide.* (Second ed.) 1967.

ARTICLES

RP, 1886 'Les études de science sociale', *Revue philosophique*, vol. 22, 1886.

RP, 1887(a) Review of Guyau: *L'irréligion de l'avenir*, in *Revue philosophique*, vol. 23, 1887.

RP, 1887(b) 'La science positive de la morale en Allemagne', Revue philosophique, vol. 24, 1887.

RP, 1889 Review of Tönnies: *Gemeinschaft und Gesellschaft*, in *Revue philosophique*, vol. 27, 1889.

RP, 1895 'Crime et santé sociale', *Revue philosophique*, vol. 39, 1895.

AS, 1897(a) Preface to *Année sociologique*, vol. 1, 1896–7.

AS, 1897(b) Review of Köhler: *Zur Urgeschichte der Ehe*, in *Année sociologique*, vol. 1, 1896–7.

RP, 1897 Review of Labriola: *Essais sur la conception matérialiste de l'histoire*, in *Revue philosophique*, vol. 44, 1897.

RB, 1898	'L'individualisme et les intellectuels', *Revue bleue*, vol. 10, 1898.
AS, 1898	'Note sur la morphologie sociale', *Année sociologique*, vol. 2, 1897–8.
AS, 1899	Review of Ratzel: *Anthropogeographie*, in *Année sociologique*, vol 3, 1898–9.
AS, 1900	'Deux lois de l'évolution pénale', *Année sociologique*, vol. 4, 1899–1900.
RIS, 1900	'La sociologia ed il suo dominio scientifico' *Revista italiana di sociologia*, vol. 4, 1900.
AS, 1902(a)	'De quelques formes primitives de classification: contribution à l'étude des représentations collectives', *Année sociologique*, vol. 6, 1901–2.
AS, 1902(b)	Review of works by Salvemini, Croce and Sorel on the nature of history, in *Année sociologique*, vol. 6, 1901–2.
RP, 1903	'Sociologie et sciences sociales', *Revue philosophique*, vol. 55, 1903 (with P. Fauconnet).
AS, 1905	Review of Tarde: '*L'interpsychologie*', in *Bulletin de l'Institut général psychologique*, 1903. *Année sociologique*, vol. 9, 1904–5.
AS, 1906(a)	Review of works by Fouillée, Belot and Landry on the nature of ethics, in *Année sociologique*, vol. 10, 1905–6.
AS. 1906(b)	Review of Jankélévitch: *Nature et société*, in *Année sociologique*, vol. 10, 1905–6.
AS, 1912	Review of Lévy-Bruhl: *Les fonctions mentales dans les sociétés inférieures* and of Durkheim: *Les formes élémentaires de la vie religieuse*, in *Année sociologique*, vol. 12, 1909–12.
Sci, 1914	'Le dualisme de la nature humaine et ses conditions sociales', *Scientia*, vol. 15, 1914.

Introduction: Durkheim's writings in sociology and social philosophy

i. *The Division of Labour in Society*

Durkheim is ordinarily regarded, in the English-speaking world, at least, as one of the founders of modern 'empirical' sociology: as a writer whose works played a leading role in the transformation of sociology from a speculative, philosophical endeavour into a clearly-bounded discipline firmly planted in the controlled observation of empirical reality. This, indeed, represented one of Durkheim's most frequently stated ambitions. But he never lost sight of broader philosophical questions, and held that it should be one of the functions of sociology to throw new light upon old philosophical debates. As he himself wrote: 'Having begun from philosophy, I tend to return to it; or rather I have been quite naturally brought back to it by the nature of the questions which I met with on my route.'[1]

Durkheim's earliest writings are rooted in an attempt to establish a critique of two major streams of social thought (which, of course, embodied numerous, complex and overlapping subdivisions), namely that formed by political economy, and utilitarian philosophy more generally, on the one hand, and that represented by the various schools of 'idealist holism' on the other.[2] The latter tradition, at least in Durkheim's treatment of it in his early writings, includes various apparently discrepant sorts of social thought – such as, for example, that of Comte, and of German authors such as Schmoller and Schäffle. What such writers as these shared in common, as it seemed to Durkheim, is the assumption, either implicit or explicit, that the positive valence of moral 'ideals' provides the major impetus to the evolution of human society. This emphasis gives their works certain distinctive merits, as compared with political economy and utilitarianism. Firstly, in contrast to the latter schools, they accentuate the *historical* nature of man. Whereas utilitarian philosophy places man outside of

history, seeking to interpret human social action in terms of
a-temporal concepts of utility and the pursuit of self-interest,
these latter authors, in their various ways, stress that social life
can only be understood in terms of an historical perspective.
Secondly, as a related premise, and again in contradistinction to
the utilitarians, they hold that society is a unity which displays
characteristics that cannot be reduced to those of its component
individuals. Moreover, this unity is primarily *moral*: that is, is
formed of the moral ideals which have evolved with the development of society.

Utilitarian individualism, however, in Durkheim's view, is by
no means without significance for social theory. For it reflects and
gives expression to social trends of fundamental importance. That
is to say, it is an intellectual expression of the fact that there has
been an historical movement towards the increasing emergence
of 'individualism', in some sense, during the course of the development of society from its primitive to its more advanced forms.
This is a phenomenon which, according to Durkheim, must be
grasped theoretically: but rather than being treated as the starting-
point of analysis, it is itself something which has to be explained.
Such an explanation is not provided, however, by the perspectives
of either of the two general traditions of social thought. Each of
these tends to treat its own standpoint as exclusive of, and wholly
opposed to, that of the other. Thus utilitarian theory justly gives
prominence to the emergence of individualism, but mistakenly
attempts to formulate an abstract social theory on this basis: in
fact, a society composed of egoistic, or self-seeking, individuals,
would be no society at all. We must therefore reject the notions
that 'the collective interest is only a form of personal interest', and
that 'altruism is merely a concealed egoism'.[3] The second group
of thinkers, on the other hand, quite correctly criticises these
assumptions, and shows that society has properties *sui generis*:
more specifically, that the moral ideals which form the core
of social unity cannot be derived solely from any principle of
individual utility. But, in doing so, they fail to appreciate the ways
in which the nature of these ideals have changed over the course
of history. The important task which has to be undertaken is that
of reconciling in an adequate fashion the (valid) point that society
always embodies collective ideals which surpass the experience
and activities of the individual, with the point (which is also valid)
that, in the course of social development, traditional values seem
to become increasingly dissolved, thus ceding more and more
freedom of action to each individual member of society.

There is another important consideration relating directly to these issues, bearing in an immediate fashion upon the role of moral ideals in society. As Kant always stressed, morality possesses an imperative, or obligatory, quality. Durkheim accepts that the obligatory element is indeed of key importance in all moral phenomena: and this is again something which is completely ignored in utilitarian theory. The good cannot be identified with the optimisation of individual satisfactions. On the other hand, in the writings of those who identify obligation as the fundamental property of morality, the imperative quality attributed to moral rules is emphasised to the exclusion of that property given prominence by the utilitarians – the intrinsic satisfaction which is normally derived from faithful adherence to the prescriptions entailed in moral ideals. Each of these characteristics of moral ideals, Durkheim concludes, must be brought within the scope of an attempt to understand the central function which moral rules have within the organisation of society. This understanding, in turn, can only be accomplished by following the lead of some of the German authors, and founding a 'science of morality'. Such a science should be a sociological science: that is to say, it should be grounded in the empirical analysis of the concrete forms of moral ideal which have existed in different societies at particular periods of history. Rather than proceeding according to the habitual mode of philosophers, who have sought to discover a single, absolute criterion of morality (e.g., that the 'good' equals the 'useful'), and then have 'applied' this to the various types of historical society, we must start off by studying moral rules as they really exist in society, in all their complexity. The endeavour to contribute to the founding of a sociological 'science of morality' very rapidly led Durkheim to a concern with the nature of sociology and of social phenomena more generally; but he always conceived of his contributions to sociology as being primarily focussed within the more specialised field of the 'sociology of moral facts'. As he wrote in 1900: 'Instead of treating sociology *in genere*, we have always concerned ourselves systematically with a clearly delimited order of facts: save for necessary excursions into the fields adjacent to those which we were exploring, we have always been occupied only with legal or moral rules, studied in terms of their genesis and development...'[4]

Thus Durkheim's first major work, *The Division of Labour in Society* (1893), was conceived as 'an attempt to treat the facts of moral life according to the method of the positive sciences'.[5] The book squarely faces the issues which he saw as problematic in the works of the philosophers dealt with in his early writings. While the book rests upon the sort of dichotomy between traditional and modern society which was a commonplace in the literature of the time, Durkheim saw its main contribution as lying in its specification of the moral characteristics of the *latter* type of society. Hence he subtitled the work, on its first appearance, 'A Study of the Organisation of the Advanced Societies'. Writers such as Comte and many others have perfectly well identified the basic feature of the moral order of traditional societies: this consists of a strongly marked set of consensual values, expressed in terms of religious symbolism. But Comte failed to explain and to adequately analyse the properties of the emergent modern social order which has replaced, or is in the process of replacing, traditionalism. Thus his 'positive stage of society' turns out to be, in large part, a reversion to the traditional order, a sort of revitalised Catholicism. An inability to perceive the depth of the *contrast* between the traditional and the modern form of society is the characteristic failure of the various forms of 'idealist holism'. Those who do accept the significance of this contrast, on the other hand – the utilitarian thinkers – fail to understand that underlying the contrast must nevertheless be continuity: that the dissolution of the traditional order has not led to a society which can be reduced to an aggregate of individuals each pursuing their particular 'best interests'.[6] Even those authors who have dealt most directly with the relationship between the traditional and the modern, such as Tönnies, whatever the validity of their treatment of the traditional order, relapse into utilitarianism in seeking to delineate the essential character of the advanced social type.

In reviewing Tönnies' *Gemeinschaft und Gesellschaft*, at the time when he was working on *The Division of Labour*, Durkheim makes this point explicitly.[7] He states his general acceptance of the dichotomy established by Tönnies: there are certainly fundamental differences between the 'lower' and the 'advanced' societies. Furthermore, he acknowledges that Tönnies' formulation of the nature of *Gemeinschaft* is essentially correct. But the latter's assessment of the properties of *Gesellschaft* is entirely unsatisfactory. According to Durkheim, Tönnies' picture of *Gesellschaft* is of a moral order in which the 'collective life resulting from internal spontaneity', characteristic of traditional society, has been lost. Therefore, Tönnies assumes, the only collective identity in *Gesellschaft* stems from the unity which the state imposes upon the egoistic life of men in civil society. In Durkheim's view, while we should recognise the depth of the opposition between the traditional and the modern order, we must nevertheless also see that 'there is in our contemporary societies a truly collective activity which is just as natural as that of the smaller societies of previous ages'.[8] In *The Division of Labour*, Durkheim sought to resolve this seeming paradox, by showing that 'individualism' *itself* is a moral phenomenon; and that, although it is quite distinct from the 'egoism' of the utilitarians, it also contrasts dramatically with the moral structure of the traditional order.

According to the thesis of *The Division of Labour*, the simpler societies are founded upon a strongly defined moral consensus, an enveloping *conscience collective*. There are four principal dimensions along which we can analyse the properties of the *conscience collective* in such societies, and each of these characteristics undergoes change in the course of social development, as the division of labour expands, and society becomes more complex. These concern the *volume, intensity, rigidity* and the *content* of the beliefs and values which compose the *conscience collective*. The first refers to the degree to which the perspectives or attitudes held by the individual are identical to those held by all the other members of the same society: or, in other words, how far the individual consciousness is simply a 'microcosm' of the *conscience collective*.[9] The degree of 'intensity' of the constituent elements of the *conscience collective* concerns the extent of the emotional and intellectual hold which these beliefs and values exert over the perspectives of the individual. This can vary, in a certain measure, independently of volume: but in general it is the case that the more 'enveloping' the *conscience collective*, the greater the intensity which it has. 'Rigidity' pertains to how clearly defined are the beliefs and associated social practices which are prescribed (and proscribed) by the *conscience collective*. Again, this tends to be closely connected to the first two dimensions. The lower the volume and intensity of collective beliefs and values, the more ambiguously and vaguely defined are the rules of conduct which stem from them: the individual must 'interpret' how they apply to any concrete situation which he is confronted with. The fourth dimension, the changing 'content' of the *conscience collective* is in a certain sense the most significant, although Durkheim did not fully elaborate its implications until after the publication of *The Division of Labour*. The essential point is, however, established in that work: that 'if there is one truth that history teaches us beyond doubt, it is that religion embraces a smaller and smaller portion of social life. Originally it pervades everything; everything social is religious...'[10]

Thus, in traditional societies the *conscience collective* tends to be high in volume, intensity and rigidity; and its content is religious in character. The unity of such a society, in other words, is to be found in the fact that there exists a strongly defined set of values and beliefs which ensures that the actions of all individuals conform to common norms. Durkheim calls this 'mechanical' solidarity, but not with the implication that such solidarity is in some way produced artificially by its component individuals. Rather, the term indicates an analogy with simple organisms, which have a mechanical structure in this sense, such that each cell is wholly comparable to every other, and such that a cell or group of cells can split away without destroying the unity of the parent organism.[11] Where mechanical solidarity is the basis of social cohesion, therefore, there is a concomitantly low level of individuation: that is to say, since every individual is a microcosm of the collective type, only restricted opportunity is offered for each member of the society to develop specific and particular personality characteristics. This dominance of the individual by the collectivity is indexed by the nature of the punishment which is meted out when a man deviates from the rigidly specified codes of conduct which are prescribed by the *conscience collective*.[12] Repressive sanctions are collective both in their source, and in their expression. A repressive sanction is a response to the highly intense emotions which are generated in the majority of individuals when a man transgresses the ideals embodied in the *conscience collective*. It is an expression of anger on the part of the community, the avenging of an outrage to morality.

There is a fundamental distinction between 'individuation' and 'individualism'. The growth of individuation presupposes a decline in the volume, intensity and rigidity of the *conscience collective*: individuals are able to develop their own particular propensities and inclinations to the degree to which these are freed from the control of the moral homogeneity of the community. But this in turn entails a transformation in the *content* of collective moral ideals: the decline of traditional religion and the emergence of what Durkheim calls variously 'moral individualism' or the 'cult of the individual'. The main thesis of *The Division of Labour* is that while individuation is a necessary concomitant of the dissolution of traditional society, it implies, not the complete eradication of the *conscience collective*, but its transmutation in the form of the development of new moral ideals: those comprised in the 'cult of the individual.'[13] Thus the 'cult of the individual' provides a moral validation of the specialised division of labour. The values and beliefs composing moral individualism, stressing as they do the dignity and worth of the human individual, emphasise that each man should develop his talents and capacities to their fullest extent: 'In the same way as the ideal of the less developed societies was to create or maintain as intense a shared life as possible, in which the individual was absorbed, our ideal is constantly to introduce greater equality in our social relations, in order to ensure the free unfolding of the socially useful forces.'[14]

In these terms, Durkheim sought a resolution of the issues dominating his earlier writings. The utilitarian thinkers, according to him, have rendered a major service to moral science in having shown that the modern social order is intrinsically committed to relationships which 'result, not from external and imposed arrangements, but from a free internal elaboration'. Their major errors, however, are to suppose that this situation can be 'deduced logically from the concept of the individual in itself'[15] and that therefore it presupposes the dissolution of collective moral ideals as such. That is to say, they fail to recognise the essential difference between individuation and moral individualism. The latter is a product *of* the development of society, and is morally validated by the existence of values whereby 'the individual becomes the object of a sort of religion'.[16]

But it is equally fallacious to suppose that this transformed type of moral consensus can play the same part in the contemporary social order which the *conscience collective* played in traditional societies. The condition of social unity in these societies is that the *conscience collective* ranks highly upon each of the first three dimensions indicated above; on the other hand, the condition of the emergence of moral individualism is precisely its weakening in each of these three respects. Moral individualism comprises beliefs and values which are the product of the collectivity, but these are far more diffuse in form than those embodied in the moral consensus characteristic of the traditional order. Thus those who believe that a strongly formed moral consensus is a prerequisite to social unity in the modern type of society, as it was in the traditional order, are as mistaken as are the utilitarians in holding that 'individualism' presupposes the dissolution of all collective moral ideals. The process of development from traditional to modern society must therefore have involved a profound set of institutional changes, which have fundamentally modified the basis of social unity. This involves, of course, the progressive displacement of mechanical by 'organic' solidarity.

Traditional societies typically have a simple, segmental

structure, consisting of aggregates of family or clan groups. Because there is only a rudimentary division of labour, each such group is a functionally equivalent and independent productive unit. The expansion of the division of labour, which entails the formation of ties of economic *interdependence* between producers, thus implies the breakdown of the segmental structure. This is a process which occurs with the growth of 'moral' or 'dynamic' density – the expansion of the range of contacts between previously isolated small-scale social communities. Thus formerly separate communities become linked within a single economic system. The growth of differentiation in the division of labour, according to Durkheim, functions to reduce the social conflicts which otherwise tend to arise when two sets of equivalent producers are in competition for scarce resources. Thus a given population of individuals whose interests would be mutually exclusive, in some determinate measure, if they were all farmers, are able – indeed, obliged – to live in co-operation with one another, if some become manufacturers, who then enter into economic exchange with the agrarian producers.[17] The growth of social differentiation, and of large-scale societies, with an urban rather than a rural base, also promotes the rise of private property. The collective property characteristic of traditional societies is the material counterpart of the form of *conscience collective* upon which their unity is founded; hence the accelerating growth in dynamic density, and the concomitant changes in the *conscience collective* which occur with the diversification of perspective and outlook enforced by the division of labour, lead increasingly to the dissolution of the old forms of collective property. Even in the modern world, however, these still have an important residue: the inheritance of property through the family, according to Durkheim, is a survival of primitive rights of communal property (and, as such, is destined shortly to disappear).

Organic solidarity thus consists in the ties of co-operation between individuals or groups of individuals which derive from their occupational interdependence within the differentiated division of labour. Durkheim uses the term 'organic' solidarity in order to stress that the organisation of developed societies resembles the structure of an advanced organism, in which the functioning of the organism depends upon the reciprocal relationships which the various specialised organs of the body have with each other. In these organisms, of course, the removal of an organ will hamper the workings of the body, or even put an end to its existence altogether – in contrast to the case with the simple organism. The solidarity produced by the division of labour is as 'spontaneous' as that deriving, in traditional societies, from the moral consensus of the *conscience collective*. It is not, and cannot be, purely 'economic', but has a moral character; however, since individuals now occupy a large number of different positions within the division of labour, this is a morality of co-operation, which necessarily takes a distinct form from that characteristic of mechanical solidarity. This is indexed by the increasing prominence which is assumed by restitutive law relative to repressive law.[18] In contrast to the latter, restitutive law does not have an expiatory character, but consists in a return in state. The prescriptions involved in restitutive law, covering individual rights, do not stimulate the collective anger characteristic of repressive sanctions. Thus their application demands the formation of specialised agencies for the administration of law, in contrast to the repressive sanctions of the traditional community, which are normally administered diffusely through the kin group. There comes into being, therefore, the whole juridical apparatus of courts and tribunals which characterises the modern legal system. The sphere of repressive law does not, of course, disappear altogether: it remains fundamental in regard to the values embodied in moral individualism, and consequently is applied to acts, such as murder, which transgress these values.

The Division of Labour isolates a subtle connection between individuation and individualism, a shifting polarity between 'man in particular' and 'man in general'. The individual within the small community, in the early phase of social development, is unconscious of the general attributes which, as a man, he shares with the whole of humanity. The social world outside his own community is alien to him. His particularity, considered in relation to *other* societies of which he himself has only a vague awareness, is collective: what he shares with others is the attributes of the specific societal group of which he is a member. As the division of labour expands and mechanical solidarity declines, the individual no longer shares the same characteristics as all other individuals in his society: he is more and more a particular, differentiated personality. But at the same time as he becomes particularised within the group, he grows increasingly aware of the properties which he possesses in common with the rest of mankind. Moral individualism stresses the rights and capacities of the individual *in abstracto*, of 'man' in general. Thus for Durkheim there is no paradox in asserting that men become more conscious of their generic characteristics as human beings to the degree to which they become more aware of themselves as separate and distinct personalities.

The analysis given in *The Division of Labour* demonstrates, in Durkheim's view, that organic solidarity is the essential basis of the modern social order; there can be no return to the form of solidarity which is typical of traditionalism. It is fundamentally important to recognise, however, that organic solidarity, at the present juncture, is emergent rather than fully actualised. The modern world is still in a transitional phase. This is what has helped to mislead both the idealist and utilitarian thinkers. The former still cast their eyes back to previous times, seeking to re-establish the moral consensus of traditional society; and a sufficient number of elements of traditionalism survive to allow this position to have a certain plausibility. The utilitarians, on the other hand, have developed their theories on the basis of generalising from other areas of society, where the traditional moral forms have been dissolved but have not yet been replaced by new moral prescriptions. This is particularly the case with certain sectors of industrial life, which are in an anomic state: that is to say, which have broken away from the moral bonds of traditionalism, but which have not yet become subject to new and more appropriate moral regulation.

The anomic condition of the division of labour, which is reflected both in the occurrence of industrial crises and in class conflict, is directly connected with the mode in which the expansion of occupational differentiation destroys the integrity of the local community. In the traditional community, production is oriented to a specific, and known, set of local needs; and, even where manufacture is quite highly developed, master and worker typically work side by side in the same shop. With the growth of the division of labour, however, and the formation of the large-scale market, each of these conditions becomes undermined. A dislocation is introduced between producer and consumer, because there is no longer a direct tie between the volume of production and the known needs of the market: thus crises of overproduction occur. This is evidence, according to Durkheim, 'that at certain points in the organism certain social functions are not adjusted to one another'.[19] Similarly, the growth of large-scale industry, which is attendant upon the development of national and international markets, fragments the unity of the small enterprise, establishing two broad classes, capital and labour, which stand in confrontation with one another. But rather than holding, with Marx, that these two sets of phenomena are to be traced to the intrinsic properties of the division of labour itself, Durkheim asserts that they derive from the fact that the division of labour is *incompletely* developed. This is true in two senses. Firstly, that there is insufficient regulation of the occupational sectors comprising the division of labour: both economic and moral regulation. He agrees with the socialists that economic co-ordination of market functions is necessary to cope with the sort of dislocation evinced in crises. But sheerly economic regulation is not enough. What is of crucial importance is that there should be moral regulation, that there should be moral rules which specify the rights and obligations of individuals in a given occupation in relation to those in other occupations. The emergence of such moral regulations, however, presupposes the occurrence of further changes in the structure of the division of labour – changes which are already in progress, but need to be further advanced. This is the second strand of Durkheim's argument and it is of considerable significance. The elimination of the anomic division of labour is impossible while there are still major inequalities in the distribution of opportunities for occupational attainment. Moral regulation of the division of labour only becomes adequately developed in so far as it is 'spontaneous', which means that individuals have to be able to fill occupational positions which accord with their talents and capabilities, and which, therefore, they will accept as legitimate. But this situation of equality of opportunity cannot prevail where the class system inhibits the chances of large masses of attaining positions commensurate with their abilities:

> If one class of society is obliged, in order to live, to take any price for its services, while another is absolved from such a necessity – thanks to resources which it possesses, but which are not intrinsically expressive of any social superiority – the latter is able unjustly to force the former to submit to its dictates. In other words, there must be unjust contracts as long as there are rich and poor at birth.[20]

This 'forced division of labour', however, can be abolished if the hereditary transmission of property is ended: and this is a process which has already been set under way by the very expansion of the division of labour itself. Durkheim does not envisage here a society in which either private property or inequality will be eliminated. Both will persist, but the existing relation which tends to pertain between them will become reversed: instead of the former determining the latter, access to material rewards will be governed by the distribution of natural inequalities. There are 'internal' inequalities of capacity and aptitude which, according to

Durkheim, are ineradicable. 'External' inequalities, on the other hand, can and will become dissolved with the further development of the division of labour: 'labour is divided spontaneously only if society is constituted in such a way that social inequalities exactly express natural inequalities.'[21]

ii.   *Moral individualism and the theory of religion*

The Division of Labour is Durkheim's fundamental work. It establishes a framework of thought which remained at the basis of all his later writings, although he never again returned to problems of such broad compass as those dealt with in that book. His subsequent works are certainly far more than a mere gloss upon the conclusions reached in *The Division of Labour.* He modified and complemented these conclusions in substantial measure; but his ensuing contributions are virtually all elaborations of themes which are originally to be found there. This is especially true of the main connecting thread in his writings, the development of his conception of moral authority. Here *The Division of Labour* sets out the underlying perspectives: that there is both *continuity* and *contrast* in the transition from traditional to modern society. The continuity is given in the necessary persistence of moral ideals and codes of conduct which order the functioning of society. The contrast is expressed in the transformation of the nature of these ideals and prescriptions which occurs with the movement from mechanical to organic solidarity. But a number of latent problems, particularly concerning the nature and origins of 'moral individualism', were left only partially resolved by *The Division of Labour.*

These received a clearer formulation in the light of two concerns in Durkheim's subsequent work which at first sight appear startlingly disparate: an attempt to approach the analysis of certain fairly concrete socio-political issues on the one hand, and a deepening interest in primitive religion on the other. The first was stimulated by a resurgence of political and economic cleavages in France in the closing years of the nineteenth century.[22] These years saw an important revival of radical socialism and, in 1898, the outbreak of public controversy over the Dreyfus Affair. Durkheim gave a course of lectures on socialism in 1895–6[23] and, about two years later, published an article explicitly dealing with certain general issues raised by the Dreyfus case.[24] But, at about the same period, he came into close contact with the work of the English anthropologists, such as Frazer, Tylor and Robertson-Smith, and through them gained a new appreciation of the significance of religion in traditional society. This stimulated the appearance of a number of comprehensive articles in the *Année sociologique* dealing with various aspects of primitive religion and eventually culminated in the publication of *The Elementary Forms of the Religious Life* in 1912. Apparently far distant from one-another, these two sets of writings complement each other in an integral way: the first led him to clarify the institutional basis of moral individualism, as rooted in the state and the occupational associations (*corporations*), while the second allowed him to identify, in a precise way, the origins of moral authority in the sacred phenomena created by society. He did not finish a systematic exposition of the general implications of these insights, although he was working upon such an exposition at the time of his death; but the connections between them, at least in outline, can be reconstructed without difficulty.

In his lectures on socialism, Durkheim makes a primary distinction between 'communism' and 'socialism'. This is a differentiation which is closely bound up with the general standpoint which he previously worked out, since it turns directly upon the contrast between egoism and individualism. Communism is utopian theory, often presented in fictional form, as in More's *Utopia* itself, and reoccurs periodically throughout history, because it is essentially a response to human egoism and greed – which, in some degree, are eternal, and constitute 'a chronic illness of humanity'.[25] Since, according to communist authors, private property is the source of egoism, communist theory involves the supposition that those responsible for the administration of society, the governing class, should be separated from economic functions, and more generally, leads to an emphasis upon the positive virtues of asceticism. Communism, for Durkheim, *must* be an unreal image, a dream of an unattainable society, for the reason that egoism cannot be extirpated from human conduct: in fact, the range of egoistic inclinations tends to grow as society develops, and individuation becomes more pronounced. While communist ideas interweave with the early history of socialism, the latter is historically specific and is tied to a very particular combination of social conditions: those which are identified in *The Division of Labour* as being the transitional phase between mechanical and organic solidarity. Socialism is a response to the state of deregulation of industry. Socialism has appeared for the reason that

in the most advanced societies of present-day Europe, production appears to be unrelated to consumption needs; or that industrial centralisation seems to have given birth to enterprises too large for society to ignore; or that the incessant changes produced by technology, with the resultant social instability, rob the worker of all security and place him in a state of inferiority which prevents him from concluding equitable contracts; it is on this and other similar evidence that socialism bases its demands for reform of the contemporary order.[26]

The Division of Labour established that class conflict is a symptom rather than a cause of the 'anomie' and the 'forced' division of labour. This is formally substantiated in the lectures on socialism: class conflict, Durkheim insists, is not a defining element in socialism, but is a derivative of its primary characteristic, which is that of advocating a fusion of economic and governmental functions. Thus in Marx's writings, according to Durkheim, the working-class movement is regarded only as a vehicle for the attainment of the more essential aim of the socialisation of production. For while communism is founded upon an ascetic attitude, socialism is based upon the notion that the wealth generated by human industry, if appropriately organised, can both free and satisfy the potentialities and needs of mankind.

The significance of socialism is twofold: that it recognises that the advanced societies are passing through a major stage of transition which demands the emergence of new social forms; and that it perceives that some kind of regulation or control of the 'free' play of market forces is necessary in the nascent new society. The limitation in socialist doctrine is that the regulation which it advocates is purely economic in character. The conception of the abolition of the 'political' and of the disappearance of the 'state' really implies that the state should have only economic functions: that, in Saint-Simonian terms, government should be the 'administration of things' and not the 'administration of men'. But, in Durkheim's view, in advocating this conception, socialism in fact shares the premise of its main opponents, utilitarianism and political economy, holding that society can be treated as an *economic* process. The only important difference is that, while the latter believe that this operates spontaneously, the former consider that economic life has to be consciously directed. The disjunctions and conflicts in the division of labour are not simply to be explained in terms of too much economic regulation (political economy), or too little (socialism), but derive from the very predominance of the 'economic' over the 'social': more specifically, that not merely economic change, but the moralisation of economic relationships, is what is demanded.

In one of his earliest publications,[27] Durkheim reached the conclusion that, contrary to the thesis of the utilitarians, there is no direct and necessary correlation between human 'happiness' and the advance of economic prosperity. If the effect of providing for wants is simply to stimulate further wants, then the distance between desires and their satisfaction has not been reduced by this advance, but perhaps even widened. This conclusion is further substantiated in *The Division of Labour*, where it is affirmed that melancholy suicide only appears with the dissolution of the traditional society – a thesis elaborated in detail in *Suicide*. Since it shares with utilitarianism the assumption that the wealth generated by human industry can satisfy the range of human needs, socialism must be subjected to the same basic criticism: it ignores the fact that, if society creates and extends human faculties, it must at the same time also make them concrete and realisable, which entails that they be defined and ordered by moral regulation. This is the core of the theory of anomie, as this is initially stated in *The Division of Labour* and amplified in *Suicide* and the lectures on socialism. The needs of animals are defined biologically, and hence their limits are also set biologically. The same is true, although not in such a clearly-defined fashion, with the biological needs of the human organism: 'Everyone recognises that the needs of the body are limited, and that consequently physical pleasure cannot increase indefinitely.'[28] But this is not the case with needs and desires of a spiritual kind, which are not given in the structure of the organism, but which are derived from the benefits conferred by society. There is no necessary limit, for example, to the desire of a man to accumulate riches; consequently, it is possible that the more wealth he accumulates, the more dissatisfied he becomes, because the horizon of his ambitions expands. But Saint-Simon, and later socialist thinkers, have failed to perceive this. To them

> it appears that the way to realise social peace is to free economic appetites of all restraint on the one hand and on the other to satisfy them by fulfilling them. But such an undertaking is contradictory. For these appetites cannot be appeased unless they are limited and they cannot be limited except by something other than themselves. They cannot be regarded as the only purpose of society since they must be subordinated to some end which surpasses them and it is only on this condition that they are capable of being really satisfied...Unlimited need contradicts itself. For need is defined by the goal it aims at and if unlimited has no goal – since there is no limit...an appetite that nothing can appease can

be a source of suffering. Whatever one does, it is never slaked.[29]

These moral bounds were provided by religion in former ages. Mediaeval Christianity, for example, instructed believers that there was a natural hierarchy in society, thus helping the poor to accept their lot and reminding the rich that they owed certain obligations to their social inferiors. This has been swept away, however, with the demise of traditional society. Economic life and the ambitions which it generates have been released from the narrow moral confines to which they were previously subject. Consequently, what is needed is the re-emergence of moral regulation in industry.

Durkheim's views on this point have frequently been interpreted as implying a heavily authoritarian doctrine and, as such, have been the object of much criticism.[30] Most such criticism, however, has been based upon a serious misreading of Durkheim's position in this regard. In calling for a remoralisation of industry in the face of the problem of anomie, he in no way argues for a revival of the sorts of restricted moral boundaries which pertained in former times. On the contrary, the essential lesson of *The Division of Labour* is that such a reversion is impossible. Both in *The Division of Labour* and in the series of lectures on the state and industry, which he gave first at Bordeaux and then, toward the latter part of his career, at the Sorbonne in Paris, he reiterates that this necessary remoralisation can only be achieved within the context of the furtherance of profound institutional change in society. The decline in the rigid control of the *conscience collective*, the increase in human sensibilities promoted by the growth in individuation, together with the expansion of moral individualism, means that men can never again be satisfied with the limitations which were imposed upon them in prior ages. This is why the elimination of the anomic division of labour is necessarily linked to the abolition of the forced division of labour.

In his writings on the state and politics, Durkheim documents in some detail the changes which are presupposed by the transition to organic solidarity and the concomitant ideals of moral individualism. These ideals can only be concretely realised within an institutional order in which the functioning of organic solidarity is mediated by the dual influence of the state and the occupational associations. The need for the development of the occupational associations is logically implied in Durkheim's theory of organic solidarity:

Where restitutive law is highly developed, there is a professional morality for each occupation. Within each specific group of workers there is a diffusion of attitudes which have to be complied with, even though they are not enforced by legal sanctions. Each order of functionaries shares customs and prescriptions which they cannot contravene without incurring the censure of the *corporation*.[31]

But this insight was not developed – at least, not in print – until the publication of the famous Preface to the second edition of *The Division of Labour*, where the nature and role of the occupational associations is specified. Their task is to control the moral ties that bind the various segments of industry which co-operate with each other in the division of labour. This is most definitely not accomplished by the existing trade unions, which are primarily bodies organised with the sole object of furthering the interests of their members in specific opposition to the interests of others. The *corporations* have to be legally defined entities, which are affiliated with each other, and which operate within the general umbrella of the state. They will establish and sanction the ethics appropriate to each occupational category, and provide a focus for the moral consciousness of the workers within that category. In a general way, they will resemble the mediaeval guilds, but without manifesting the same inflexible and reactionary character: this will be possible because of the co-ordination with the directive functions of the state.

As in his analysis of the division of labour in general, in his thinking on the modern state Durkheim sought to differentiate his views from those of the idealist philosophers on the one hand and from utilitarianism (and socialism) on the other. The former, particularly those influenced by Hegel, give the state a pre-eminence over society which, in Durkheim's eyes, is quite illegitimate. In fact, the state is always rooted in civil society, and even the most autocratic and apparently self-sufficient state in fact draws its strength from society. This is recognised by the utilitarians and socialists, but they go too far in the other direction, believing that the state is simply parasitic upon civil society – and therefore they argue that, in the near future, the state is due to 'disappear'. This latter hypothesis, Durkheim points out, is entirely inconsistent with the trend of social development. All the evidence indicates that the size and the functions of the state expand with the growth of the division of labour. We must accept, therefore, that the enlargement of the sphere of activities of the state is an inevitable concomitant of the development of modern society.

But this seems to present a major difficulty. How is the expansion of the scope of the state to be reconciled with the growth of individual freedoms which, according to Durkheim, is also necessarily stimulated by the progression of the division of labour? He attempts to resolve this problem in terms of a definite conception of the nature of the tasks of the modern state and a specification of the system of democratic government which is generated by the combined action of the state and the occupational associations. For Durkheim, the state is a moral agency. It is a body of officials whose role is to articulate and to focus the collective representations which are the product of the society which it serves. The state is, as he sometimes says, the brain of the social organism. Its primary function is to give a clear expression to the currents of thought and feeling in the 'lower layers' of society. But the state is not limited to simply making these collective attitudes articulate, it also plays an active role in canalising and directing policies which translate these attitudes into practice. As such it leads as well as being led. This is what explains how it is that the expansion of the state can go hand in hand with the growth of the rights of the individual: because the task of the state is precisely that of implementing and realising the ideals embodied in moral individualism. Individualism 'is not a theory: it lies in the realm of practice, not in that of speculation'.[32]

The first and most basic condition for this action of the state is that given in *The Division of Labour*: that society must have broken away from the confines of segmental structure. In traditional societies which do possess a state, it is usually despotic in character, because it partakes of the sacred, 'suprahuman' qualities of the *conscience collective*, and thus separates itself in high degree from the mundane activities of individuals in civil society.[33] In his lectures on the state, Durkheim emphasises again the integral connection between individuation and the development of large-scale society and the differentiated division of labour:

> There is no doubt that when society is small, when it surrounds every individual on all sides and at every moment, it does not allow him to develop in freedom. If it is always present and always operating, it leaves no room for his initiative. But it is no longer the same when society has reached sufficient dimensions. When it is made up of a vast number of individuals, a society cannot exercise over each one a control which is as close, vigilant, or effective as when it is concerned only with a small number. A man is far more

free in the midst of a crowd than in a small group. Hence it follows that individual diversities can develop more easily; that collective tyranny declines and individualism establishes itself as a reality and, in time, the reality becomes a right.[34]
But this tyranny can also exist *within* a developed society, if the secondary groups, such as the *corporations* themselves, assume too great an autonomy over the activities of the individual. If they are balanced by the power of the state, however, the individual is protected from this domination; and vice versa, the sphere of authority of the occupational associations offsets the possibility of state autocracy. If the power of the state is not counterbalanced by other agencies, it readily becomes detached from the interests of those in civil society: 'it is out of this conflict of social forces that individual freedoms are born.'[35]
But, for Durkheim, what makes such a society 'democratic' is not primarily the balancing of powers which is provided for by the juxtaposition of the state and occupational associations in the modern order, but the channels of communication which this organisation of society opens up between its various component parts. In elaborating his conception of democracy, he decisively rejects the classical notion. In a large-scale society, it is quite out of the question for the mass of the population to participate in any direct way in government. Moreover, those cases, of small, traditional communities, which might be plausibly said to approximate to 'direct democracy', contravene one of the main desiderata of modern government: that it should be flexible and capable of leading change. The thesis that democracy is the 'self-government of society' must therefore be abandoned. The very conception of a 'political society', according to Durkheim's definition, involves a differentiation between government and governed. A democratic society, moreover, is not one in which the state is weak. If the state simply expresses the opinions and attitudes of the populace, the result is again a stagnant society: one in which there may be constant change in government personnel, but where superficial volatility on the political level cloaks an underlying conservatism.[36]
Democracy is not to be understood as a mode of minimising the power of the state, therefore, but as a means of ensuring an active interplay between the state and the rest of society. In every society there are collective currents of change, modifications of belief and attitude, which take place at the level of infrastructure: in the 'lower layers' of society. A society can be called 'democratic', according to Durkheim's usage, to the degree to which a reciprocal relation is established between these 'unconsciously'

evolved movements and the more articulate and deliberate activities of the state.

The classical theorists of democracy, according to Durkheim, had a dim perception of this, because when the state is weak, it is necessarily in close touch with the attitudes and feelings expressed in society in general, since the activities of the state merely follow the dictates of these attitudes and feelings. But in reality the existence of close ties of communication between state and civil society does not entail that the state should not be strong: only given a strong state is it possible for democracy, in Durkheim's sense of the term, to come into being. Democracy is thus a condition in which, as he puts it, 'society can achieve a consciousness of itself in its purest form'.[37] A democratic system of government renders accessible to conscious decision and rational deliberation social processes which, in former times, were the product of occurrences which escaped rational human control. The occupational associations play an essential role in this, as the main intervening groups between the individual and the state. These groups constitute the primary channel of communication between the state 'consciousness' and the infrastructure. Durkheim thus suggests that the occupational groups should be accorded an openly political role. The system of direct representation should be replaced by one in which the *corporations* would be organised as electoral bodies, intermediary between the mass of the population and the representative assemblies of government. Direct representation tends to produce a situation in which the achievement of real social change is difficult, because the parties are compelled, if they wish to obtain power, to conform in a docile manner to the views of the electorate. This again removes the independent sphere of decision-making which Durkheim sees as necessary to counter the 'relentless traditionalism' into which society otherwise tends to lapse.

This conception of democracy was undoubtedly worked out by Durkheim in closest possible connection with his examination of the nature of religion in traditional society. Three major propositions are documented in *The Elementary Forms of the Religious Life*: that religion is society becoming 'conscious of itself', although in a symbolically transmuted form; that the representations created in religion are thus the initial source out of which all subsequent forms of human thought have become differentiated; and that, as creations of the superior being which is society, religious symbols are accorded a peculiar respect or veneration which is denied to the properties of the profane world. Each of

these propositions helps to elucidate the contrast *and* the continuity between the social and moral structure of traditional
society and that of the developed type. Religion is the symbolic
self-consciousness of society, but in a form which is not truly
accessible to the very men who create it: the forces which are
generated by human association are represented in the individual
mind as the product of supernatural essences or beings. The process of social development changes this and allows men to become
rationally aware of the principles which govern the natural and
the social world. Within society itself, democratic organisation,
such as Durkeim describes it, is the institutional means whereby a
maximum of rationality may be attained in societal self-consciousness. The social consciousness of traditional society can be compared to the intellectual processes of the lower animals, which are
rudimentary and unthinking; that of developed society, by contrast, is articulate and deliberated:

> there are two ways in which a human being can receive help
> from external forces. Either he receives it passively, uncon-
> sciously, without knowing why – and in this case, he is noth-
> ing more than a thing. Or, he is aware of what these forces
> are, of his reasons for submitting and being responsive to
> them. . .Because there is a constant flow of communication
> between themselves and the state, the state is for individuals
> no longer like an external power that imparts a wholly
> mechanical impetus to them. . .It is and must be a centre
> of new and original ideas which must put the society in a
> position to conduct itself with greater intelligence than when
> it is swayed merely by diffuse sentiments working on it.[38]

But neither the cognitive nor the moral elements which today
dominate the human consciousness are simply 'given' in the mind
(as is suggested in Kantian philosophy). The very categories of
conceptual thought, as *The Elementary Forms* shows, were
originally elaborated as religious ideas; and the same is true of
the forms of morality. Thus moral individualism has its proximate
source in the ideals which Christianity embodied. The Christian
ethic contrasts both with the major Eastern religions and with the
paganism of Greece and Rome. Indian Hinduism and Buddhism,
Durkheim admits, have reached a high level of rationalisation,
resting upon 'a whole theory of the world'; they have 'attempted
to give pantheism a rational and systematic form'.[39] This shows
that science and philosophy may reach a high level of development
without being accompanied by the growth of moral individualism,
since the latter barely exists in traditional India. Individualism

was rather more highly developed in the Ancient World, but even there it was never more than rudimentary as compared with the Christian societies of Western Europe. Classical religion was polytheistic and was primarily directed externally, towards the rituals which were believed to ensure the regular functioning of the universe. Christianity substituted for this an integral ethic which placed the emphasis upon the state of grace of the believer and thereby obliged him to maintain a continual internal scrutiny of his intentions and motivations.[40] In so doing, it served to draw a separation between the human and the natural world and to make the self-fulfilment of the individual, in relation to his divinely appointed tasks, the major ideal:

It was the first [religion] to teach that the moral value of actions must be measured in accordance with intention, which is essentially private, escapes all external judgements and which only the agent can competently judge. The very centre of the moral life was thus transferred from outside to within and the individual was set up as the sovereign judge of his own conduct having no other accounts to render than to himself and to his God. . .It is thus a singular error to present individualistic morality as antagonistic to Christian morality; quite the contrary, it is derived from it.[41]

The Elementary Forms demonstrates that the existence of gods is not essential to religious phenomena: in fact, that all moral phenomena, being the product of society, possess a certain 'sacred' quality. This is therefore true of the ideals comprised in moral individualism, as Durkheim makes clear in his article written during the course of the Dreyfus controversy. Individualism has been attacked, he points out, as being hostile to morality in general, and to Christian morality in particular. But the latter accusation is absurd, for the very reason that moral individualism is derived from the Christian ethic and continues it, but in a rationalised form. The more general charge rests upon a similar misunderstanding, confusing egoism and moral individualism. While it may be true that the individuation which accompanies the growth of moral individualism necessarily produces an increase in egoism, it is fundamentally mistaken to see egoism as the source of moral individualism. The latter is a collective product and is quite distinct from egoism: far from being based upon self-seeking, it is founded upon sentiments of respect for others and for the dignity of men in general. Each individual, in a sense, incarnates these sacred sentiments, but they are not created by him. The motive force of moral indivi-

dualism is hence not 'the glorification of the self', but rather
'sympathy for all that is human, a wider pity for all sufferings,
for all human miseries, a more ardent desire to combat and
alleviate them, a greater thirst for justice'.[42] This modern 'cult
of the individual' is certainly in some respects quite different
from the religions characteristic of previous forms of society;
but it has the same sacred properties. It is worth quoting Durkheim's conclusion on this matter in some detail:

> We know today that a religion does not necessarily imply
> symbols and rites in the full sense, or temples and priests.
> All this external apparatus is merely its superficial aspect.
> Essentially, it is nothing other than a system of collective
> beliefs and practices that have a special authority. Once a
> goal is pursued by a whole people, it acquires, as a result of
> this unanimous adherence, a sort of moral supremacy which
> raises it far above private goals and thereby gives it a
> religious character. On the other hand, it is clear that a
> society cannot hold together unless there exists among its
> members a certain intellectual and moral community. How-
> ever, having recalled this sociological truism, one has not
> advanced very far. For if it is true that religion is, in a
> sense, indispensable, it is no less certain that religions change,
> that yesterday's religion could not be that of tomorrow.
> Thus what we need to know is what the religion of today
> should be.
>
> Now, all the evidence points to the conclusion that the
> only possible candidate is precisely this religion of humanity
> whose rational expression is the individualist morality. . .
> as a consequence of a more advanced division of labour, each
> mind finds itself directed towards a different point of the
> horizon, reflects a different aspect of the world and, as a
> result, the contents of men's minds differ from one subject to
> another. One is thus gradually proceeding towards a state of
> affairs, now almost attained, in which the members of a single
> social group will no longer have anything in common other
> than their humanity, that is, the characteristics which con-
> stitute the human person in general. . .This is why man has
> become a god for man and is why he can no longer turn to
> other gods without being untrue to himself. And just as each
> of us embodies something of humanity, so each individual
> mind has within it something of the divine, and thereby
> finds itself marked by a characteristic which renders it
> sacred and inviolable to others. The whole of individualism

lies here. That is what makes it into the doctrine that is currently necessary. For, should we wish to hold back its progress, we would have to prevent men from becoming increasingly differentiated from one-another, reduce their personalities to a single level, bring them back to the old conformism of former times and arrest, in consequence, the tendency of societies to become ever more extended and centralised and stem the unceasing growth of the division of labour. Such an undertaking, whether desirable or not, infinitely surpasses all human powers.[43]

The conception of religion which is set out in *The Elementary Forms* thus has to be understood within the context of the theory of social development which forms the general framework of Durkheim's work. Thus while, of course, the book can be treated for some purposes as an independent and self-contained study of primitive religion, its broad significance in Durkheim's writings can only be adequately understood in these terms. Although, as the conclusion of the book puts it, there is something in the 'sacred' which is eternal and which survives the changing forms of religion in history, there are nonetheless profound differences between primitive religion and the modern 'cult of the individual'. In specific and conscious opposition to those of his contemporaries who called for a religious revival, Durkheim emphasised that there can be no regression to traditional deism.

The Elementary Forms fills, in some considerable detail, a major gap in *The Division of Labour*. In the latter work, as has been mentioned previously, Durkheim set himself the principal task of establishing the nature of the moral forms appropriate to the *modern* type of society, accepting that (apart from the nature of crime and punishment) the characteristics of mechanical solidarity had already been satisfactorily determined by other authors. But he came to see later that this was by no means the case, and *The Elementary Forms* provides a penetrating analysis of two basic features of the functioning of mechanical solidarity which were left aside in the former work: the origins of the symbolic content of the *conscience collective*; and the institutional framework – of ritual and ceremonial – which creates and recreates these symbols.

Each of these elements is built into the very definition of religion which is offered at the beginning of *The Elementary Forms*. Religion consists of a set of symbolic beliefs – beliefs relative to 'sacred' things. But it is not only this. There is no religion which is not also oriented to *action*, which does not possess a set of accepted ritual practices; in short, there is no religion without a church. *The Elementary Forms* develops partially separable explanations for each of these characteristics of religion. What distinguishes the 'sacred' is that it exists in polar opposition to the 'profane'. The specific quality of religious beliefs is that they presuppose a division of the universe into two parts: those phenomena which are regarded by men as being integral to mundane, everyday life, and those which are the subject of special attitudes of awe and reverence. The essential point is that this is an absolute division. No object or being can pass directly from one world to the other without undergoing certain ritual procedures which transform it – rites of initiation or purification. In totemism, which Durkheim takes as the simplest form of religious system, there are three sorts of sacred objects: the emblem or representation of the totem, such as is carved upon wood, etc.; the totem itself; and the members of the totemic clan. Of these, the representation of the totem is the most sacred. The reason for this is that each of these classes of objects draws its religiosity from an external force: that of society. Since the totemic emblem, in the mind of the member of the group is the most essential symbol of the identity of the clan, it possesses the highest religious power. The clan group, the prototype of society in general, manifests the two properties characteristic of the divine: it claims his obligation and his respect. Hence the equation is reached that the sacred force – or, when it becomes personalised, god – is a symbolic representation of society, of the social force which the individual subjectively evaluates as emanating from a being who is quite separate from and superior to himself. From the totemic emblem, the religious force becomes diffused to the object which is thus represented: the totemic object itself.

The individual member of the collectivity derives his religiosity from the manner in which the sacred force is created. This is a crucial step in Durkheim's argument, linking the symbolic aspect of religion with its necessary correlate, that of practice. The sentiment of the divine is evoked in collective ceremonial, during which, as a result of the intense emotionality and involvement which is generated, the individual feels himself swamped by action of an entity superior to himself. Although this force emanates from the collective assembly, it only realises itself through the consciousness of the individual, who feels it to be both transcendent over him and yet immanent within him. Hence the individual member of the group is represented as participating in the sacred properties of the totemic cult. The equation 'god equals society' has to be understood in this dynamic sense: the divine power is the symbolic representation of the creative capacity, the autonomous self-generating force, of the collectivity. It is only within the framework of the collectivity, according to Durkheim, that the individual is raised above the level of sensory experience which he shares with the other animals. Every individual possesses a definite sensory equipment which permits him to make various sorts of perceptual discriminations among stimuli which he receives from the external world. But there is a basic difference between the (biologically given) capacity to make such discriminations and the (socially given) capacity to formulate classifications of phenomena. The mode in which phenomena are sorted into logical classes is not predetermined either by some principle of structure implicit in reality itself, or by some faculty intrinsic to the human mind. The life of the animal is bound by its immediate sensory environment, and is a formless continuity of shifting images; that of man extends both in time and in space far beyond the environment in which he finds himself at any particular moment. It is his participation in the collectivity which introduces a stable order into the universe and which creates the *concepts* of time and space. The point about the concept of 'time', for example, is that it is discrete from the personal experience of the individual: it is not 'his' time, but refers to a measuring scale which is impersonal. This can only have been arrived at, therefore, by reference to the experience of the collectivity: the concept of time thus referred originally to the periodic movements of society, as manifest in regularised ceremonial and rite. What is true of the categories of time and space can be generalised to all other concepts. A concept is 'impersonal': it is not specific to any one individual, but is shared by all members of the collectivity. There is an absolute gulf between concept and sensation.[44]

Conceptual thought is thus religious *by origin*. In the collective representations of primitive religion there are fused together nascent conceptions of science, poetry and art. The various 'branches' of intellectual activity only become differentiated out of this original set of representations with the growth of social differentiation in the division of labour and the consequent fragmentation of the integral *conscience collective* of primitive society. The differentiation of intellectual life accompanies the evolving differentiation in moral ideas. In indicating this, Durkheim takes some pains to emphasise that the theory set out in *The Elementary Forms* is not to be regarded as merely another version of a 'mechanical materialism', in which ideas are treated as 'reflections' of social reality and hence as mere epiphenomena. There is no universal relationship between systems of ideas and their infrastructures: the nature of this relationship is contingent upon the level of advancement of society.

What is universal, what does persist throughout the successive forms assumed by societies in the course of their development, is the transformative effect of the collectivity upon individual experience. Although shown in its most 'elementary' and therefore in its most direct and vital manifestation in primitive religion, this is the condition of everything which elevates man above an animal existence:

As Rousseau demonstrated long ago: deprive man of all that comes to him from society and he is reduced to his sensations. He becomes a being more or less indistinct from an animal. Without language, essentially a social thing, general or abstract ideas are practically impossible, as are all the higher mental functions. Left to himself the individual would become dependent upon physical forces. If he has been able to escape, to free himself, to develop a personality, it is because he has been able to shelter under a *sui generis* force; an intense force since it results from the coalition of all the individual forces, but an intelligent and moral force capable, consequently, of neutralising the blind and amoral forces of nature.[45]

Human freedom consists in the liberation of man from domination of phenomena which are not subject to his rational control. These phenomena are of two sorts: the irrational impetus of his own inner passions which, if not subject to rational mediation, make man the plaything of arbitrary and transient desire and expose him to the aimlessness of anomie; and the external forces of nature. In the early phases of development of society, the submergence of the individual by the *conscience collective* ensures that anomie remains latent. With the process of social development, as man masters and humanises nature and thus increasingly delivers himself from subjection to the vicissitudes of the material world, the declining strength of the *conscience collective* and especially the demoralisation of industry itself open up the possibility of his subjection to his own, uncontrolled, desires. In a state of anomie, man is not free, because he is not master of himself. Freedom, according to Durkheim, does not consist in being able to give expression to every wish or whim; but in the autonomous control of reason over human conduct. This applies to the very evolution of human society. In traditional society, where the *conscience collective* is strong, the individual is subject to the tyranny of the group: deviation from the strictly defined moral prescriptions is severely punished. The development of the differentiated modern type of society allows for the progressive growth of individual liberties. It is a basic error, however, to suppose that this is the emancipation of the individual *from* society; on the contrary, the very prerequisite for this emancipation is the transfiguration in human existence produced by society. Thus there is no inherent opposition between 'regulation' and 'freedom': the first is the condition of the second. For Durkheim, the existence of any form of society necessitates the existence of moral regulation, and what is demanded of the individual by the obligations entailed in this does not always accord with his private wishes or inclinations: hence morality implies sanctions. But this is by no means to hold that this necessary moral regulation takes the same form in all types of society. The emergence of moral individualism and the associated structural changes in the division of labour certainly do not signify that the individual 'tears himself from society', or is no longer dependent upon it, but they do mean that there is 'a transformation of the social ties', such that the individual 'is joined to (society) in a new manner. . .because society sees him in a new manner and wishes this change to take place'.[46]

This perspective, of course, does rest upon a generalised conception of the nature of moral authority, one which Durkheim only fully clarified in the course of his work in connection with the writing of *The Elementary Forms*. There is an essential distinction, as he came to see, between moral codes and other forms of rules which an individual observes. There are various sorts of rules, such as rules of hygiene, which an individual may keep to, simply in order to avoid the noxious consequences which are likely to result from his failure to conform to them. If a man does not keep away from a source of infection, he will probably contract disease. In such an instance, the outcome of his action follows as a direct consequence of his having neglected a rule of quarantine. The case with moral rules is quite different. Here the penalty which the offender suffers for his violation is not 'given' as a consequence of his act. This is shown by the fact that an identical action, having the same effective outcome, is regarded differentially in varying circumstances: the killing of one man by another, for example, may receive positive moral approbation in times of war, but be stringently punished in peace-time. A moral sanction is thus altogether distinct from the material consequence which follows the violation of a precautionary rule; it is the content of the rule *itself* which stimulates a primitive reaction. But when an individual acts in accordance with a moral ideal, he does not normally do so simply in anticipation of the unpleasant results which would be incurred if he acted differently. If morality always possesses the characteristic of obligation, it also has the property of positively impelling individuals to conform to its prescriptions. Thus moral phenomena have a dual quality, each aspect of which has been emphasised separately by different schools of moral philosophy. Kantian idealism, for its part, has emphasised the aspect of duty or obligation; utilitarian philosophy has stressed the aspect of the intrinsic satisfaction which is gained from moral conduct. In fact, in most moral acts, these are fused: 'desirability and pleasure permeate the obligation'.[47]

iii. *Durkheim's conception of sociological method*

Durkheim's ideas upon the scope of sociology and the nature of sociological method are ordinarily associated almost exclusively with his controversial work, *The Rules of Sociological Method.* Although it is true that any examination of his conception of the distinctive attributes of sociology and sociological procedure must depend largely upon this source, he wrote quite widely on these matters in various other articles, short discussions and reviews,[48] and these serve as a valuable corrective to, and amplification of, the often heavily polemical statements in the synthetic work. Moreover, he stressed that the ideas set out in *The Rules* should not merely be looked at *in abstracto*, since they were developed in conjunction with the more concrete investigations detailed in his other major works and represent only a theoretical exposition of the concrete principles applied there.

According to Durkheim, there are two main strands in the development of sociology: each has contributed, and is contributing, to the formation of sociology as an independent and autonomous discipline. These are social philosophy, on the one hand, and the various specialist social scientific disciplines such as economics, jurisprudence, and geography on the other. Sociology has gradually developed, as a discipline conscious of its own separate identity, out of the diffuse subject-matter of social philosophy: the most distinctive contributors to this process are such authors as Montesquieu, Comte and Spencer. But the works of such men, even where, as in the case of the latter two authors, they have attempted to delimit the tasks of the specific discipline of 'sociology', have remained bound to overall philosophies of history. Thus, in Comte's work, everything is subsumed within the conception of the evolutionary 'law of the three stages'; similarly, in the writings of Comte's immediate successor, Herbert Spencer, social phenomena are not studied 'for their own sake', but only in order 'to show how the evolutionary hypothesis can be verified in the social world.'[49] Nevertheless, Spencer's writings prepared the stage for the final emergence of sociology as a scientific discipline. However, while the general conception of sociology, its tasks and its subject-matter, was created from within social philosophy, the development of the other closely related disciplines is equally important. Disciplines such as economics, jurispudence, etc. have developed largely in separation from each other, as well as from sociology. But each relate to the life of man in society, and thus can only gain by becoming permeated by a general understanding of the mode in which the particular social institutions with which they deal relate to other institutional sectors of society. The immediate problems facing the youthful science of sociology, consequently, are twofold: to free itself from the last vestiges of philosophy, in order to become a study firmly grounded in empirical reality (a process which, as has been mentioned previously, by no means excludes *using* sociological insights in order to cast new light upon traditional problems of philosophy); and to integrate and expand the findings of the particular social sciences by informing them with sociological concepts and methods.

The history of sociology, Durkheim frequently states, has been dominated by French authors: its roots lie in the traditions of social thought which stretch back through Comte to Rousseau, Montesquieu and Condorcet. Whatever the various philosophical and political differences which have divided these authors, they have all fostered the conception that society can and must be studied as a phenomenon given in nature, and which is thus of the same order as the phenomena studied by the natural sciences. According to Durkheim, this is the single most essential conception which must precede the formation of an autonomous discipline of sociology. Although these previous thinkers, implicitly or explicitly, adopted this principle, they did not consistently adhere to it in practice. For acceptance of this principle means that social reality cannot be adequately grasped by the philosopher who refuses to immerse himself in detailed empirical study. It demands that the sociologist must approach his subject-matter with the same reserve as the natural scientist does; its properties can no more be presumed to be 'known' prior to factual investigation than those of the areas of reality studied in the natural sciences. Thus the 'system-building' of earlier writers must be abandoned in favour of a more cautious and circumspect method.

The two precepts which are formulated in *The Rules*, that social facts are to be treated as 'things' and that they must be, initially, conceptualised and examined in terms of their 'external', observable properties, have to be understood against this background. The first proposition simply states, although in a bluntly polemical fashion, that the subject-matter of sociology belongs to the realm of nature and consequently is not refractory – as many who deny the very possibility of sociology claim – to study by methods which parallel those which have been applied to the examination of the material world. Social phenomena are not merely plastic creations of the will of the observer, but share the properties of physical objects in the sense that they exist independently of his observation of them. He cannot, therefore, discover their characteristics either by *a priori* reasoning, or by introspective examination of his own consciousness. But, in relation to many areas of social reality, it has been assumed that such methods are perfectly appropriate. A good example is provided by the study of moral norms. Up to the present, ethical theorists have proceeded as if the empirical study of the diverse forms of morality which exist in different societies were entirely irrelevant to their concerns. They construct abstract ethical doctrines, but they have no empirically grounded sociology of moral life. The properties of moral conduct cannot be known, however, unless they are studied in concrete detail. To consider social facts as 'things', therefore, is the first prerequisite of sociology. In holding this, Durkheim does not argue, of course, that social reality is not distinct from natural reality in other respects: this is not to relapse into any sort of crude materialism. The conception that the social realm is part of nature, according to him, is in no way incompatible with the equally valid conception that notions such as 'purpose', 'idea' and 'value' are specific to human conduct.

> Undoubtedly social life is composed of values and values are properties added to reality by human consciousness; they are wholly the product of psychic mechanisms. But these mechanisms are natural facts, which can be studied scientifically; these evaluations which human judgement makes of things depend upon causes and conditions which can be discovered inductively.[50]

If it be conceded that the basic properties of social phenomena cannot be determined in advance of their empirical investigation, it follows that the sociologist cannot be satisfied with the ordinary, lay definitions of them. As Durkheim makes clear in each of his major works, the definition of the particular subject-matter to be studied in any given piece of research is a matter of prime importance. *The Division of Labour, Suicide* and *The Elementary Forms* all proceed from such initial definitions. His insistence upon this point again stems from a desire to clearly set off his own position from that of most prior authors. In sociology, there is a particular temptation to adopt popular concepts without subjecting them to critical examination, since the phenomena to which they relate are part of everyday experience. But popular usage is not only shifting and ambiguous; it may be based upon classifications which, from the scientific point of view, are simply erroneous. Thus the correct procedure for the sociologist, when approaching a given area of social reality, is to establish a preliminary conceptualisation which is constructed from 'common external characteristics' possessed by the phenomenon in question.[51] This is Durkheim's stated approach, for instance, in *The Division of Labour*, in setting up a definition of 'crime', which is considered to be any act which has the 'external characteristic' of evoking a punitive reaction from society. 'External', in this context, is not to be directly equated with '*physically* observable', i.e. does not exclude states of consciousness. The sense of Durkheim's discussion on this point makes it fairly clear that he is speaking of characteristics which are observed (in a preliminary way) when different concrete acts or occurrences are examined to decide whether or not they can appropriately be classified together. That is to say, rather than imagining that we can grasp the 'essence' of a given area of social reality by some kind of deductive or introspective procedure, we must seek a conceptualisation from an an initial survey of cases which might plausibly fall within a common class. This method, Durkheim suggests, frequently leads us to reach definitions which differ from those employed in popular language. Thus his definition of 'suicide', as any case of death 'resulting directly or indirectly from a positive or negative act of an individual against himself, which he knows must produce this result',[52] cross-cuts the separation which is often made between 'suicide' and 'self-sacrifice' in conventional usage.[53]

The emphasis that social phenomena must be treated as 'facts in nature' emerges strongly also in Durkheim's discussion of 'externality' as a delimiting characteristic of the 'social' as com-

pared to the 'psychological'. What is true of the scientific observer confronting social reality, Durkheim asserts here – that
social phenomena are not the creations of his own will – is also
true of any given individual member of society. This can be
shown to be so from two, related, aspects. The first is that every
individual is born into an already existing society, which moulds
his own development. The second is that the particular individual
is no more than a single element in a vast system of social relationships. The reality which is thus expressed cannot, therefore, be
understood in terms of the sorts of concepts appropriate to psychology: concepts which refer to the individual consciousness.
But 'externality', thus understood, while it helps distinguish
sociology from psychology, is not a sufficient criterion to delimit
the scope of the subject-matter of sociology, because phenomena
which do not fall directly within its purview, such as geographical
or climatic influences, are external realities in the same sense.
The crucial distinguishing characteristic of social facts is to be
found in their obligatory character. Social facts are modes of
human conduct which are enforced upon the individual member
of a group in virtue of that membership. The type case of such
obligation is moral obligation. Contravention of a moral code
brings into play sanctions against the individual. While he may
flout a moral prescription, its obligatory force makes itself felt by
the effort which this costs him and the consequences which he
suffers. The resistance which is offered when an individual deviates from the prescription is an *index* of its obligatory character.
The actual manifestation of sanctions is not, of course, in any
way a necessary characteristic of any given social act: in most
cases men accept the obligation as legitimate and do not have to
be externally constrained to behave in the appropriate manner.
While Durkheim makes this point in *The Rules*, he does not stress
it, and he later noted that his critics had frequently misunderstood
his position in this respect:

Since we have made constraint the external criterion by
which social facts can be most easily recognised and distinguished from the facts of individual psychology, it has been
assumed that, in our view, physical constraint is essential
to social life. In reality, we have never considered it to be any
more than the material and manifest expression of an internal and deep-rooted phenomenon which is wholly ideal:
this is *moral authority*.[54]

In seeking, then, to draw the boundary between sociology and
psychology, Durkheim does not imply that the former discipline

must eschew any reference to states of consciousness. The point is that social phenomena cannot be studied either by the concepts or with the methods of individual psychology, which looks at the individual as an isolated subject. The data which form the subject-matter of sociology are no more to be regarded as epiphenomena of the individual consciousness than the latter can be regarded as epiphenomena of the nerve-cells of the brain. But society is just as dependent for its existence upon its composite elements, conscious, willing individuals, as mental phenomena are upon the organic structure of the brain. In saying that social facts are 'external' to individuals, Durkheim states, he does not wish to make the 'absurd' assertion that society has some sort of separate physical existence to the individuals who compose it.[55] A combination of units yields new properties which cannot be derived from the study of any one of these units considered in isolation:

> Whenever any elements combine and, by the fact of their combination, produce new phenomena, it is plain that these phenomena are not given in the elements, but in the totality formed by their union. The living cell contains nothing but mineral particles, just as society contains nothing but individuals; it is obviously impossible for the phenomena characteristic of life to exist in the atoms of hydrogen, oxygen, carbon and nitrogen. . .The hardness of bronze is not in the copper, nor in the tin, nor the lead, which served to create it and which are soft and malleable bodies; it is in their mixture. The fluidity of water and its nutritional and other properties are not in the two gases of which it is composed, but in the complex substance which they form by their association.[56]

In interpreting Durkheim's attitude towards psychology, it is evidently important to bear in mind the state of development of that discipline at the time at which he wrote. The sort of 'social psychology' which existed was the 'collective psychology' advanced by some contemporary German thinkers, which in fact, was really an anthropology of culture. Durkheim recognises this in agreeing that, if this is what is meant by 'social psychology', he would have no objection to substituting the latter term for sociology. For the study of collective representations is a principal task of sociology. What did not exist during his lifetime was a social psychology which, while accepting that social organisation possesses its own distinctive attributes, sought to understand the interconnections between society and the individual personality. Psychology embraced two sorts of endeavour: the newly formed discipline of experimental psychology and the old type of speculative, philosophical psychology, based upon unsystematic introspection. While disapproving of the latter, Durkheim accepts the legitimacy and the necessity of a 'positive' science of psychology and even instructs sociologists that they can only gain from becoming acquainted with its major findings. But it is altogether another thing to imagine that the properties of society can be derived from the study of the isolated individual – which is the method followed by both experimental and philosophical psychology. This can easily be demonstrated in the example of the explanation of suicide: while psychology may tell us a great deal about the personality characteristics of the individual suicide, it is powerless to tackle the problems that are posed by the differential patterns of suicide rates which can be discerned between different societies, or between different strata within the same society. The explanation of such phenomena has to be attempted by reference to social factors.[57]

Many of those authors who have called themselves 'sociologists' and have, in principle, accepted the autonomous character of sociology, have in fact frequently slipped into reductive, psychological explanations of social phenomena. Such explanations are usually teleological in form, implying that the existence of a given social institution can be understood in terms of its having been set up in order to satisfy certain psychological needs. Thus religion, for instance, is 'explained' as deriving from the anxieties generated by dreams, or social life itself is 'explained' as the result of an instinct of gregariousness. But such interpretations, even if they can be shown to have some degree of validity as descriptions of psychological states, typically invert the order of causation: 'These sentiments, then, result from collective organisation, far from being its basis.'[58] To avoid such illegitimate teleology, Durkheim insists that functional and causal explanation must be separated. 'Function' must also be carefully distinguished from 'purpose' for the very reason that social phenomena are not normally created for consciously formed purposes; or rather, that the actual social function of a given piece of social conduct may be quite different from the felt motivations of those who participate in it. Functional interpretation, Durkheim makes clear, is basic to sociological method. When we compare different societies, we find that similar functional relationships constantly appear. But he is equally insistent upon the basic significance of causal or historical analysis. Change is ubiquitous in human society; man must be studied in his becoming: 'history is not only the natural framework of human life; man is a product of history. If one separates man from history, if one tries to conceive of him outside time, fixed and immobile, one takes away his nature.'[59] But the sociologist must reject the conception, held by many historians, that history is a unique series of events which allows of no systematic classification. The historical method must be applied in sociology within an evolutionary framework, which recognises that societies can be classified into different types and thus can be grouped at varying levels along a scale. This is not a unilineal scale, but can be conceived like a tree, having numerous branches stemming from a central trunk.[60]

Such a typology of society is essential to the use of the comparative method, which is the primary means of empirical verification in sociology. Comparative assessment of data drawn from a number of societies cannot be validly interpreted if no attention is given to the degree of development of the societies in question; a form of educational institution, for instance, which has a certain function in one type of society may be nothing more than an irrelevant survival in a society of a more developed type. A typology of society is also necessary to be able to distinguish social 'normality' from 'pathology'. The attempt to make such a distinction is one of Durkheim's most persistent concerns throughout his writings, although it has been largely disregarded by subsequent interpreters of his work. In his very earliest writings, Durkheim showed a concern to break through the traditional dilemma of ethics: the apparent dichotomy between what 'is' and what 'ought to be'. Rejecting Kantian dualism, he was nevertheless not prepared to accept the alternative solution of a total philosophy of history, which seemed to him to be incompatible with the sociological perspective. The conception of normality and pathology, conceived on analogy with the notions of health and disease as applied to the biological organism, offered a middle path between these two. While scientific analysis cannot reveal to us any transcendent values, what it can do is to demonstrate what is 'normal' to any given societal type. The main problem underlying *The Division of Labour*, for example, is conceived in these terms: as an attempt to discover whether the ideals of moral individualism are simply aberrant deviations, symptomatic of a pathological social condition, or whether they are genuinely founded in the necessary demands of a new societal type. Durkheim concludes, of course, that the latter is the case: those pathological elements which can be discerned in the contemporary situation originate from the transitional state in which modern society finds itself.

Following his previously stated methodology, Durkheim argues that an initial criterion of normality can be derived from the 'external' characteristic of the degree of 'generality' of the phenomenon in question. In most cases, when first approaching the study of a given social item, it can be assumed that, if that item is found in all, or the majority, of cases belonging to a particular societal type, it is normal to that type. Further analysis may demonstrate, however, that this initial assumption is not in fact justified: the real test of the normality of a social phenomenon is whether or not it is founded in the conditions of existence of the societal type in question. This may be shown by the demonstration that the phenomenon fulfils a specific function. But there are also instances where a normal element in a particular type has no distinguishable function, but is simply 'given' in its structure. This is the case, for example, with the radical physiological side-effects which the process of giving birth has upon the female body. These have no specific function, but are unavoidable in the normal process of parturition.[61] When a type of society is undergoing change, it is common to find that there are phenomena which are generally distributed but which are no longer 'normal', since they are survivals from the previous phase of its development. In periods of transition, only close sociological analysis can demonstrate what properly belongs to the past and what is the emergent form which is preparing the future.

In these terms, Durkheim seeks to apply factual analysis to the resolution of moral and practical dilemmas. In his eyes, this is the most significant contribution which sociology can offer to modern man. As he states several times in his writings, academic research is worthless if it yields no eventual practical outcome. This method makes possible the introduction of rationality into the formulation of practical policy:

Our method has. . .the advantage of regulating action at the same time as thought. If the desirable is not subject to observation but can and must be determined by a sort of mental calculus, no limit, so to speak, can be set for the free inventions of the imagination in search of the good. For how may we assign to perfection a limit? It escapes all limitation, by definition. The goal of humanity recedes into infinity, discouraging some by its very remoteness and, by contrast, arousing others who, in order to draw a little nearer to it, quicken the pace and plunge into revolutions. This practical dilemma may be escaped if the desirable is defined in the same way as is health, and if health is something that is defined as inherent in things. For then the object of our efforts is both given and defined at one stroke. It is no longer a matter of pursuing desperately an objective that retreats as one advances, but of working with steady perseverance to maintain the normal state, of re-establishing it if it is threatened and re-discovering its conditions if they have changed. The duty of the statesman is no longer to violently push society toward an ideal that seems attractive to him, but his role is that of physician: he prevents the outbreak of illnesses by good hygiene and he seeks to cure them when they have appeared.[62]

The use of the criteria of normality and pathology, in other words, places realisable limits upon the anomic boundlessness of aspirations for change. Such a viewpoint inevitably laid Durkheim open to the accusation of favouring an inherent conservatism and critics were not slow to make this charge.[63] He makes two points in answer to such an admonition. The first is that the method sometimes leads to unusually radical conclusions. This is the case, for example, with his conclusion that a certain, specifiable level of crime is a normal condition of functioning of every type of society. The second is that the use of this procedure allows us to help to actually *achieve* change, because it allows us to identify what are the nascent developments which are occurring and shows us what has to be done to foster them. Certainly it is true, he agrees, that this method teaches us that established social forms cannot be changed overnight, by a single stroke. For Durkheim, real social change is evolutionary, not revolutionary: those societies – such as nineteenth-century France itself – which have experienced the greatest number of revolutionary upheavals tend in fact to be stagnant and resistant to change. Rapid political changes mask an underlying stasis. If, however, we can isolate the real forces making for change, we can further their development: and this is precisely what the sociological analysis of emergent trends makes possible.

iv.   *The contemporary interpretation of Durkheim's sociology*

In 1938, introducing his account of Durkheim's work, Alpert remarked that, although Durkheim's writings were well-known in the English-speaking world, they were not known well. Since that date, Durkheim's writings have become even more familiar to sociologists in the United States and in this country, but it is still debatable whether their proper significance has been fully recognised. Two connected sorts of 'interpretation' of Durkheim's writings have dominated the secondary literature. The first, written from a point of view sympathetic to Durkheim, treats his work as primarily a prolonged attempt to deal with the 'problem of order'. The second, which is critical of him, considers his writings as an endeavour to produce an authoritarian theory of moral discipline. These two types of interpretation are actually closely connected, since both treat Durkheim as a writer concerned above all with the origins of *consensus* in society and thus as largely unconcerned with the analysis of change and conflict. But this implies a view of the corpus of Durkheim's writings which is, at best, a highly slanted view of his major interests and his principal conclusions.

Talcott Parsons' discussion of Durkheim's work in his *The Structure of Social Action* is undoubtedly the single most important analysis to appear in English: it has set the tone for most subsequent secondary accounts and has heavily influenced the direction of more specific pieces of research which have taken their theoretical lead from Durkheim – such as the vast literature occupied with the elaboration of the notion of 'anomie'. In seeking to demonstrate the occurrence of a convergence of thought between several leading thinkers of the turn of the twentieth century, Parsons concentrates upon the supposed unfolding of Durkheim's attempts to resolve the 'Hobbesian problem of order': that is, how society avoids the 'war of all against all'. Durkheim's various attacks upon this problem in works written at different stages of his career show, according to Parsons, that 'there is a fundamental change, from one set of sharply formulated ideas to another'.[64] The views set out in *The Division of Labour*, while focussing Durkheim's later writings, represent essentially only a preliminary solution to the problem of order and are fundamentally ambiguous. At this stage he hesitated between holding that the *conscience collective* simply disappears with the transition to organic solidarity and that its content becomes changed.[65] Later, it became increasingly clear to him, according to Parsons, that the second theorem is the valid one and his thought subsequently increasingly devolved upon a concern with what he previously relegated as solely relevant to traditional societies: mechanical solidarity. By this route, he came to appreciate the significance of consensual values as the most important determinant of 'order'. This process of change in Durkheim's thought, in Parsons' view, was accompanied by significant developments on the methodological level. Beginning from a radically positivistic position, implicit in *The Division of Labour* and systematised in *The Rules,* he initially sought to define the subject-matter of sociology by erecting a clear-cut dichotomy between the 'inner' propensities of the individual and the 'external' character of social facts. The category of the 'social' here is merely residual: it shares the 'external' and 'constraining' characteristics of non-social phenomena, such as those of the physical environment, or those of heredity. But Durkheim was forced to abandon this position, at least implicitly, in the light of the analyses developed in *Suicide* and subsequent works. The outcome of these was to show that sociology cannot ignore the subjective perspective of the individual; Durkheim's earlier position involved a confusion between society as 'external' to the flesh-and-blood individuals who compose it (a completely untenable notion if pushed to its logical conclusion: that society is in some way physically distinct from its component individuals) and the (valid) supposition that the properties of social organisation are *analytically* separable from those of the individual personality.

Parsons' account remains the most penetrating analysis of Durkheim's writings which has yet been made. But it contains several major deficiencies and misrepresentations – some of which have only become fully apparent with the publication of a number of key works by Durkheim of which only fragments were available when *The Structure of Social Action* was written (including, principally, *Leçons de sociologie*). In the first place, it ignores the political and more general social background to Durkheim's writings. Durkheim did not ever play a very direct role in the politics of his time in the way in which, for example, Max Weber did; but it is hardly possible to understand adequately the nature of his concerns in his sociological writings without relating them to the concrete problems of his day, as he perceived them. To ignore these might be defensible in a work concerned purely with intellectual analysis: but it is not acceptable when the professed objective of the account is to examine the changing character of Durkheim's writings during the latter's lifetime. The direction of Durkheim's evolving interests was by no means dictated by purely intellectual dilemmas, but was significantly affected by external social and political changes.[66] In this respect, *The Structure of Social Action* must be subjected to its own critique. One of the principal themes of the work is that positivism – conceived as 'the doctrine that positive science is man's sole significant cognitive relation to external reality'[67] –

cannot provide a satisfactory framework for social theory. But *The Structure of Social Action* itself proceeds just as if the intellectual developments it analyses were the result of purely 'scientific' problems which each thinker struggled with in the evolution of his thought.

This is directly connected with a serious flaw of omission in Parsons' account: that it almost completely ignores Durkheim's discussion of the 'forced division of labour'. Although the true significance of this discussion is perhaps only completely elucidated in *Leçons de sociologie*, the theme is clearly stated in *The Division of Labour*. It is not enough to say that this is simply dismissed by Durkheim as an 'abnormal form' of the division of labour: as he recognises, the abolition of the forced division of labour demands a major process of institutional reorganisation – later detailed as centring upon the interrelationship between the state and occupational associations. Parsons' interpretation places almost the whole weight of his analysis away from Durkheim's theory of institutions; yet the latter once described sociology as the science of institutions and their functioning. The nature of the *institutional* change from mechanical to organic solidarity is a basic problem in his writings. This must be emphasised, even though it is certainly true that, as regards his own personal work, he sought to concentrate his efforts primarily in the area of the 'science of morality'.

Parsons' concentration upon the presumed changes occurring in Durkheim's work inevitably tends to minimise the significance of *The Division of Labour* as providing a general framework within which the rest of the latter's writings may be set. The book is treated mainly as representative of a passing phase in Durkheim's thought, rather than as being the outline of a scheme which is basic to the whole of his life's activity. The result is that Durkheim's consistent emphasis upon development is left aside almost completely and his work is portrayed as an a-historical quest to come to grips with the 'problem of order'. But far from the 'problem of order' having been 'Durkheim's central problem from an early stage',[68] it can perfectly well be said that it was not a problem for Durkheim at all. The central issue informing his writings was that of change: in common with virtually all the other major social thinkers of his generation he was preoccupied above all with the confrontation between the dissolving 'traditional' society and the emergent 'modern' type. It is quite true that, if one looks to the social background to his writings, the disastrous defeat in the Franco-Prussian war and the subsequent exhibitions of barbarism involved in the repression of the Commune, which created an indelible impression upon the French bourgeois consciousness, profoundly influenced Durkheim's intellectual outlook; and he accepted the need for the consolidation and reunification of the country. But, in common with his liberal contemporaries, he also saw in this situation the possibility, even the necessity, of achieving real social change. The earlier part of the nineteenth century, in his assessment, in spite of having been disturbed by political turmoil, had brought little significant structural change in French society. The task at hand, therefore, was that of promoting the concrete social changes which would actualise the ideals which were formed, but not implemented, in the 1789 Revolution. On the intellectual level, this is manifest in the prominence which is given in Durkheim's writings to the nature of moral individualism and its relationship to the institutional structure of organic solidarity.

By abstractly contrasting moral consensus (the existence of 'common values') with anomie (the dearth of such values), Parsons' account blankets out Durkheim's overriding concern with the distinctions between the moral and institutional structure of the modern social order and that found in traditional forms. The problem of anomie cannot be separated from the effects of the transformation of the division of labour, as Durkheim assesses them. The polarity is not primarily between the existence of moral consensus and its absence, but between the rigid moral conformity of the traditional *conscience collective* and the looser, more institutionally complex, structure of organic solidarity – together with the fact that contemporary societies are still in a transitional phase. Moreover, Durkheim specifically calls into question the meaningfulness of the 'Hobbesian problem' in the sense in which Hobbes himself posed it. For Hobbes (as for Rousseau) 'there is a break in continuity between the individual and society. Man is thus naturally refractory to social life; he can only resign himself to it when forced'.[69] Such a conception, Durkheim says, has to be rejected as simply involving an untenable starting-point for social theory. This is a view which is already stated in *The Rules*: Durkheim insists here that what he means by 'obligation' or 'constraint' is not an 'external force', as is the case with Hobbes and Rousseau in their theories of the relationship between the state and civil society. For Durkheim, this 'obligation' is at the same time 'spontaneous' and subjectively acceded to, at least in the vast majority of circumstances, by the individuals who submit to it. In the light of this it is difficult to accept Parsons' charac-

terisation of the crudely positivistic position which he holds
Durkheim to adopt in *The Rules*. Parsons interprets the object of
Durkheim's polemic in that work as being utilitarian individualism
alone, whereas in fact, as in the case of *The Division of Labour*,
Durkheim is concerned to counterpose his own viewpoint both
to utilitarianism and to holistic idealism, the latter being the
conception which treats 'social life as the logical development of
ideal concepts'.[70] Although it can hardly be maintained that
Durkheim's formulation of the nature of social phenomena in
The Rules is satisfactory, it is nevertheless considerably less naïve
than Parsons' account would suggest.

In rejecting the label of 'positivist' (although his understanding
of this term is rather different from Parsons' usage), in *The Rules*
Durkheim explicitly affirms that his objective is to synthesise and
thereby to transcend utilitarianism and idealism, without relapsing
into any sort of materialistic standpoint. Thus the 'external' and
'obligatory' character of social facts is stressed as against both of
these schools of thought. But what distinguishes social phenomena
from other 'external' phenomena, as Durkheim recognises from
the beginning, is the 'ideal' or 'spiritual' character of the former:
'Is not the essence of idealism contained in the idea that psychological phenomena cannot be directly derived from organic
phenomena?'[71] Moreover, in some of his earliest writings, published prior even to *The Division of Labour*,[72] Durkheim makes
clear that the properties of the 'social' are emergent characteristics:
in other words, are created by the organisation of individuals in
society and necessarily have their 'substratum' in the individual
consciousness. Finally, it should be pointed out that the analysis
given of the relationship between individuation and moral individualism set out in *The Division of Labour* gives a concrete
illustration of the fact that in Durkheim's writings 'obligation'
or 'constraint' are not to be identified sheerly with 'restriction'
or 'denial': that is, are not to be interpreted as simply placing
limits upon a range of potential individual actions in a given
situation. It is the development of moral individualism (given
the institutional infrastructure of organic solidarity) which makes
possible the freedoms of thought and action associated with
increasing individuation. 'Obligation', in other words, as a moral
phenomenon not only sets 'boundaries' to human action, but also
shapes and propels it. This is the sense of Durkheim's assertion
that 'obligation' and 'spontaneity' are not opposites, but are fused
together in human conduct.

Although Parsons' account of Durkheim's work in *The Structure of Social Action* is basically a favourable one, those more recent interpretations which have taken a strongly critical stance towards Durkheim's sociology have leaned heavily upon premises similar to those adopted by Parsons. Some examples in the recent literature are the works by Horton and Zeitlin,[73] but perhaps the most penetrating is that of Coser.[74] According to Coser, Durkheim's intellectual background is steeped in 'conservative' thought: 'his whole contribution to theory was itself a result of his concern as a conservative with the conditions of the French society of his time. The problem of order preoccupied Durkheim from his earliest writings to the last pages of the *Introduction à la morale*, a paper he wrote shortly before his death'.[75] The distinctive feature of conservative thought, Coser states, is the belief that man is naturally antipathetic to society and thus that he must be constrained to accept it by some kind of repressive force. This 'pessimistic' view of human nature can be contrasted with a contrasting 'liberal or radical' standpoint which holds to the perfectibility of man through social change. The theory of anomie, in Coser's view, links Durkheim definitely with the 'pessimistic' conception: true morality consists in renunciation of desire. This is exactly analogous to the position underlying the ideas of Freud; the imperious demands of the id must be strictly controlled by the super-ego for society to be possible. Since Durkheim was so convinced of the need for repressive discipline, he failed to consider whether there might not be differing degrees of repression in different forms of society. Durkheim's 'conservative' emphasis, Coser seeks to show, is nowhere more clearly reflected than in his sociology of education, where he holds that the teacher should be a strict disciplinarian and should exert complete control over the conduct of his pupils; Durkheim was utterly opposed to any sort of education which attempts to develop the individual propensities of the child or which allows him any degree of free initiative in the schoolroom. From this conception flow a group of other fundamental weaknesses in Durkheim's work: that he sees society only as a 'whole', neglecting sub-groups within it; that he ignores the role of political power; that he is blind to the fact of social conflict; and that he treats the 'social question' (i.e., the problem of class conflict) not in relation to the differential distribution of wealth or property, but purely as a moral issue, as a matter of curbing the appetites of the lower strata of society.

Many secondary writers have, like Coser, drawn a comparison between Durkheim's sociology and Freud's theory of culture. The comparison is, in fact, in very large degree, quite misleading.

Whereas for Freud the need for repression of individual drives increases with the growth of civilisation, according to Durkheim – in an important sense, at least – the reverse is the case. It is simply untrue to hold, as Coser does, that Durkheim was unable to perceive that there are varying degrees of 'repression' in different types of society. Far from denying this proposition, Durkheim makes it the very cornerstone of his theory. Quite in contrast to Freud, it is the very progression of societal development which makes possible the extension of the range of human freedoms. In traditional society, there is only a minimal degree of individuation and the individual is subject to the tyranny of the *conscience collective*. The key to Durkheim's whole life's work is to be found in his attempt to resolve the apparent paradox that the liberty of the individual is only achieved through his dependence upon society. It is mistaken to identify Freud's 'repression' with Durkheim's 'obligation', for this reason.

Durkheim's analysis of education in reality demonstrates this very clearly. As with other parts of his work, this has to be placed in an historical context: one which is sketched out in considerable detail in *L'évolution pédagogique en France*.[76] Systems of education are dependent upon the nature of the broader society of which they form part; consequently, they become changed as society changes. Modern education, therefore, cannot be founded upon the same sort of discipline as that of prior ages. Of course, since he rejects the conception that moral conduct can spring solely from the wants or desires of the individual, Durkheim also discounts the view that the impetus to education can emerge from the wants or desires of the child. The teacher must hold a morally superior position to the child and in fact function as society's representative. But, just as in history, individual freedoms are created by society, so a similar process can and should operate in the development of the individual child. Modern education thus must be responsive to the ideals of moral individualism: 'once the individual personality has become an essential element of the intellectual and moral culture of humanity, the educator should take into account the germ of individuality that is in each child'.[77] This entails that educational practice should become rational: that is, informed by pedagogical theory which is grounded in sociology and psychology. For the educational environment today can no longer be bound to inflexible rules, because it has to be adapted to a society which is rapidly changing and which constantly generates new ideas and needs.

Coser's interpretation follows that of Parsons in failing to connect Durkheim's theory of anomie to his conception of the social changes which must accompany the development of moral individualism. It is significant that Parsons holds that, in terms of his distinction between 'communism' and 'socialism', Durkheim himself belongs to the first rather than to the second category and Coser states bluntly that 'Durkheim always rejected socialism. . .'[78] Each of these propositions is quite clearly mistaken. Certainly, for Durkheim, communism correctly asserts that social life necessarily must involve the curtailment of egoism; but communism is an imaginative fiction rather than a realistic programme for the alleviation of the practical problems faced by contemporary society. Socialism, by contrast, is born out of the social conditions generated by the transition from mechanical to organic solidarity. While the socialist thinkers fail to perceive that the programme for social reform cannot be purely economic, they do understand that there must be a profound reorganisation of society as a consequence of the decline of the traditional order. It is true that Durkheim never formally aligned himself with a socialist party, or indeed with any political party. Moreover, he rejected every type of revolutionary thought and derided the claims of Marxists to have founded a 'scientific socialism'. But he accepted what he took to be the basic premises of all forms of socialism, whether reformist or revolutionary: that regulation of industry is necessary to overcome the dislocations caused by the present conditions of economic production; and that this is inseparably linked to the demands of the underprivileged for greater justice in the distribution of economic rewards. The moral consolidation of the differentiated division of labour cannot be achieved without the occurrence of changes which conform to these two principles of socialism.

In Durkheim's view, this entails an extension of the role of the state: the state cannot 'disappear', as is envisaged in socialism, through the merging of the 'political' and the 'economic'. But civil society is not to be subordinated to the state. Again, in the light of his discussion of this matter, it is hardly justified to argue that Durkheim gives no concern to the analysis of political power, or that he ignores the conflicts which can stem from the distribution of divergent interests among sub-groups within society as a whole. In *The Division of Labour*, Durkheim treats political power as directly dependent upon the degree of development of the division of labour: despotism is a product of relatively undeveloped forms of society. Despotism is simply a 'transformed communism';[79] the autocratic ruler embodies in his person the moral dominance of the *conscience collective* and thus the repressive sanctions which are called into play for deviation from its dictates appear as political sanctions wielded by the autocrat. But those who regard his control over these sanctions as the *source* of his power, Durkheim argues, are in error. His power derives from the fact that he is the personification of the moral authority of the *conscience collective*: it is not his power which creates the form of the society which he dominates, but the society which creates that power. The appearance of despotism in the relatively early stages of development of society, according to Durkheim, is in fact not contrary to the thesis that the growth of the division of labour leads to the progressive expansion of moral individualism. The emergence of despotism is rather to be regarded as an initial stage in the formation of individualism. The ruler, in subjecting others to his authority, is himself partially freed from subjection to the dictates of the collective morality of the community: 'A source of initiative is thus opened up which did not previously exist. There is thereafter someone who can create new phenomena and even, to some degree, depart from collective customs. Equilibrium has been broken.'[80]

In *The Division of Labour*, however, Durkheim argues that this autocratic power then declines progressively with the further growth of the individualising tendencies of the division of labour which it helps to promote. Although the sphere of the state grows with the advancing complexity of society, autocratic forms of political domination disappear. He later came to see this view as too simple and, without abandoning the suppositions underlying it, modified it to account for the fact that the degree of centralisation of political power may vary, in certain measure, independently of the degree of complexity of society.[81] The formation of autocratic political power is not merely a reflection of the *conscience collective* and therefore only a primitive phenomenon but, in more developed societies, tends to come into being whereever there are not secondary groups in society whose authority can counterbalance that of the state. Hence the importance of the political role of the occupational associations, as a counterweight to the domination of the state.

According to Durkheim's account of social development, change tends to occur progressively: not through radical social revolution, but through slow accretion. But this does not happen without conflict, as he explicitly stresses; nor does he condemn all such conflict as 'pathological'. Thus, in criticising Montesquieu's conception of social development, he notes that Montesquieu 'fails to see that every society embodies conflicting factors, because it has gradually emerged from a past form and is tending toward a future one'.[82] Such conflict is a necessary condition of social change and is the more extreme to the degree to which a radical reorganisation of a given type of society is taking place. Those who are in the vanguard of such a confrontation with an established order are normally branded as 'criminals' by the latter; but, in attacking the existing order, they are in fact the harbingers of newly developing social forms. This is not, however, true of all conflict: particularly in major periods of transition, there tend to occur conflicts and dissensions which are symptomatic of the need for social change, but which do not themselves directly contribute to it. This is the case with class conflict in contemporary society. Class conflict certainly stems from the transformations which have already taken place in social and economic life. Moreover, class struggles also give some indication of necessary changes which must take place as regards the sectional interests of the groupings involved: that the power of inherited property must be abolished and the barrier to free mobility between the classes removed. But class conflict is definitely not, as is claimed in revolutionary socialism, the vehicle whereby the necessary social reorganisation can be attained; rather than promoting the required social and moral restructuring of industry, class conflict inhibits the chances of its occurrence.

The 'orthodox' interpretation of Durkheim, such as advanced by Parsons from the sympathetic side, and by Coser from the critical standpoint, thus largely ignores basic aspects of Durkheim's writings and misconstrues other parts. As filtered through Parsons' works, this interpretation has formed one major strand built into the theoretical parameters established by 'structural-functionalism', which has dominated sociology for the past two or three decades. Those who have mounted a critique of structural-functionalism, in opposing 'consensus theory' by 'conflict theory', have implicitly accepted the same interpretation. The debate has been a sterile one and it is increasingly apparent that social theory must move in a new direction. This in turn demands a reappraisal of the leading themes in the writings of those thinkers who established the main theoretical and conceptual foundations of modern sociology at the turn of this century. Durkheim must certainly rank among the foremost of these.

REFERENCES (where page references alone are given, these refer to parts of the present book)

1 From a letter to Davy, quoted in Georges Davy: 'Emile Durkheim', *Revue française de sociologie*, vol. I, Jan.–March, 1960, p. 10.
2 For a more extended discussion of Durkheim's early writings, see my 'Durkheim as a review critic', *Sociological Review*, vol. 18, 1970, pp. 171–196; and *Capitalism and Modern Social Theory*. Cambridge, 1971, pp. 65–71.
3 'La science positive de la morale en Allemagne', RP, vol. 24, 1887, part I, p. 38.
4 'La sociologie en France au xixe siècle', *Revue bleue*, vol. 13, 1900, part 2, p. 648.
5 DTS, p. xxxvii.
6 See pp. 90–2.
7 See pp. 146–7.
8 Pp. 146–7.
9 Pp. 138–9.
10 DTS, p. 143.
11 The context in which Durkheim discusses Tönnies' typology, in his review of *Gemeinschaft und Gesellschaft*, indicates fairly clearly that Durkheim chose to contrast 'mechanical' with 'organic' solidarity in part to deliberately separate himself from Tönnies' distinction. Tönnies, according to Durkheim, does tend to imply that, whereas in *Gemeinschaft* solidarity is 'organic', meaning 'spontaneous', in *Gesellschaft* it is 'produced mechanically', that is, 'artificially', by the 'external action of the state' (p. 146).
12 Durkheim refined his thinking on this matter subsequent to the publication of *The Division of Labour*. See pp. 128–35.
13 Several of the leading secondary accounts of Durkheim's work fail to see the basic significance of this proposition. cf. my article 'Durkheim's political sociology', *Sociological Review*, vol. 19, 1971.
14 DTS, p. 381.
15 *Ibid.* p. 380.
16 *Ibid.* p. 147.
17 Pp. 153–4.
18 See pp. 135–7.
19 DTS, p. 344.
20 DTS, p. 378.
21 P. 182.
22 See 'Durkheim's political sociology', *loc. cit.*

23 Subsequently published in 1928. (In English as *Socialism and Saint-Simon*. Ohio, 1958.)
24 'L'individualisme et les intellectuels', *Revue bleue*, vol. 10, 1898, pp. 7–13. A full translation appears in Steven Lukes: 'Durkheim's "Individualism and the Intellectuals"', *Political Studies*, vol. 17, 1969, pp. 19–30.
25 Soc., p. 74.
26 P. 169.
27 'Suicide et natalité, étude de statistique morale', *RP*, vol. 26, 1888, pp. 446–7.
28 DL, p. 238.
29 P. 176 and Soc., pp. 239–40.
30 See *Capitalism and Modern Social Theory*, pp. 224–32.
31 DTS, p. 206.
32 LS, p. 73.
33 See pp. 194–5.
34 P. 200.
35 P. 202.
36 See 'Durkheim's political sociology', *loc. cit.*
37 P. 199.
38 LS, pp. 109–11.
39 *Ibid.* p. 72.
40 See pp. 239–40.
41 'L'individualisme et les intellectuels', p. 11.
42 *Ibid.* p. 9.
43 *Ibid.* p. 11.
44 See pp. 264–6.
45 SP, p. 55.
46 P. 115.
47 SP, p. 79.
48 See, for example, pp. 51–63.
49 P. 53.
50 P. 63.
51 RMS, p. 45.
52 Su, p. 5.
53 Halbwachs later claimed that such a distinction should, in fact, be upheld. Maurice Halbwachs, *Les causes du suicide*. Paris, 1930, pp. 451–80.
54 FE, p. 298.
55 Su, p. 320.
56 Pp. 69.
57 Durkheim's *Suicide*, on its first appearance, sparked off a prolonged controversy in French sociology. See my 'The suicide problem in French sociology', in Anthony Giddens (ed.), *The Sociology of Suicide*. London, 1971.

58   RMS, p. 132.
59   'Introduction à la morale', RP, vol. 89, 1920, p. 89.
60   P. 129.
61   P. 104.
62   P. 105.
63   See, for example, pp. 44–8.
64   Talcott Parsons, *The Structure of Social Action*. Glencoe, 1949, p. 304.
65   For a similar analysis, see Robert A. Nisbet, *Emile Durkheim*. Englewood Cliffs, 1965, p. 37 and *passim*.
66   See 'Durkheim's political sociology', *loc. cit.*
67   Parsons, *op. cit.* p. 421.
68   *Ibid.* p. 307.
69   P. 99.
70   RMS, p. vii.
71   *Ibid.*
72   See 'Durkheim as a review critic', *loc. cit.* pp. 173–8.
73   John Horton, 'The de-humanisation of anomie and alienation', *British Journal of Sociology*, vol. 15, 1964, pp. 283–300; Irving M. Zeitlin, *Ideology and the Development of Sociological Theory*. Englewood Cliffs, 1968.
74   Lewis A. Coser, 'Durkheim's conservatism and its implications for his sociological theory', in Kurt H. Wolff, 'Emile Durkheim *et al.*', *Essays on Sociology and Philosophy*. New York, 1960, pp. 211–32. See also the earlier essay, by Robert A. Nisbet, 'Conservatism and sociology', *American Journal of Sociology*, vol. 58, 1952, pp. 165–75.
75   Coser, *op. cit.* p. 213.
76   See pp. 205–15.
77   ES, p. 105.
78   Coser, *op. cit.* p. 216.
79   DTS, p. 173.
80   *Ibid.* p. 172.
81   See pp. 193–4.
82   MR, p. 107.

1. The field of sociology

A science which has only just come into existence necessarily has at the outset only an uncertain and ill-defined sense of the area of reality that it is about to approach, of its extent and its limits. It can gain a clearer picture only to the degree that it acquires a procedure to guide its research; and the heightened awareness of its subject matter that it obtains in this way is of the greatest importance. For the task of the scientist is the more secure the more orderly it becomes; and the more methodical it is, the more accurate is the account that he can render of the territory he is penetrating.

Sociology has reached the stage at which it is opportune to make every effort to bring about such an advance. If some reactionary critics, inadvertently influenced by the prejudice which always hinders the formation of a new science, reproach sociology for not knowing the precise subject-matter with which it intends to deal, they can be told that such ignorance is inevitable in the early phases of research, and that our science came into being only very recently. It must not be forgotten, especially in view of the popularity of sociology today, that fifteen years ago it would scarcely have been possible to enumerate as many as ten individuals who could, properly speaking, be called 'sociologists'. We must add to this that it is asking too much of a science to define its subject-matter with excessive precision, for the part of reality that it intends to study is never precisely separated from others. In fact, in nature everything is so closely interconnected that there can be neither a complete division, nor too precise boundaries, between the various sciences. Nevertheless, it is important that we should obtain as clear an idea as possible of what constitutes the domain of sociology, where this domain is to be found, and what indices allow us to recognise the complex of phenomena with which we must deal. However, we must refrain from establishing boundaries in those areas which are necessarily indeterminate. This problem is all the more urgent for our science, because unless we are careful, its province may become infinitely extended: for there is no phenomenon – from physicochemical ones to properly social facts – which does not take place *in* society. Thus we must accurately distinguish social facts, and show what it is that gives them their identity, if we are to avoid reducing sociology to nothing but a conventional label applied to an incoherent collection of disparate disciplines.

RIS, 1900, pp. 127–8

Whether he proceeds by deduction or by induction, Montesquieu follows a methodological rule that modern science must not overlook.

Social phenomena are usually classified according to considerations which might appear at first sight to be wholly unconnected. Religion, law, morality, trade, and administration seem, indeed, to differ in nature. This explains why each class of phenomena was for a long time treated separately – and sometimes still is: as though it could be examined and explained by itself, without reference to the others, just as physicists do not take colour into consideration when dealing with weight. It is not denied that one class of phenomena is related to the others; but the relationships are regarded as merely incidental, so that, as the inner nature of the phenomena cannot be ascertained, it seems safe to disregard the relations between them. For example, most moralists deal with morality and rules of conduct as though they existed in isolation, and do not bother to consider the economic character of the societies in question. Those who deal with the subject of wealth maintain, in a similar way, that their science, namely political economy, is completely autonomous and can be carried on without paying any attention to the system of rules that we call morality. One could give many such examples.

Montesquieu, however, saw quite clearly that all these elements form a whole and that if each is considered separately, without reference to the others, they cannot be understood. He does not separate law from morality, trade, religion, etc., and above all he does not detach them from the form of society, which affects all other social phenomena. However widely they differ, all of these phenomena express the life of a given society. They are the elements or organs of the social organism. Unless we try to understand how they harmonise and interact, it is impossible to know their functions. We shall fail even to identify their nature, for they will seem to be distinct realities, each with its independent existence; whereas they are actually parts of a whole. This attitude accounts for certain errors that are still made by many authors. It explains why many political economists have regarded personal interest as the only principle of society and why they have denied that the legislator has the right to intervene in activities related to trade and industry. Conversely, though for the same reason, moralists have generally regarded property rights as fixed and immutable, whereas they actually depend upon extremely varied and changing economic factors.

This error had to be dispelled before social science could develop or even come into existence. The various disciplines dealing separately with different forms of social phenomena did indeed prepare the way for social science; it was from them that it originated. But social science, in the strict sense, came into being only when it was clearly perceived that the branches mentioned above were bound together by strict necessity and were parts of a whole. Such a conception, however, could not arise until it was realised that all events in society are related. In pointing to the interrelatedness of social phenomena, Montesquieu foreshadowed the unity of our science – although his view of the matter was still confused. Nowhere does he say that the problems he deals with might form the subject-matter of a definite science, embracing all social phenomena and having a method and a name of its own. And yet, without being aware of the implication of his efforts, he gave posterity the first sample of such a science. Although he did not consciously draw the conclusions implicit in his principles, he paved the way for his successors who, in instituting sociology, did little more than give a name to the field of study which he inaugurated.

MR, pp. 102–5

. . .sociology could only become conscious of itself within philosophical thought, far from the specialised disciplines and their influence. Even this characteristic depended upon causes of too profound a nature for it to have lost all *raison d'être* by the time at which the first beginnings of organisation of the science appeared. This is why we should not be surprised to meet with it in Comte's immediate successor, Spencer. It is obvious that Spencer wrote sociology as a philosopher, because he set out, not to study social facts in themselves and for themselves, but to show how the evolutionary hypothesis can be verified in the social realm. But, by that very token, he found himself in a position to complete or to correct the general conceptions of Comtean sociology upon important points. Although Comte had definitely integrated societies in nature, the exaggerated intellectualism which permeated his doctrine accorded poorly with this rule, which is fundamental to all sociology. If scientific evolution determines political, economic, moral and aesthetic evolution, there is a great distance between sociological explanation, and that which is applied in the other natural sciences, and it is difficult to avoid slipping into ideology. In showing that, in different forms, a single law dominates the social and the physical world, Spencer linked societies more directly with the rest of the universe. He made us aware that, below the phenomena which occur on the surface of the *conscience collective,* and which express the products of deliberated thought, there operate obscure forces which do not move men through the sort of logical necessity which connect the successive phases of scientific development to one-another. From another aspect, Comte did not accept that there were a diversity of social types. According to him there existed only one society, human association in its entirety; and particular states represented only different moments in the history of this single society. Sociology thus found itself in a situation unique among the sciences since it had as its object an entity which was the only one of its type. Spencer cleared up this anomaly by showing that societies, like organisms, can be classed into forms and types and, whatever the value of the classification which he offered, the principle, at least, deserved to be maintained and has survived. Although they were formulated philosophically, these two reforms hence constituted invaluable acquisitions for the science.

But if this mode of conceiving and of doing sociology was certainly, at a given moment, necessary and useful, this necessity and usefulness was only temporary. In order to come into being, and even to make progress initially, sociology needed to lean upon philosophy; but in order to really become itself, it was absolutely necessary for it to assume another character.

The very example of Comte himself can serve to prove this: for, because of its philosophical character, the sociology which he constructed did not at all satisfy the conditions which he himself demanded of every positive science.

In fact, of the two parts of the science which he distinguished, statics and dynamics, he really only treated the second. Moreover, from his point of view, this was the more important, since if there were, according to him, social facts distinct from purely individual phenomena, this is above all because there is a progressive evolution of humanity; that is to say because the work of each generation survives it, and comes to be joined to that of the generations which follow it. Progress is the social fact *par excellence*. Now social dynamics, in his exposition, shows none of 'that continuity and that fruitfulness' which, according to Comte's own remark, constitute 'the most definite criteria of all truly scientific conceptions': for Comte himself considered it to be virtually completed by his own work. Indeed, it is contained entirely in the law of the three stages, and, once this law has been discovered, one cannot see how it would be possible to add to it, to extend it and, even less, what different laws could be discovered. Hardly having been founded, the science would already be closed. In fact, those of Comte's disciples who were strictly attached to the content of the doctrine were able to do nothing more than to reproduce the propositions of the master, sometimes illustrating them by new examples, but without these purely formal variations ever having constituted real discoveries. This is what explains the lack of development of the properly Comtist school after Comte; the same formulas were ritually repeated without any progress being realised. The fact is that a science cannot live and develop when it is reduced to a single and unique problem upon which a great mind now and then makes its mark. In order for it to progress, it must be resolved into a progressively expanding number of special questions, in such a way as to make possible the co-operation of different minds and of successive generations. It is only on this condition that it will acquire the collective and impersonal character without which there is no scientific research. Now the philosophical and unitary conception which Comte made of sociology is opposed to this division of labour. Moreover, his social dynamics is at bottom only a philosophy of history, remarkable for its novelty and profundity, but not different in type from that of previous philosophies. It is a matter of perceiving the law which governs 'the necessary and continuous movement of humanity', and which alone makes it possible to introduce into the succession of historical events the unity and continuity which they lack.

RP, 1903, pp. 469–71

There still exist a number of thinkers who do not believe in the future of sociology. Their favourite argument is that they do not perceive that it has any clear objective, divisions, or programme. They mistrust a science which is announced to the world as a newcomer without historical antecedent. And in this they are quite right – if it were really true, as has sometimes been said, that sociology dated from Auguste Comte. If it was born out of nothing, at that instant, we would share this justifiable mistrust. Revolutions and immediate creations no more exist in the world of science than they do in the world of things. Every being which is born capable of life is the product of a long evolution. But it is an illusion to believe that sociology dates from yesterday and is the fruit of brilliant improvisation. It existed at all times, in a latent and diffuse state. The great service which was rendered by Comte and his school was simply to show the unity of these apparently incoherent researches, to give to social science a name and an individuality, and to integrate it within the system of positive sciences. At all times, economic phenomena, the state, law, morality and religion have been studied scientifically, thus giving birth to five sciences which can rightly be called sociological.

However, it is necessary for them to remain worthy of this designation, which all too frequently they forget. Social science, states Maurice Block, 'only sees *men*, in abstraction from that external tie which is called the state'. In other words, so-called 'social' science should study men by supposing that they do not live in society. It would be better, in fact, to give it another name. We are told that state and society are two different things. Yes, but on one condition: that the state is seen as a wholly external tie, an artificial system which is superimposed upon society, but does not derive from it. This is the simplistic conception of Rousseau, which the economic school stubbornly adhere to, even after a century of experience which has hardly been favourable to the theory of the *Social Contract*. Things are far more complex. A society is not a collection of individuals which an enormous and monstrous machine keeps united and compressed against each other by the use of force. No, solidarity comes from the inside and not from the outside. Men are attached to one another as naturally as the atoms of a mineral and the cells of an organism. The affinity which they hold for each other is based upon sympathy, a feeling the germs of which can be discerned in animal societies; this expands, diversifies, and becomes transformed with progress, but it is no less natural to man than egoism, to which, in the interests of simplicity, the economists would reduce the human mind. Now, at each moment in its development, this solidarity is expressed externally by an appropriate structure. The state is one of these structures. The state is the external and visible form of sociability. To abstract from it is thus certainly, as we have said, to suppose that men do not live in societies. It is to take as an axiom that there is not and cannot be more than external contacts and transient relationships between men, determined by the necesarily fortuitous connections of interest. It might be objected that abstraction is a legitimate procedure of science. Certainly. But to abstract is to take out of reality a part which one isolates: it is not to create a mental construction out of nothing. Now, the man and society which are conceived of by the economists are purely imaginary, and correspond to nothing in reality. The sociologist will therefore consider economic facts, the state, morality, law and religion as so many functions of the social organism, and will study them as phenomena which occur in the context of a definite, bounded society. From this point of view, things immediately take on a different aspect. By the same token, as we have already seen, political economy loses its autonomy, because one cannot study one social function wholly in isolation from others.

RP, 1886, pp. 78–9

SOCIAL AND NATURAL PHENOMENA

A discipline may be called a 'science' only if it has a definite field to explore. Science is concerned with things, realities. If it does not have a datum to describe and interpret, it exists in a vacuum. Separated from the description and interpretation of reality it can have no real function. Arithmetic is concerned with numbers, geometry with space and figures, the natural sciences with animate and inanimate bodies, and psychology with the human mind. Before social science could begin to exist, it had first of all to be assigned a definite subject-matter.

At first sight, this problem presents no difficulty: the subject-matter of social science is social things: that is, laws, customs, religions, etc. Looking back in history, however, we find that no philosophers ever viewed matters in this way until quite recently. They thought that all such phenomena depended upon the human will and consequently failed to realise that they are actual things, like all other things in nature; they have their own specific properties, and these call for sciences which can describe and explain them. It seemed to them sufficient to ascertain what the human will should strive for and what it should avoid in established societies. Hence what they strove to discover was not the nature and origin of social phenomena, not what they actually are, but what they ought to be; their aim was not to offer us as valid a description of nature as possible, but to present us with the idea of a perfect society, a model to be imitated. Even Aristotle, who was far more concerned with empirical observation than Plato was, aimed at discovering, not the laws of social existence, but the best form of society. He begins by assuming that the sole objective of society should be to make its members happy through the practice of virtue, and that virtue lies in contemplation. He does not establish this principle as a law which societies actually follow, but as one which they should act upon in order that human beings may fulfil their specific nature. Certainly he does turn later to historical facts, but with little purpose other than to pass judgement upon them, and to show how his own principles could be adapted to various situations. The political thinkers who came after him on the whole followed his example. Whether they wholly disregard reality or pay a certain amount of attention to it, they all have a single purpose: to correct or transform it completely, rather than to know it. They take virtually no interest in the past and the present, but look to the future.

MR, pp. 29–31

The proposition according to which social facts are to be treated as things – which is the very foundation of our method – is one which has stimulated great opposition. It has been considered paradoxical and scandalous for us to assimilate the realities of the social world to those of the external world. Such criticism involves a singular misunderstanding of the meaning and application of this assimilation: the object of this was not to reduce the higher to the lower forms of being, but on the contrary to claim for the higher forms a degree of reality at least equal to that which is readily granted to the lower. We do not say that social facts are material things, but that they are things by the same right as material things, although they differ from them in type.

Just what is a 'thing'? A thing differs from an idea in the same way as that which we know from without differs from that which we know from within. A thing is any object of knowledge which is not naturally controlled by the intellect, which cannot be adequately grasped by a simple process of mental activity. It can only be understood by the mind on condition that the mind goes outside itself by means of observations and experiments, which move progressively from the more external and immediately accessible characteristics to the less visible and more deep-lying. To treat the facts of a certain order as things thus is not to place them in a particular category of reality, but to assume a certain mental attitude toward them; it is to approach the study of them on the principle that we are absolutely ignorant of their nature, and that their characteristic properties, like the unknown causes on which they depend, cannot be discovered by even the most careful introspection.

With the terms thus defined, our proposition, far from being a paradox, could almost pass for a truism if it were not too often misunderstood in the human sciences and especially in sociology. Indeed, one might say in this sense that, with the possible exception of the case of mathematics, every object of science is a thing. In mathematics, since we proceed from simple to more complex concepts it is sufficient to depend upon mental processes which are purely internal in character. But in the case of 'facts' properly so called, these are, at the moment when we undertake to study them scientifically, necessarily unknown *things* of which we are ignorant; for the representations which we have been able to make of them in the course of our life, having been made uncritically and unmethodically, are devoid of scientific value, and must be discarded. The facts of individual psychology themselves have this character and must be seen in this way. For although they are by definition purely mental, our consciousness of them reveals to us neither their real nature nor their genesis. It allows us to know them up to a certain point, just as our sensory knowledge gives us a certain familiarity with heat or light, sound or electricity; it gives us confused, fleeting, subjective impressions of them, but no clear and scientific notions or explanatory concepts. It is precisely for this reason that there has been founded in the course of this century an objective psychology whose fundamental purpose is to study mental facts from the outside, that is to say as things.

This is all the more necessary in the case of social facts, for consciousness is even more helpless in knowing them than in knowing its own life. It might be objected that since social facts are our own creations, we have only to look into our own mind in order to know what we put into them and how we formed them. But, in the first place, the greater part of our social institutions was bequeathed to us already formed by previous generations. We ourselves took no part in their formation, and consequently we cannot by introspection discover the causes which brought them into being. Furthermore, when we have in fact collaborated in their genesis, we can only with difficulty obtain even a very confused and a very distorted perception of the true nature of our action and the causes which determined it. When it is merely a matter of our private acts we know very imperfectly the relatively simple motives that guide us. We believe ourselves disinterested when we act egoistically; we think we are motivated by hate when we are yielding to love, that we obey reason when we are the slaves of irrational prejudices, etc. How, then, should we be able to discern with greater clarity the much more complex causes from which collective acts proceed? For, at the very least, each one of us participate in them only as an infinitesimal unit; a huge number of others collaborate with us, and what takes place in these other minds escapes us.

Thus our principle implies no metaphysical conception, no speculation about the fundamental nature of being. What it demands is that the sociologist put himself in the same state of mind as physicists, chemists, or physiologists, when they enquire into a hitherto unexplored region of the scientific domain. When he penetrates the social world, he must be aware that he is penetrating the unknown. He must feel himself in the presence of facts whose laws are as unsuspected as were those of life before the development of biology; he must be prepared for discoveries which will surprise and disconcert him.

RMS, pp. xii–xiv

[Written in review of a work by Jankélévitch concerned with the philosophy of social science.]

Here is yet another book of philosophical generalities on the nature of society – generalities in which it is difficult to discern a close and familiar acquaintance with social reality. Nowhere does the author give the impression that he has entered into direct contact with the facts which he discusses; for we do not believe that the general ideas which he develops are illustrated by a single concrete example, nor applied to a single precise and defined sociological problem. Whatever the skill in argument, or the literary talent, of an author, one cannot denounce too strongly the scandal of a method which flouts in this way all our customary scientific procedures but which, nonetheless, is becoming a very frequent practice. We no longer accept today that one can speculate upon the nature of life without having first been initiated in biological technique; by what privilege should it be permissible for the philosopher to speculate about society, without taking account of the detail of social facts?

The object of the book is to demonstrate that the social sciences are not 'sciences in the true sense of the word, that is to say, assimilable to the natural sciences', and that the phenomena with which they are concerned with are not part of the framework of natural phenomena, but constitute 'something, if not opposed, at least, different'. The author does not mean to understand by this, however, that society is outside of nature, 'not recognising any law, any rule, never repeating itself, and only making itself manifest through a series of hazards and accidents'. He readily sees that such a society is impossible; but he considers nevertheless, that man, as a social being, has the power to resist nature, to escape from laws, to modify them, and to add to them in pursuit of the realisation of certain ends. It is, therefore, the very principle of Comtean sociology and, more generally, of all scientific sociology, which is placed in contention.

As to the demonstration of the thesis, it is contained completely in the two following arguments, which the author reiterates in different forms, but without essential variation. In his exposition, these are often confused; but, although they are of a kind such as to lend themselves to mutual suport, we believe that there is some point in distinguishing them and considering them separately.

All the things in nature derive from the category of being; all that can be said of them is that they are, and that they are what they are. This is why the natural sciences have no other objective than to allow us to know *what is*; they do no more than express the real, such as it is manifest to us. But when man appears on the scene, and consequently the society which man is inseparable from, there also appears a new category, which is that *of value*. We do not confine ourselves to knowing what things are; we declare them to be good, bad, indifferent, etc., according to whether they accord or do not accord with our desires, or do not affect them in any way. Here we thus add to nature a property which is not intrinsic to it. We superimpose upon the natural point of view, which is that of science, a new point of view, which is the human point of view. The natural sciences are hence unable to know things from this second aspect. Now social life is solely made up of values; religious, moral, juridical, economic, and artistic values. Everything, in society, is considered in relation to man. Objects which are materially, as regards their physical properties, of the poorest sort, can have an incomparable social prestige and price, if human judgement attributes it to them. From which it follows that the social sciences cannot be assimilated to the natural sciences.

In the second place, social phenomena can only be explained *historically*; they are all the result of an evolution. Now, what does the idea of evolution imply? That things do not remain identical with themselves: that something new, which did not exist before, comes into being, appears at a given moment; and social evolution is an uninterrupted succession of new phenomena of this kind. Nature, on the contrary, is, by definition, that which does not change, that which is ever immutable. The subject-matter of the natural sciences is that which repeats itself identically; their role is to discover the laws which are always and everywhere the same, to efface differences, and to show the uniformity beneath the apparent diversity. On this point again, consequently, it does not seem as though they can serve as a model for the social sciences; for history never repeats itself.

From these considerations, it follows that the teleological point of view must predominate in the disciplines which deal with society. If we properly understand the author, they must above all take as their object the construction of ideal ends, to determine what must be valued, and what are – or rather how it is appropriate to consider – the different human values. As to the method which has to be followed in order to proceed to this consideration, no indication is given us.

We are very much afraid that this whole fabric of argument simply rests upon a confused notion.

The author seems to accept as obvious that there only exists one nature, that is to say, physical nature, and that to refuse to admit a radical heterogeneity between the social and the natural sciences is to admit *ipso facto* that the social fact is completely reducible to the properties of matter. For him, nature is the totality of cosmic forces, and it is for that reason that nature and humanity are always presented in his book in antithetical form. Thus understood, the naturalist thesis is easy to refute. The only thing is, that it has never been held, in this form, by any sociologists of any authority: and it would be quite extraordinary that it should have received much credence, because it has as its corollary the very negation of sociology. In any case, since Jankélévitch accords us the honour of choosing us as the principle contemporary representative of the thesis which he opposes, we may be permitted to say that the whole of our work protests against this Eleatic monism. If we have said that societies are in nature, we have sought with no lesser determination to show that social nature is *sui generis*, that it is irreducible, not only to physical nature, but even to the psychic nature of the individual. To declare that societies are natural things, that collective events submit to necessary laws, is thus not to hold that there is nothing new or different in the world. No-one has made greater efforts than us to show that the characteristic changes in social life are quite real and that, in a general way, the diversity of things is no mere appearance. In this, moreover, we do no more than to follow the path opened up by the founder of positive sociology, by Auguste Comte, who even went so far as to point to a radical discrepancy between the different realms of nature, and even between the different animal species. If, therefore, as every indications shows, it is indeed our method which Jankélévitch intended to oppose in his book, either he is poorly acquainted with it, or he has mis-understood it. It is possible that we are in error, and that one cannot, without contradiction, reconcile the naturalist thesis and the principle of the specificity of social things; but, on the other hand, in order to establish the contrary thesis, one must not forget or ignore the fact that this reconciliation has been attempted by the very doctrine which is claimed to be refuted.

And moreover, one cannot readily see how the character by which our author distinguishes social facts prevents us from treating them according to methods comparable to those em-ployed by the natural sciences. Undoubtedly social life is com-posed of values, and values are properties added to reality by human consciousness; they are wholly the product of psychic mechanisms. But these mechanisms are natural facts, which can be studied scientifically; these evaluations which human judgement makes of things depend upon causes and conditions which can be discovered inductively. There is thus here the subject-matter of a whole group of sciences which, as with the sciences of physical nature, move from given effects to the causes upon which those effects are dependent: such is the object of the social sciences. And it is only when we know better, in fact, in what these creations and these classifications of values have con-sisted in the past, what are the mental processes which they result from, the agencies of these processes, etc., that it will be possible to substitute for these empirical, instinctive, evaluations, which are made in an unreflective fashion, more considered and rational methods.

AS, 1906(b), pp. 171–4

THE SUBJECT-MATTER OF SOCIOLOGY

When I carry out my obligations as brother, husband, or citizen, when I comply with contracts, I perform duties which are de-fined, externally to myself and my acts, in law and in custom. Even if they conform to my own sentiments and I feel their reality subjectively, this reality is still objective, for I did not create them, I merely received them through my education. How many times it happens, moreover, that we are ignorant of the details of the obligations incumbent upon us, and that in order to get to know them we must consult the law and its authorised interpreters! Similarly, the church-member found the beliefs and practices of his religious life ready-made at birth; if they existed before him, they existed externally to him. The system of signs I use to express my thought, the system of currency I employ to pay my debts, the instruments of credit I utilise in my commercial relations, the practices followed in my profession, etc., function independently of whatever use I make of them. If one were to take, one after the other, all of the individuals who compose society, the preceding statement could be repeated of all of them. Here, then, are ways of acting, thinking, and feeling that present the remarkable property of existing outside the individual consciousness.

These types of conduct or thought are not only external to the individual but are, moreover, endowed with an imperative and coercive power, by virtue of which they impose themselves upon him, independent of his individual will. Of course, when I conform to them wholeheartedly, this coercion is felt only slightly, if at all, as it is unnecessary. But it is nevertheless an intrinsic characteristic of these facts; this is shown by the way in which it asserts itself as soon as I attempt to resist it. If I attempt to violate legal rules they react against me so as to prevent my act if possible, or to nullify my violation by restoring the damage, if it has been carried out but can be rectified; or to demand expiation if it cannot be compensated for otherwise.

Thus we are able to conceptualise in a precise way the field of sociology. It comprises only a limited group of phenomena. A social fact is to be recognised by the power of external coercion which it exercises or is capable of exercising over individuals; and the presence of this power can be recognised in turn either by the existence of some definite sanction or by the resistance offered against every individual act that tends to contravene it. However one can also define it in terms of its diffusion within the group, provided that, in following our previous remarks, one takes care to add as a second and essential characteristic that it exists independently of the individual forms it assumes in its diffusion. This last criterion is actually, in certain cases, easier to apply than the preceding one. In fact, the constraint is easy to identify when it expresses itself externally by some direct reaction of society, as is the case in law, morals, beliefs, customs, and even fashions. But when it is only indirect, like the constraint which is exercised by an economic organisation, it cannot always be so easily detected. Generality combined with externality may, then, be easier to establish. Moreover, this second definition is but another form of the first; for if a mode of conduct whose existence is external to individual minds becomes general, this can only be brought about by its being imposed upon them.

Every scientific investigation is directed towards a well-defined group of phenomena, which fall within a single category. The first step of the sociologist, therefore, must be to define the things he treats, in order that his subject-matter may be clearly known. This is the first and most indispensable condition of all proof and verification. A theory can really be tested only if we are able to recognise the facts of which it is intended to give an account. Moreover, since this initial definition determines the very subject-matter of science, this subject-matter will or will not be a thing, depending on the way in which the definition is constructed.

In order to be objective, the definition must obviously deal with phenomena not as mental ideas but in terms of their inherent properties. It must characterise them by an element integral to their nature, not by their conformity to some sort of intellectual ideal. Now, at the very beginning of research, when the facts have not yet been analysed, the only ascertainable characteristics are those external enough to be immediately visible. Those that are more deep-lying are no doubt more significant, and their explanatory value is greater; but they are unknown to science at this stage, and they can be anticipated only by substituting some hypothetical conception in the place of reality. The material included under this fundamental definition must be sought among the external characteristics of phenomena. Moreover, it is clear that this definition must include, without exception or distinction, all phenomena which manifest the same characteristics; for we have no reason nor any means of choosing between them. These properties are our only clue to reality: consequently, they must be given complete sovereignty over the way in which facts are grouped. We possess no other criterion which could even partially justify any exception to this rule.

We may lay down as a principle that social facts are capable of objective representation to the degree that they are completely detached from the individual facts expressing them. In effect, the degree of objectivity of a sensation is proportionate to the degree of stability of its object; for objectivity depends upon the existence of a constant and identical point of reference to which the representation can be referred, and which makes it possible to eliminate everything which is variable and subjective. But if the points of reference themselves are variable, if they constantly differ in relation to each other, there is no common standard, and we have no way of distinguishing between those impressions which are external and those that are subjective. So long as social life is not separated from the particular events of which it is comprised, and has no separate existence, it will present this dilemma. As these events differ among themselves and change in time, and as social life is inseparable from them, they communicate their change-ability to it. Social life then consists of free currents which are constantly in the process of transformation, and cannot be fixed by the observer. The scholar cannot approach the study of social reality from this aspect. But we know that it possesses the power of crystallisation without ceasing to be itself. Apart from the individual acts to which they give rise, collective habits find expression in definite forms: legal rules, moral regulations, popular proverbs, social conventions, etc. As these forms have a per-manent existence and do not change with the different applica-tions made of them, they constitute a fixed object, a constant standard of reference for the observer, which excludes subjective impressions and purely personal observations. A legal regulation has an intrinsic identity, and there are no two ways of looking at it. Since these practices are merely social life consolidated, it is legitimate, except where there are contradictory indications, to study the latter through the former.

When, then, the sociologist undertakes the investigation of a given order of social facts, he must endeavour to consider them from an aspect that is isolated from their individual manifesta-tions. It is this principle that we have applied in studying the diverse forms of social solidarity and their evolution, through the medium of the legal structure which expresses them. In the same way, an attempt to distinguish and classify the different types of family on the basis of literary descriptions given us by travellers and sometimes by historians, is exposed to the danger of con-fusing the most diverse forms and of relating together the most dissimilar types. If, by contrast, the legal structure of the family and, more specifically, the right of succession, are taken as the basis of classification, these are objective criteria which, while not infallible, will prevent many errors. Let us suppose we wish to classify the different sorts of crime. We would have to try to reconstruct the modes of life and the occupational practices that are followed in the different worlds of crime. One would then recognise as many criminological types as there are different forms of this organisation. To come to grips with customs and popular beliefs, one must take account of the proverbs and epigrams that express them. No doubt, in proceeding thus, we leave the concrete substance of collective life temporarily outside the realm of science; and yet, however changeable and unstable it may be, its unintelligibility cannot be assumed *a priori*. But in order to follow a methodical course, we must establish the initial bases of science on solid ground and not on shifting sand. We must approach the social realm at those points at which it offers the best access to scientific investigation. Only later will it be possible to push research further and, by successive approximations, to encompass, little by little, this fleeting reality, which the human mind will perhaps never be able to grasp completely.

RMS, pp. 3–4, 11–12, 33–5 and 44–6

For the Manchester school, political economy consists in the satisfaction of the needs of the individual, particularly his material needs. In this conception, therefore, the individual is the sole end of economic relationships; it is through him and also for him that everything is accomplished. As for society, this is a mental construct, a metaphysical entity which the scholar can and must neglect. What is called by that name is simply the coming into contact of all the individual activities; it is a composite in which there is nothing more than the sum of its components. In other words, the major laws of economics would be exactly the same even if there had never been either nations or states in existence; they presuppose only the presence of individuals who exchange their products. One sees that the liberal economists are, at bottom, unconscious disciples of Rousseau, whom they reject as in error. They recognise, it is true, that the condition of isolation is not the ideal; but, like Rousseau, they see in the social tie nothing more than a superficial connection, determined by the convergence of interests. They conceive of the nation only as an immense society, through the action of which everyone receives exactly as much as he gives, and in which one remains only as long as one profits from it. It also seems to them good that things should be thus: for too intense a collective life would quickly become a threat to that individual independence which to them is the most precious thing in the world. Moreover, the more consistent among them have not hesitated to declare that national sentiments are only the residue of prejudices which one day are destined to disappear. In these conditions, economic activity can have no other origin than egoism, and as a consequence political economy becomes radically separated from morality – if indeed humanity retains any moral ideals, once one has dissolved every social bond.

RP, 1887(b), p. 37

2. Methods of explanation and analysis

EMERGENT PROPERTIES

Whenever any elements combine and, by the fact of their combination produce new phenomena, it is evident that these phenomena are not given in the elements, but in the totality formed by their union. The living cell contains nothing but mineral particles, just as society contains nothing but individuals; it is obviously impossible, however, for the phenomena characteristic of life to exist in the atoms of hydrogen, oxygen, carbon, and nitrogen. For how could the properties of life exist within inanimate elements? How, moreover, would the biological properties be divided among these elements? These properties could not exist equally in all the elements because the latter are different in nature; carbon is not nitrogen and consequently can neither possess the same properties nor have the same role. It is similarly inadmissible that each of the principal aspects or characteristics of life be manifest in a different group of atoms. Life could not thus be subdivided; it is a unity, and consequently its basis be only the living substance in its totality. It is in the whole, not in the parts. The inanimate particles of the cell do not feed themselves, reproduce – in a word, live – only the cell itself can do so. What we say of life could be repeated for any type of compound. The hardness of bronze is not in the copper nor in the tin, nor the lead, which served to create it, and which are soft and malleable bodies; it is in their mixture. The fluidity of water and its nutritional and other properties are not in the two gases of which it is composed, but in the complex substance which they form by their association.

Let us apply this principle to sociology. If, as we may accept, the synthesis *sui generis* which every society constitutes yields new phenomena, differing from those which take place in the individual consciousness, we must also admit that these facts reside exclusively in the very society itself which produces them, and not in its parts – that is, its members. Thus they are in this sense external to individual minds considered as such, in the same way as the distinctive characteristics of life are external to the mineral substances composing the living beings. These new phenomena cannot be reduced to their elements without contradiction in terms, since, by definition, they suppose something other than that contained by these elements. Thus we have a new justification for the separation which we have established between psychology proper, which is the science of the individual mind, and sociology. Social facts do not differ from psychological facts in quality only: *they have a different substratum.* They do not develop in the same milieu; and they do not depend on the same conditions. This does not mean that they are not themselves also psychic in a certain way, since they all consist of ways of thinking or acting. But the states of the *conscience collective* are different in nature from the states of the individual consciousness; they are representations of another sort. The mentality of groups is not the same as that of individuals; it has its own laws. The two sciences are hence as clearly distinct as two sciences can be, whatever connections there may be otherwise be between them.

Nevertheless, on this point a distinction can be made which will perhaps throw some light on the discussion.

That the *substance* of social life cannot be explained by purely psychological factors, that is to say, by states of individual consciousness, seems to us to be perfectly evident. Indeed, what collective representations express is the way in which the group thinks of itself in its relation to objects which affect it. Now the group differs from the individual in its constitution, and the things that affect it are of a different nature. Representations or concepts that express neither the same subjects nor the same objects cannot derive from the same causes. To understand the way in which a society represents itself and the world around it, we must consider the nature of the society and not that of the individuals. Even the symbols which express these conceptions change with the society.

If, for example, it conceives itself to be descended from a totemic animal, it is in the form of one of those special groups called 'clans'. If the animal is replaced by a human ancestor, but similarly mythical, it is because the clan has changed its nature. If, over and above local or family divinities, it creates others on which it believes itself to be dependent, it is because the local family groups of which it is composed have tended to concentrate and unite; the degree of unity which is presented by divinities corresponds to the degree of unity attained at the same moment by the society. If society condemns certains modes of conduct, it is because they transgress certain fundamental sentiments which derive from its constitution, as those of the individual derive from his physical temperament and his mental organisation. Thus, even if individual psychology had no more secrets for us, it could not give us the solution to any of these problems, since they relate to orders of facts of which it has no knowledge.

We must not be surprised, moreover, if other phenomena in nature display, in other forms, the very character by reference to which we have defined social phenomena. This similarity simply derives from the fact that both are real things. For everything that is real has a definite nature that asserts itself, that must be taken into account and is never completely overcome, even when we manage to neutralise it. And, fundamentally, this is the most essential element in the idea of social constraint. For all that it implies is that collective ways of acting or thinking have a reality outside the individuals who, at any moment of time, conform to it. These are things which exist in their own right. The individual finds them already formed, and he cannot act as if they did not exist or were different from how they are. He is therefore obliged to take account of them. It is difficult (we do not say impossible) for him to change them to the degree to which they share in the material and moral supremacy of society over its members. Of course, the individual plays a role in their genesis. But for a social fact to exist, several individuals, at the very least, must have contributed their action; and it is this combined action which has created a new product. Since this synthesis takes place outside each one of us (for a plurality of consciousnesses enters into it), its necessary effect is to fix, to institute outside us, certain ways of acting and certain judgements which do not depend on each particular will taken separately. Thus it has been pointed out that there is a term, which, provided that one extends the ordinary meaning somewhat, expresses this mode of reality quite well: this is 'institution'. One can, indeed, without distorting the meaning of this expression, call *institutions* all the beliefs and modes of conduct instituted by the collectivity. Sociology can then be defined as the science of institutions, their genesis and functioning.

RMS, pp. xvi–xviii and xxii

If, once they come into being, ideas continue to exist independently, without being perpetually contingent upon the arrangement of neural centres, if they are capable of reacting directly upon each other and combining according to their own laws, then they are realities which, while maintaining a close relation with their substratum, are to a certain extent independent of it. Certainly their autonomy can be no more than relative; there is no realm of nature that is not tied to others. Nothing could be more absurd than to elevate psychic life into a sort of absolute, derived from nothing and unconnected with the rest of the universe. It is obvious that the state of the brain affects all intellectual phenomena and is the immediate cause of some of them (pure sensation). But, on the other hand, it follows from what has been said earlier that ideational life is not inherent in the intrinsic nature of nervous matter, since it exists partly by its own force, and has its own particular modes of existence. An idea is not simply an aspect of the condition of a neural element at the particular moment that it occurs, since it persists after that condition has passed, and since the relations of the ideas are different in nature from those of the underlying neural elements. It is something quite new, which certain characteristics of the cells certainly help to produce but do not suffice to constitute, since it survives them and shows different properties. To say that the mental state does not derive directly from the cell is to say that it is not comprised within it, that it forms itself in part outside it and is to that extent exterior to it. If it was a direct derivative it would be within the cell, since its reality would come from that source alone.

When we said elsewhere that social facts are in a sense independent of individuals and exterior to individual minds, we simply confirmed for the social world what we have just established for the psychic world. Society has for its substratum the mass of associated individuals. The system which they form by uniting together, which differs according to their geographical disposition and the nature and number of their channels of communication, is the base from which social life arises. The representations which form the framework of social life derive from the relations between the individuals thus combined, or from the secondary groups that are between the individuals and the total society. If there is nothing extraordinary in the fact that individual representations, produced by action and reaction between neural elements, are not inherent in these elements, there is nothing surprising in the fact that collective representations, produced by action and reaction between individual minds that form the society, do not derive directly from the latter and consequently surpass them. This conception of the relationship which unites the social substratum and the social life is wholly comparable to that which indisputably exists between the physio-logical substratum and the psychic life of individuals – if, that is, one is not going to deny the existence of psychology in the proper sense of the word. The same consequences should then follow on both sides. The independence and relative externality of social facts in relation to individuals is even more directly apparent than is that of mental facts in relation to cells of the brain, for the former, or at least the most important ones, clearly bear the marks of their origin. While one might perhaps dispute the statement that all social facts, without exception, impose themselves from outside upon the individual, it is hardly possible to doubt that this is the case with religious beliefs and practices, the rules of morality and the innumerable precepts of law – that is to say with all the most characteristic manifestations of collec-tive life. All these are expressly obligatory, and this obligation is the proof that these modes of action and thought are not the creation of the individual but come from a moral power above him, that which the mystic calls 'god' or which can be more scientifically conceived. The same law is found at work in the two fields.

If the characteristics of obligation and constraint are so essen-tial to these eminently social facts, it is to be expected that they will be found, if less obviously, in other social facts. It is im-possible for phenomena of the same nature to differ to the extent that some come to the individual from without and others are the result of an opposite process. We should like here to correct a false interpretation that has been made of our thought. When we said that obligation and constraint are the characteristics of social facts, we had no intention of giving a summary explanation of the latter. We wished simply to point to a convenient sign by which the sociologist can recognise the facts falling within his field.

SP, pp. 32–5

SOCIOLOGY AND PSYCHOLOGY

We have shown that social facts, like all natural phenomena, are not to be explained simply by showing that they serve some end. When it has been proved satisfactorily that the progressively more accomplished social organisations which have succeeded one another in the course of history have had the effect of increas-ingly satisfying certain of our fundamental desires, we have still not shown at all how these social organisations originated. The fact that they were useful does not tell us what brought them into being. Even if we were to explain how we came to conceive of them and to plan them in advance so as to picture to ourselves the services we could expect from them – already a difficult problem in itself – the wishes that led to their creation still did not construct them out of nothing. In short, even admitting that social organisations are the necessary means of attaining a desired objective, the question remains unanswered: from what source and by what means have these been created?

We arrive, therefore, at the following principle: *The determining cause of a social fact must be sought among antecedent social facts and not among states of individual consciousness.* Moreover, we can easily see that everything which has just been said applies to the determination of the function as well as to the cause of social phenomena. The function of a social fact can only be social, that is to say, it consists in the production of socially useful effects. No doubt it may and does happen that it also serves the individual. But this fortunate outcome is not its immediate cause. We can thus complete the preceding proposition by saying: *The function of a social fact must always be sought in its relation to some social end.*

It is because sociologists have often misunderstood this rule and have considered social phenomena from too psychological a point of view that many of their theories seem too vague, imprecise, and far removed from the specific character of the things they are intended to explain. The historians in particular, who treat social reality directly and in detail, could hardly have failed to sense how powerless these over-generalised interpretations are to explain the relation between their data; and their frequent mistrust of sociology has been, no doubt, partly produced by this circumstance. This is not to say, of course, that the study of psychological facts is not indispensable to the sociologist. If collective life does not derive from individual life, the two are nevertheless directly related; if the latter cannot explain the former, it can at least aid in the former: it can at least aid in its explanation. First, as we have shown, it is indisputable that social facts are produced by an elaboration, *sui generis*, of psychological factors. In addition, this very action is similar to that which takes place in each individual consciousness and which transforms the primary elements (sensations, reflexes, instincts) of which it is originally constituted. It is not without reason that it has been said that the self is itself a society, by the same right as the organism, although in a different sense; and long ago psychologists showed the great importance of the factor of *association* in the explanation of mental life.

Psychological training, more than biological training, constitutes, then, a necessary preparation for the sociologist; but it will not be useful to him except on condition that he emancipates himself from it after having received it, and then goes further by special sociological training. He must abandon psychology as the centre of his operations, as the point of departure for his excursions into the sociological world to which they must always return. He must establish himself in the very heart of social facts, in order to observe them directly, asking the science of the individual mind only for a general preparation and for useful suggestions where these are needed.

RMS, pp. 109–11

Perhaps these comparisons will clarify why we insist so strongly upon the distinction between sociology and individual psychology.

It is simply a matter of introducing and making acceptable in sociology a conception parallel to that which is tending to prevail more and more in psychology. During the last decade considerable advance has been made in that science. Interesting efforts have been made to establish a psychology which is actually 'psychological', without any other qualifying adjective. The old introspectionists were content to describe mental phenomena without trying to explain them; psycho-physiology explained them but dismissed their distinctive traits as unimportant. A third school is coming into being which is trying to explain them without destroying their specificity. For the former school mental life certainly had a nature of its own, but it was one that lifted the mental out of the world of reality, and placed it above the ordinary methods of science. For the second school it was of no intrinsic significance, and the role of the scientist was to pierce this superficial layer in order to arrive at the underlying realities. Neither school recognised anything more than a thin curtain of phenomena which, according to the first, was readily visible to the conscious mind and to the second, was lacking in any consistency. Recent research has shown us that it is far better to conceive of it as a vast system of *sui generis* realities made up of a great number of mental strata superimposed upon each other, far too profound and complex for the conscious mind to penetrate, far too specialised to be accounted for by purely physiological considerations. We thus characterise psychological facts by their *spirituality*. This seemed in the past to be either above or below the attentions of science, but has itself become the object of a positive science; between the ideology of the introspectionists and biological naturalism, a psychological naturalism has been founded, the legitimacy of which the present work will, perhaps, help to demonstrate.

A similar transformation should take place in sociology, and it is towards this goal that all our efforts are directed.

SP, pp. 45–7

[Written in review of Tarde's attempt to found an 'interpsychology'.]

Towards the end of his life, Tarde liked to replace the term 'collective psychology' by that of 'interpsychology'. The first expression seemed to him to be ontologically suspect, as it appears to imply that there is a psychology proper of the collectivity. Since, according to the author, there is no reality apart from the actions and reactions exchanged between individuals, it is necessary that the name of the science itself should indicate that it has no other object. It is not the case that all interpsychic relations are social. The impressions which the sight of another person can evoke in me have nothing social about them. There must be in addition an action exercised by one mind upon another mind, having the effect of producing in the latter a certain mental state. But neither is every reciprocal mental act social; there are some which are rather obstacles to the social tie, for example, hatred, or fear, or the appetite of a cannibal. Only suggestion involving sympathy, confidence, or obedience, has a truly social character.

One can already see how arbitrary and confused this notion is. First of all, if interpsychology really comprises phenomena which are not social, it is certainly a poor method which mixes within the same category two categories of phenomena which are so clearly distinct. Moreover, why refuse to allow that sentiments such as fear and hatred can have the character of social facts? If hatred separates, it also unites, in the same way as, if sympathy unites, it separates. These two occurrences are correlative with each other; and what an unsatisfactory definition it is which places them in two distinct categories, and attributes them to two different sciences!

This conception is even arbitrary in the division and the framework of the science. The major problems which the science is to be concerned with are the following: 1. The effect of an individual upon an individual. 2. That of an individual upon an assembled crowd, and vice versa. 3. That of an individual upon a public or a diffuse crowd, and vice versa. But in order to study the effect of an individual upon a crowd, or of a crowd upon an individual, it is necessary first to know what a crowd is, and how its mentality is formed. Can the genesis of this mentality be reduced to simple inter-individual actions? This question cannot be settled in advance, when the science has not yet got under way. Evidently the author supposes that the crowd is made by a leader: this simplification disposes of any difficulty, but cannot, however, be accepted as evidence. Now this is exactly the problem; one wonders whether Tarde has any inkling of it.

Let us add in conclusion that these problems are singularly vague, and it is difficult to see how it is possible to approach them methodically. In what way, by what observations, are we to approach the study of the influence of an individual upon an individual, of an individual upon a crowd, etc? Are we going to limit ourselves, as has been done up to now, to collecting a few freely adapted anecdotes? Is this the way to carry out scientific work? There are crowds of all sorts, publics of all sorts; each one has its own particular way of reacting. It would be necessary to distinguish these, to find some way to observe objectively the way in which they behave, and to look for the conditions in relation to which they vary. But such special and definite researches immediately direct thought in quite a different direction from vague interpsychology.

One will find at the end of Tarde's article a proof of the circle in which his thinking moves. According to him, as we already know, all social phenomena derive 'from the unilateral or reciprocal effect of the contact of minds': imitation is the fundamental type of such an effect. Now, without having perceived the vicious circle, the author indicates in concluding his work that this effect is itself promoted or hindered by social causes. In other words, imitation, the source of social life, itself depends upon social factors; it presupposes what it produces. Men only act upon each other, for example, in such a way as to produce social facts, when there is already a sufficient moral homogeneity between them, which is a result of life in common. Men imitate their superiors, but superiority is already a social institution; so it is the case that the word 'imitation' is empty and explains nothing. We must discover why men imitate, and the causes which lead men to imitate, to obey each other, are already social.

AS, 1905, pp. 133–5

HISTORY, FUNCTION AND CAUSE

History can only be a science on condition that it raises itself above the particular; but then it is the case that it ceases to be itself, and becomes a branch of sociology. It merges with dynamic sociology. History can remain a distinct discipline only if it confines itself to the study of each individual nation, taken by itself, and considered at the different moments of its development. But it is then no more than a narrative, which is mainly practical in objective. Its function is to put societies in a position to remind themselves of their past; it is the most distinctive form of collective memory. Having distinguished these two conceptions of history, it should be added that, more and more, they are destined to become inseparable. There is no longer any conflict between them but only a difference in degree. Scientific history, or sociology, must be founded upon the direct observation of concrete facts and, on the other hand, national history, history as art, can only gain through being penetrated by the general principles arrived at by the sociologist. For in order for a people to know its past well, it is still necessary to select from the multitude of phenomena in order to retain only those which are particularly vital; and in order to do that, we must have criteria, thus presupposing comparison. In the same way, in order to be able to discover with greater certainty the way in which the concrete events in a definite period of history are linked together, it is useful to know the general relationships of which specific relationships are instances and as if so many applications. There is not in reality, therefore, two separate disciplines, but two different points of view which, far from excluding each other, mutually presuppose each other. But this is no reason to confuse them, and to attribute to one what is a characteristic of the other.

AS, 1902(b), pp. 124–5

As soon as history becomes a comparative discipline, it is indistinguishable from sociology. Sociology, in turn, not only cannot do without history but needs historians who are, at the same time, sociologists. As long as sociology has to sneak like a stranger into the historical domain in order in some way to steal from it the facts in which it is interested, it cannot derive much profit from it. Finding itself in an unfamiliar context, one in which it has no roots, it is almost inevitable that sociology should be unable to perceive, or should see only vaguely, that which it actually has the greatest stake in observing with particular clarity. The historian, on the other hand, is accustomed to dealing with historical fact and handles it with ease. Thus, however antagonistic they may be, these two disciplines naturally tend to move toward one another, and everything suggests that they will be called upon to fuse into one common study, which recombines and unifies elements of both. For it appears equally impossible that the historian – the student whose role it is to discover facts – should neglect the comparisons which make use of this material, as that the sociologist, who compares them, should neglect how they have been discovered. To produce historians who know how to see historical facts as sociologists do, or – which amounts to the same thing – to produce sociologists who have mastered all of the techniques of history, is the objective which must be striven for from both sides. In this manner, the explanatory formulas of sociology will progressively extend to the whole universe of social facts, instead of reproducing only their most general outlines; and, at the same time, historical scholarship will become meaningful because it will be employed to resolve the most important problems which face mankind.

AS, 1897(a), p. iii

It is a very widely held notion that whoever occupies himself with practical matters must partly turn himself away from the past in order to concentrate the whole weight of his attention upon the present. Since the past is no more, since we have no effect upon it, it seems that it can merely have the interest of curiosity for us. It is, so it is believed, the domain of scholarship. It is not what was, but what is, which we must know and, better still, it is what is tending to happen that we must seek to predict in order to be able to satisfy the needs which impel us....In point of fact, the present, in which we are invited to enclose ourselves, is nothing if taken alone; it is no more than the prolongation of the past, from which it cannot be separated without in large part losing its whole meaning. The present is formed of countless elements, which are so completely entangled with one another that it is not easy for us to perceive where one begins and the other finishes, what each one is, and what connections there are between them; thus immediate observation gives us only an incoherent and confused conception of them. The only way to distinguish and to separate them, and hence to introduce a little clarity into this confusion, is to seek in history how they came progressively to be conjoined one to the other, to combine and acquire an organised form. In the same way as our perception of matter made it appear to us as homogeneous mass, until scientific analysis showed us its true composition, so the direct perception of the present does not allow us to suspect its complexity, until it has been revealed to us by historical analysis. But what is even more dangerous is the undue importance which we are thus prone to attribute to the aspirations of the present moment, when we do not submit them to control. For, precisely because they are of the present, they hypnotise us, absorb us, and prevent us from being aware of anything other than ourselves. The awareness which we have of something which we need is always very strong; hence it tends to assume a preponderant place in our minds, and throws all else in the shadow. Completely enveloped by the object towards which we are directed by our desires, it appears to us as the most precious thing in existence, that which matters above everything, the ideal to which all else must be subordinated. Now very often what we want in this way is not more essential, or is less essential, than that which we have; and we thus risk sacrificing really vital necessities to passing and secondary needs.

EPF, pp. 22–3

To show how a fact is useful is not to explain how it was created or why it is as it is. The uses which it serves presuppose the specific properties characterising it, but do not create them. The need we have of things cannot give them their specific nature, or cause them to come into being. It is to causes of another sort that they owe their existence. The idea we have of their utility may indeed motivate us to put these forces to work and to elicit from them their characteristic effects, but it will not enable us to produce these effects out of nothing. This proposition is evident so long as it is a question only of material, or even psychological, phenomena. It would be equally undisputed in sociology if social facts, because of their extreme intangibility, did not – mistakenly – appear to us without all intrinsic reality. Because we usually see them as purely mental constructions, it seems to us that they may be produced at will whenever we find it useful. But since each one of them is a force, which dominates the individual, and since it has its own characteristic nature, it is not true that they can be brought into existence merely by an effort of the will. It still necessitates the development of forces capable of producing this specific force. To revive the spirit of the family, where it has become weakened, it is not enough that everyone understand its advantages; the causes which alone can produce it must be made to act directly. To give a government the authority which it needs, it is not enough to sense that this authority is necessary; we must have recourse to the sources from which all authority is derived. We must, namely, establish traditions, a common spirit, etc.; and for this it is necessary again to go back along the chain of causes and effects until we find a point where human action may effectively intervene.

What shows plainly the dualism of these two orders of research is that a fact can exist without serving any end, either because it has never been adjusted to any vital end or because, after having been useful, it has lost all utility while continuing to exist by force of habit alone. There are, in fact, more survivals in society than in the organism. There are even cases where a practice or a social institution changes its function without thereby changing its nature. The rule, *Is pater est quem justae nuptiae declarant*, has remained in our code essentially the same as it was in the old Roman law. But while its purpose then was to safeguard the property rights of a father over children born to the legitimate wife, it is rather the rights of children that it protects today. The custom of taking an oath began by being a sort of legal test and has become today simply a solemn and imposing formality for a witness. The religious dogmas of Christianity have not changed for centuries, but the role which they play is not the same in our modern societies as it was in the Middle Ages. Thus, the same words may serve to express new ideas. It is, moreover, a proposition true in sociology, as in biology, that the organ is independent of the function – in other words, while remaining the same, it can serve different ends. The causes of its existence are thus independent of the ends it serves.

However, we do not wish to argue that the impulses, needs, and desires of men never intervene actively in social evolution. On the contrary, it is certain that they can advance or retard its development, according to the circumstances which determine the social phenomena. But even apart from the fact that they cannot, in any circumstances, make something out of nothing, their actual intervention, whatever may be its effects, can take place only by means of efficient causes. A deliberate intention can contribute, even in this limited way, to the production of new phenomena only if it has itself been newly formed or if it is itself a result of some transformation of a previous tendency. For, unless we postulate a truly providential and pre-established harmony, we cannot admit that man has carried with him from the beginning – potentially ready to be awakened at the call of circumstances – all the tendencies which conditions were destined to demand in the course of human evolution. Now a tendency is itself something objectively real; it can, then, neither be created nor modified by the mere fact that we judge it useful. It is a force having a nature of its own; for that nature to be given existence or altered, it is not enough that we should find this profitable. In order to bring about such changes, there must be causes acting which physically produce them. . .

Thus when we undertake to explain a social phenomenon, we must seek separately the efficient cause which produces it and the function it fulfils. We use the word 'function', in preference to 'end' or 'purpose', precisely because social phenomena do not generally exist for the useful results they produce. What we have to do is to determine whether there is a correspondence between the fact under consideration and the general needs of the social organism, and in what this correspondence consists, without occupying ourselves with whether it has been intentional or not. All such questions of intention moreover, are too subjective to allow of scientific treatment.

Not only must these two orders of problems be separated, but it is convenient, in general, to treat the former before the latter. This sequence, indeed, corresponds to that given in reality. It is natural to seek the causes of a phenomenon before trying to determine its effects. This method is all the more logical since the first question, once answered, will often help to answer the second. Indeed, the bond which unites the cause to the effect is reciprocal to an extent which has not been sufficiently recognised. The effect can no doubt not exist without its cause; but the latter, in turn, needs its effect. It is from the cause that the effect draws its energy; but it also restores it to the cause on occasion, and consequently it cannot disappear without the cause showing the effects of its disappearance.

RMS, pp. 90–2 and 95

SOCIAL MORPHOLOGY

The specialisation which is demanded if sociology is to become a truly positive science does not therefore entail a kind of grand construction which has no historical precedent; on the contrary, it is the natural outcome of a long development. It is not a matter of inventing and creating new disciplines, hitherto unknown, out of nothing; in large degree, it is sufficient to develop a certain number of existing sciences in the direction in which they are spontaneously moving.

But however real this spontaneous evolution, what remains to be done is not inconsiderable. The necessary preparatory work has been done, but it is not yet finished. Because scholars in the specialised disciplines are directly in contact with factual materials, they have a strong sense of the diversity and complexity of things and, consequently, they are not inclined to be satisfied with simplistic formulas and facile explanations; but, on the other hand, since they have not first taken an overall view of the ground to be explored, they are somewhat haphazard, and are not fully aware of the objective to be attained, or of the direct relationships which unite them and which make them colleagues in the same enterprise. The consequence of this is that, in many ways, they are unable to formulate a conception of their science which is really adequate to its objective.

In the first place, because these different disciplines exist in separation from each other, and almost without being aware of each other, the way in which they have divided up the social world is not always consistent with the nature of things. Thus, for example, geography and demography (or the science of population) until recently remained separate from one-another, and are only just beginning to become interrelated. However, both study the same subject-matter, in order to understand the material substratum of society; for what is it which forms the main substance of society, if it is not social space plus the population which occupies this space? In this there are two orders of phenomena which are inextricably related: a society is of greater or lesser density according to the extension of the land over which it is distributed, according to the shape of this land, the number or direction of the waterways, according to the position of the mountain ranges, etc. On the other hand, the external forms of social groups have changed over time, and it is the historian, ordinarily, who studies these changes. For example, the origin and development of rural and urban groupings is a problem which usually is considered to be the concern of history. However, in order to be able properly to understand the actual nature and function of these groups, issues which occupy the demographer, it is absolutely necessary to know about their origins, and the conditions of these. There is thus a whole group of historical studies which is inseparable from demography and consequently also from social geography. Now it is not merely to create a pleasingly ordered science that there is some point in removing these fragmentary researches from their state of isolation: rather, as a consequence of their integration, new problems are brought to light which would not otherwise be perceived. Ratzel's approach, which is characterised precisely by its sociological point of view, which forms his starting point, has successfully demonstrated this. Because he is an ethnographer and an historian at the same time as he is a geographer, he has been able to see, for example, that the diverse forms which the frontiers of countries have assumed can be classed into a certain number of different types; he has subsequently sought to determine the conditions which give rise to these. It thus seems possible to unite all the varied researches which deal with the material substratum of society within a single science; elsewhere, we have proposed to call this science *social morphology*. Conversely, it would be easy to show that other disciplines, which are only indirectly related to one-another, are confused in a way which produces an amalgam which has no intrinsic unity. Who could say precisely what the *Kulturgeschichte* of the Germans, or their *Völkerpsychologie*, or their *Volkskunde*, consist in? How could such composite researches, formed of such disparate elements, practise even a loosely defined method? For the nature of a method, being always directly related to the nature of its object, cannot be more clearly defined than the latter is.

But this same state of dispersion has another consequence, which is perhaps more general: it prevents these various sciences from being social, except in name alone. Indeed, if this term is not to be a mere label applied to them, they must be based upon the fundamental principle that all the phenomena which they are concerned with are social; that is to say, are manifestations of one and the same reality – society. The observer should retain only those which have this characteristic, and they should be explained in terms of the mode in which they derive from the nature of society, and the specific way in which they manifest this. But if the various specialists remain enclosed in their respective specialities, it is impossible for them to come to collaborate under the guidance of this fundamental notion; for since each studies only a part of the totality, which he takes to be the totality itself, he fails to reach an adequate conception of this totality, which is society. He holds that the phenomena which he is concerned with are social because they are manifestly the product of human association; but society is only very rarely considered as the determining cause of the events for which it forms the stage. We have stated, for example (in a previous section of the article), that the science of religion has made considerable progress, but it is still extremely unusual for religious systems to be treated as deter-

mined by definite social systems. Religious beliefs and practices
are still presented to us as the product of sentiments which
originate and develop in the consciousness of the individual; only
in their expression, because it is external, do they take on a social
form. Impressions left in the mind by the spectacle of the great
cosmic forces, by the experience of sleep or of death, thus form
the main substance of religion. The anthropology of law, for its
part, while declaring that law is a social function, is mainly
preoccupied with connecting it to certain qualities of human
nature in general. The writers in this school have seen in the
similarities which exist between the legal institutions of different
societies proof that man possesses a single legal consciousness;
and it is this primary and fundamental consciousness which they
have sought to discover. . .This is to posit *a posteriori* a natural
law, prior to the formation of societies, which would seem logically
to be part of the moral consciousness of every human individual.
From this point of view, social factors can only be referred to in
order to show how this primitive and universal source becomes
differentiated in detail according to particular national differences.
As to political economy, we are aware that the general propositions, which it terms 'laws', were for a very long time treated as
independent of any characteristics of time and space, and consequently of any collective states. It is true that recently, with
Bücher and Schmoller, economic science has moved in a new
direction, with their formulation of types of economy. But these
attempts are still isolated ones, and their method, moreover,
is still very unclear. In Schmoller's writings particularly we see
procedures and ideas of very different origin mingled in a rather
confused eclecticism.

Even the principle of the interdependence of social facts,
although easily accepted in theory, is far from being effectively
put into practice. The moralist still studies moral phenomena
as if they were separable from the legal phenomena of which they
are, however, merely one variety. On the other hand, it is very
rare to find jurists who realise that law cannot be understood
apart from religion, from which it has taken its major distinctive
characteristics and of which it is, in part, simply a derivation.
Conversely, historians of religion do not generally feel the need to
examine the religious beliefs and practices of different peoples in
relation to their political organisation. Sometimes, however, when
a specialist has managed to understand that the facts which he
deals with are bound up with other collective manifestations, he
feels obliged to refashion his point of view and to integrate

all the special sciences which he needs to make use of in his research. Schmoller has done this in his *Grundriss der allgemeinen Volkswirtschaftslehre*. This is a complete sociology, seen from the economic point of view. One can see how tenuous such a synthesis necessarily tends to be, since it is summarily assembled from quite heterogeneous studies, which demand an equally heterogeneous range of special skills. Only the spontaneous co-operation of all of these specific sciences can give to each one something of an accurate notion of the relations which pertain between it and the others.

Thus although these sciences are tending more and more to orient themselves in a sociological direction, this orientation still remains in many ways ambiguous and unconscious. The pressing problem which faces sociology, we believe, is that of working to make this a more conscious process, to further it, and to give it greater precision. We must make the sociological idea penetrate these different approaches which, although they no doubt arise spontaneously, do so only at a slow pace, as if groping in the dark. On this condition, the Comtean conception will cease to be an idea, and become a reality. For the unity of the social realm cannot find adequate expression in a few general philosophical formulæ, totally removed from the facts and from detailed researches. Such a unity can only operate through the agency of a body of distinct and interdependent sciences, which, however, are aware of their interdependence. Moreover, it can be foreseen that, once organised, these sciences will return with interest to philosophy what they have borrowed from it. For the shared conceptions which will emerge from the relationships established between them, which will form the core of the unity which will thus be established, will provide the subject-matter of a revitalised social philosophy, a social philosophy as positive and progressive as the very sciences whose crowning endeavour it will be.

RP, 1903, pp. 493–6

[Written in review of a work by Ratzel.]

We have already had occasion to indicate here (in the *Année sociologique*) the importance which we attribute to the work of Ratzel. Not only are his books full of interesting and ingenious ideas, but he possesses the great merit of having rescued geography from the state of isolation in which it was languishing, and of turning it into a genuinely social science; and he has therefore opened up the way to promisingly fruitful research. But we have to make the same comment about his *Anthropogeographie* which we have already made when reviewing his *Politische Geographie*. If the science which Ratzel is seeking to found is extremely thought-provoking, his objective as well as his method still remain very unclear. We have seen above (in the present review) that it is not easy to say definitely what it is exactly concerned with. Undoubtedly the theory of migratory movements is the central part of it; but many other subjects are discussed. In brief, it is concerned to study all of the influences which the soil may have upon social life in general. Now the diverse problems which present themselves according to the standpoint are much too heterogeneous to be dealt with by one science alone. The nature of the soil, climate, etc., has certainly exerted an influence over collective representations, myths, legends, the arts etc.; but it is the task of the sociology of religion to study them from this aspect. The same causes act upon the characteristics of nations: the problems posed in collective ethnology derive from this. Certain features of economic life depend upon the flora and fauna; it is the economist who should be conscious of this. The configuration of the land facilitates or inhibits the concentration of population; consequently demography cannot abstract from this phenomenon. A single scholar hence cannot be equally competent to deal with such a diverse range of problems. This is why *Anthropogeographie* leaves the reader with a rather messy impression. It provides a whole series of considerations which are worthy of further thought; but the connections between these are not always apparent. Above all only a small number of defined laws emerge from it.

Furthermore, when such a multitude of facts of every kind are surveyed with the sole aim of indicating the role which the geographical factor plays in producing them, the result is necessarily to exaggerate its importance, precisely because other factors, which also influence the development of these same phenomena, become lost to view. No doubt geographical influences are far from being of negligible significance; but they do not seem to have the sort of preponderance that has been claimed for them. They help to shape what one might call the idiosyncratic qualities of different peoples – their disposition, or the particular characteristics of their temperament and their organisation. But, to our knowledge, there is not one of the constituent elements of social types which can be accounted for in this way; in any case, we find nothing of this sort demonstrated in Ratzel's book. Moreover, how could this be possible, since geographical conditions vary from one place to another, while we find identical social types (abstracting from their individual peculiarities) at the most diverse points on the globe?

Nor is it proven that this limited influence is of the same intensity at different moments of history. It appears that it is tending to become increasingly weaker. Religious beliefs in the less developed societies show the imprint of the soil upon which they are formed; today, the truths of science are independent of any local context. Thanks to improved communications, fashions, tastes and the customs of different regions become more and more homogeneous. In order to meet this objection, and to show how societies, even the most developed, depend directly upon their territorial base, Ratzel observes that a major European nation is more seriously affected if it loses a part of its territory, even if empty of inhabitants, than if a corresponding part of its population is taken over. In effect, as nations increasingly involve the land in their life and transform it for their own use, it becomes, to the same degree, increasingly difficult to separate them from it. The only thing is, that if in this case there is indeed still a relation of dependence, it is almost the converse of that which is found originally. If now society is linked to the land, this is not because it has come under its influence, but, on the contrary because it has incorporated it within itself. Far from it being the case that society models itself upon the land, it is the land which bears the imprint of society. Thus it is not the land which explains man, it is man which explains the land; and if it remains important for sociology to be aware of the geographical factor, this is not because it sheds new light on sociology, but because the former can only be understood in terms of the latter.

AS, 1899, pp. 556–8

3. The science of morality

There is not a single system of ethics which has not developed from an initial idea in which its entire development was contained implicitly. Some believe that man possesses that idea at birth. Others, by contrast, believe that it evolves more or less slowly in the course of history. But for both schools of thought, for empiricists as well as for rationalists, this idea is the sole reality in ethics. As for the details of legal and moral rules, these are treated as if they had no existence in their own right but were merely applications of this fundamental notion to the particular circumstances of life, varied somewhat to suit the different cases. Hence, the subject-matter of the science of ethics cannot be this system of precepts, which has no reality, but must be the idea from which the precepts are derived and of which they are only diverse applications. Furthermore, all the problems ordinarily raised in ethics refer not to things but to ideas. Moralists examine the idea of law, or the ethical idea, not the nature of law and ethics. They have not yet arrived at the very simple truth that, as our representations of physical things are derived from these things themselves and express them more or less exactly, so our idea of ethics derives from the observable manifestation of the rules that are functioning under our eyes and reproduces this schematically. It follows that these rules, and not our schematic idea of them, should be the subject-matter of science, just as actual physical bodies, and not the layman's idea of them, constitute the subject-matter of physics. The result is that what is taken as the basis of ethics is in fact merely its superstructure: that is, its expression in the individual consciousness. And this method is applied not only to the most general problems of this science but also to particular issues. From the fundamental ethical concepts which are treated first, the moralist proceeds to the derived ideas of family, country, responsibility, charity, and justice; and it is always with ideas that his analysis is concerned.

                                                                    RMS, pp. 23–4

...it has certainly never been demonstrated that the whole of morality can be reduced to a single rule, and comprised within a single concept. When one thinks of the prodigious complexity of moral facts, of the ever-increasing profusion of beliefs, customs and legal prescriptions, one cannot help but find too simple and narrow any formula which is claimed to govern ethics as a whole. Even if we were to admit that there might exist, in fact, in moral life a law which is more general than any others, of which these latter are no more than different forms and particular applications, it would still be necessary, in order to discover it, to follow the conventional scientific method. These observations apply just as much to Mill as to Kant or to Spencer. Whatever efforts the latter might have made to overhaul utilitarianism, his fundamental postulate is still formulated in the same way as that of the utilitarians, holding that the objective of morality is the advancement of the life of the individual, and that the good and the useful are synonymous terms. This may possibly be the principle of morality as he would wish it to be; but it remains to be seen if it is the principle of morality as it is. Perhaps if utilitarianism were valid, moral life would be simpler and more logical; but it is no more up to the moralist to reconstruct it than to the physiologist to remake the organism. He has simply to observe it, and to explain it if possible. At least, this is how we must begin: the construction of ethical directives can only come afterwards.

But even if a single law dominated the whole of morality, and was known to us, we could not deduce from it the specific truths which are the substance of science. Deduction can only apply to very simple things, that is to say, to very general things. Since they are found everywhere, the images which portray them, being constantly repeated, become detached early on from the mass of other impressions, and become firmly organised in the mind. They form a deeply-rooted layer in the mind, an unchanging foundation. The mind can thus relate to these kinds of objects without going outside of itself; but it is not the same with complex – that is to say, concrete – things. As the representations which we have of these are the most recently developed in the evolution of the intellect, they are scarcely more than ambiguous outlines of things. Also, the mind, to some degree, makes of them what it wishes; this is why in these sorts of affairs one quite easily proves what one believes, that is to say, what one desires. Now moral phenomena are the most complex in the world; the use of deduction in relation to them is thus absolutely out of the question. Certainly Spencer is correct in saying that some modes of conduct are better than others, and that this is not the result of accident: that 'this outcome must be the necessary consequence of things'. But in order to see how they come into being, we have to uncover the causal connections which exist in reality. The connection which ties moral prescriptions to the initial fact in question is itself a fact which can only be established by observation and testing. It might be asked, if we know the nature of man and that of his social and physical environment cannot we decide how the first should adapt to the second? In certain simple cases, perhaps; but in few in which the circumstances are more complicated. In the latter, our calculations will be too little informed by fact, and the proposed adaptation will be very unlikely to be the best possible. Moreover, is it necessary to point out that we are far from knowing, even in an approximate way, the nature of man and of societies?

These theoretical considerations were necessary in order to make apparent the full novelty of the German school. It makes, in point of fact, a protest against the use of deduction in the moral sciences, and an attempt at last to introduce into them a truly inductive method. Each of the moralists whom we have mentioned (i.e. Schmoller, Wagner, Wundt, etc.) are strongly conscious of how narrow and artificial are all the ethical doctrines which have been adopted by thinkers up to the present. Kant's ethics seem to them no less inadequate than those of the utilitarians. The Kantians see in morality a phenomenon which is specific, but transcendental, and which is outside the scope of science; the utilitarians treat morality as an empirical fact, but one which has no specific properties of its own. They reduce it to this highly confused notion of 'utility', and see in it nothing more than an applied psychology or sociology. Only the German moralists consider moral phenomena as facts which are empirical and at the same time *sui generis*. Ethics is not an applied or derivative science, but an autonomous one. It has its own subject-matter, which it studies in the same way as the physicist studies physical facts, and the biologist studies biological facts; and it employs the same method. The facts with which it deals are mores, customs, positive legal prescriptions, and economic phenomena in so far as these become the object of legal provisions; it observes these, analyses them, compares them, and thus progressively moves towards the laws which explain them. No doubt it is related to psychology, since moral facts have their location within the heart of the personality of the individual; but they are distinct from psychic facts, if only by their imperative character. In addition, they are related to all other social facts, but are not to be confused with them. Ethics is not a consequence of, and as if a corollary of, sociology, but is a social science by the side of and amidst the others.

RP, 1887(b), pp. 276–8

Let us not be surprised to see a single society riven, at a given moment, by divergent or even contradictory currents. Does it not happen constantly that the individual is divided against himself: that one part of him is pulled in one direction, while all the rest is pushed in another direction? Now these divergencies, indeed, even these contradictions, are perhaps more normal in society than in the individual. Above all they are inevitable in periods of crisis and transition. . .

EPF, p. 223

[According to Wundt] The true object of morality is to make man feel that he is not a whole, but part of a whole – and how insignificant he is by reference to the plurality of contexts which surround him. Since society forms one of these contexts, and one of the most immediate, it is consequently morality which makes it possible; but it does so, so to speak, in passing, and without seeking to achieve this result. Morality results from the efforts which man makes to find a durable objective which he can attach himself to in order to find a happiness which is not merely transient. Once he has cast off his own personality so as to undertake this search, the first objects of this nature which he meets with are the family, the city and the nation, and at that point he goes no further. However these have not, because of this, any value in themselves, but only symbolise – moreover, in an imperfect fashion – the ideal which he pursues. In a word, since societies are one of the means whereby moral sentiments become realised, they engender them in the course of their functioning, and at the same time the instincts and inclinations which they are conditional upon. But these are never more than one of the transitory phases through which they pass, one of the forms which they successively assume.

But in this view one of the essential properties of morality becomes inexplicable: this is its obligatory force. Wundt recognises this characteristic in principle, but we need to show from where morality derives such authority, in whose name it commands. It is in the name of God, if one sees in it a duty given to us by the divinity; it is in the name of society, if it consists in a social discipline. But if it is neither of these, one can no longer see from where it takes the right to issue its orders. Could it be said that it is logical for the part to submit to the whole? But only the intellect is led by logic, not the will: the objective of our conduct is not the true, but the useful or the good. We are assured, certainly, that we will profit by this submission, which will cause us to find happiness. This may be so, but concern with our happiness alone can never give rise to actual imperatives. That which is desirable is not obligatory. When we have acted against our interests, however elevated they may be, the regret which we feel is not comparable to remorse. We cannot obligate ourselves; every command entails at least an eventual sanction, and consequently a superior power to us, which is capable of constraining us. Now a need, or an aspiration, is only a part of our personality and, in the normal way, is not separate from it. Wundt, moreover, recognises two sorts of imperatives, certain of which are due to constraint, and others to freedom. But who cannot see that these two words, imperative and freedom, clash when coupled together? Evidently the first is only there for reasons of symmetry and, in fact, Wundt considers that morality, in its highest form, is not obligatory. It is certainly true that men of high morality submit without difficulty and even gladly to obligation; but this does not mean that they do not feel it, that it does not exist for them. Duty, even when carried out with enthusiasm, is still duty, and no form of morality has ever been observed in which duty was not in some measure the dominant idea. But then the question remains: to whom are we obligated? To ourselves? This is simply a play on words; for what is a debt where we are at the same time debtor and creditor?

Certainly the idea which is at the basis of this doctrine is as correct as it is profound, and can be accepted by even the most empiricist ethics. It is an undoubted fact that we need to believe that our actions have consequences which go beyond the immediate moment; that they are not completely limited to the point in time and space at which they are produced, but that their results are, to some degree, of lasting duration and broad in scope. Otherwise they would be too insignificant; scarcely more than a thread would separate them from the void, and they would not have any interest for us. Only actions which have a lasting quality are worthy of our volition, only pleasures which endure are

worthy of our desires. No doubt not everyone experiences this
need in the same way; for the child and the savage, the future
hardly goes beyond the next moment. Adult and civilised man,
but of average culture, measures his future in months and years;
the more developed man sees before him ever vaster perspectives.
But all of these aspire to detach themselves from the present,
whose limitation they feel. The perspective of nothingness is an
intolerable burden to us; and since it threatens us everywhere
around, the only means of escaping it is to live in the future.
None of our ends has an absolute value, not even happiness; it is a
utilitarian who has shown this [here Durkheim refers to J. S. Mill].
If they attract us, it is because we believe them to be relative to
something other than ourselves. If this were an error, if ever we
perceived that behind these relative ends there was only nothingness, the spell which draws us to them would be broken, and our
life would be deprived of meaning and significance. If our efforts
result in nothing lasting, they are hollow, and why should we
strive for that which is futile? Moreover, individualism, because it
detaches the individual from the rest of the world, because it
confines him in himself and closes off every horizon, leads directly
to pessimism. Of what value are our individual pleasures, which
are so empty and short? This is, in fact, the greatest objection to
utilitarian and individualist ethics. But if this need is an important
factor in moral evolution, is it the essential factor in it? This is
what does not seem to us to have been demonstrated at all.
Could not one say, on the contrary: morality is first and foremost a
social function, and it is only by a fortunate circumstance, because
societies are infinitely more long-lived than individuals, that they
permit us to taste satisfactions which are not merely ephemeral?

RP, 1887(b), pp. 138–40

If orthodox economists and the moralists of the Kantian school
placed political economy outside of ethics, this is because the two
sciences seemed to them to be two separate and unrelated worlds.
But if the only distinction between them is that the one is the
container, and the other the contents, it is then impossible to
detach one from the other. One cannot understand anything of the
moral precepts which concern property, contrast, labour, etc., if
one does not know the economic causes from which they derive;
and on the other hand, one would form an entirely false idea of
economic development if one neglected the moral causes which
play a part in it. For ethics is not absorbed by political economy;
but all social functions contribute to producing the form which

economic phenomena are led to assume, even while those phenomena themselves contribute to it. For example, to the degree that a
society needs a higher productivity, so it becomes necessary to
stimulate the personal interest to a greater extent, and consequently
law and morality each recognise a greater amount of personal freedom. But, at the same time, under the influence of causes which are
only distantly connected with economic necessities, the conception of human dignity develops, and opposes excessive and premature exploitation of children and women. These protective
measures, dictated by morality, react in their turn upon economic
relations, and transform them by encouraging the industrialist
to replace human labour by that of machines...Up to the
present, for all schools of ethical theory, for the utilitarians as
for the Kantians, the problem of ethics consisted essentially in
determining the general form of moral conduct, from which they
subsequently deduced the content. They began by establishing
that the principle of morality is the good, or duty, or the useful,
and then drew from that axiom certain precepts which constituted
practical and applied morality. It follows from the writings which
we have just discussed [in the previous part of the article] that,
on the contrary, form does not pre-exist content, but derives from
it and expresses it. We cannot construct morality out of nothing
in order to impose it subsequently upon reality; rather, we must
observe reality in order to induce morality from it. We must
examine it in its multiple relations with the unending number of
phenomena in terms of which it is shaped, and which, in turn, it
regulates. If ethics is separated from these, it seems no longer to
have any basis of its own, and to float in a void. When it loses
contact with the very source of life, it becomes arid to the point of
being reduced to nothing more than an abstract conception,
entirely limited to a dry and empty formula. By contrast, if it is
allowed to remain bound to the reality of which it is a part, it
appears as a vital and complex function of the social organism.
There is hardly any event of any importance in society which
does not have repercussions upon morality and influence it. The
economists, it is true, have only drawn our attention to certain
of these which particularly interest them: but it is easy to general-
ise the conclusions which they have arrived at. This being the
case, it is just as impossible to draw a radical separation between
ethics, political economy, statistics and the science of positive law,
as it is to study the nervous system in abstraction from other
organs and other functions.

RP, 1887(b), pp. 40–3

CHARACTERISTICS OF MORAL PHENOMENA

The first question that confronts us, as in all rational and scientific research, is: By what characteristics can we recognise and distinguish moral facts?

Morality appears to us to be a collection of precepts, of rules of conduct. But there are also other rules that prescribe our behaviour. All utilitarian techniques are governed similarly by systems of rules, and we must find the distinctive characteristics of moral rules. The violation of a rule generally brings unpleasant consequences to the agent. But we may distinguish two different types of consequence: (i) The first results mechanically from the act of violation. If I violate a rule of hygiene that commands me to stay away from a source of infection, the result of my act will automatically be the contraction of disease. The act, once it has been performed, sets in motion the consequences, and by analysis of the act we can know in advance what the result will be. (ii) When, however, I violate the rule that forbids me to kill, an analysis of my act will tell me nothing. I shall not find inherent in it the subsequent blame or punishment. There is complete heterogeneity between the act and its consequence. It is impossible to discover *analytically* in the act of murder any element of the notion of punishment. The link between act and consequence here is a *synthetic* one.

Such consequences attached to acts by synthetic links I shall call *sanctions*. I do not as yet know the origin or explanation of this link. I merely note its existence and nature, without for the moment going any further.

We can, however, enlarge upon this notion. Since sanctions are not revealed by analysis of the act that they govern, it is clear that I am not punished *simply because* I did this or that. It is not the intrinsic nature of my action that produces the sanction which follows, but the fact that the act violates the rule that prohibits it. In fact, one and the same act, identically performed with the same material consequences, is punished or not punished according to whether or not there is a rule forbidding it. The existence of the rule and the relation to it of the act determine the sanction. Thus homicide, condemned in time of peace, is freed from blame in time of war. An act, intrinsically the same, which is punished today among Europeans, was not punished in ancient Greece since there it violated no pre-established rule.

We have now reached a more profound conception of sanctions. A sanction is the consequence of an act that does not result from the content of that act, but from the violation by that act of a pre-established rule. It is because there is a pre-established rule, and the breach is a rebellion against this rule, that a sanction follows.

Thus there are rules that present this specific characteristic: we refrain from performing the acts they forbid simply because they are forbidden. This is what is meant by the *obligatory* character of the moral rule. We re-discover by a rigorously empirical analysis the idea of *duty* and obligation almost as Kant understood them.

We have so far only considered negative sanctions (blame, punishment), since in these the characteristic of obligation is most apparent. There are sanctions of another sort. Acts that comform to the moral rule are praised and those who accomplish them are honoured. In this case the public moral consciousness reacts in a different way and the consequence of the act is favourable to the agent, but the mechanism of the social phenomenon is the same. As in the preceding instance the sanction comes, not from the act itself, but from its conformity to a rule that prescribes it. No doubt this type of obligation differs somewhat from the former in degree, but we have here two varieties of the same group. There are not two kinds of moral rules, negative and positive commands: these are but two types within the same class. . .

We cannot perform an act which is not in some way meaningful to us simply because we have been commanded to do so. It is psychologically impossible to pursue an end to which we are indifferent – that does not appear to us as good and does not affect our sensibility. Morality must, then, be not only obligatory but also desirable and desired. This desirability is the second characteristic of all moral acts.

SP, pp. 59–63 and 64

A rule is not a simple mode of customary action; it is a mode of conduct that we do not feel free to alter according to taste. It is in some measure – and to the same extent that it is a rule – resistant to the will. There is in it something that resists us, is beyond us and which imposes itself upon and constrains us. We do not determine its existence or its nature. It is independent of what we are. Rather than expressing us, it dominates us. Now, if it were entirely an internal state, like a sentiment or a habit, there would be no reason why it should not conform to all the variations and fluctuations of our internal states. Of course, we do set for ourselves a line of conduct, and then we say that we have set up 'rules' of conduct of such and such a sort. But the word so used generally lacks its full meaning. A plan of action that we ourselves outline, which depends only upon ourselves, and which we can always modify is a project, not a rule. Or, if in fact it is to some extent really dependent upon our will, it is also at the same time dependent on something other than our will, on something external to us. For example, we adopt a given mode of life because it carries the authority of science; the authority of science gives it its own authority. It is to science that we conform in our conduct, not to ourselves. It is to science that we bend our will.

We see in these examples what there is in the conception of rules beyond the notion of regularity: *the idea of authority.* By authority, we must understand that influence which is imposed upon us by any moral power that we acknowledge as superior. Because of this influence, we act in the way which is prescribed, not because the required conduct is attractive to us, not because we are so inclined by some innate or learned predisposition, but because there is a certain compelling influence in the authority dictating it. Voluntary obedience consists in such acquiescence. What are the mental processes at the bottom of the notion of authority, which create this imperative force to which we submit? This we shall have to investigate presently. For the moment, the question is not germane; it is enough if we have the feeling of the thing and of its reality. There is in every moral force that we feel to be superior, something that bends our will. In one sense one can say that there is no rule, properly speaking in any sphere of action, which does not have this imperative character in some degree. For once again, every rule commands. It is this that makes us feel that we are not free to do as we wish.

Morality, however, constitutes a category of rules where the idea of authority plays an absolutely preponderant role. Part of the esteem we accord to principles of hygiene or of professional practice or various precepts drawn from popular wisdom un-doubtedly derives from the authority accorded science and experimental research. Such a wealth of knowledge and human experience, by itself, imposes on us a respect that communicates itself to the bearers, just as the respect of the believer for religious things is also given to priests. However, in all these cases, if we conform to the rule it is not only out of deference to the authority that is its source; it is also because the prescribed action may very well have useful consequences, whereas contrary behaviour would entail harmful results. If, when we are sick, we take care of our-selves, following the doctor's orders, it is not only out of respect for his authority, but also because we hope thus to be cured. There is involved here, therefore, a feeling other than respect for authority. There enter quite utilitarian considerations, which are intrinsic to the nature of the act and to its outcomes, possible or probable. It is quite otherwise with moral rules. No doubt, if we violate them, we risk unfortunate consequences: we may be censured, blacklisted, or materially hurt, either in person or with reference to our property. But it is certain and incontestable fact that an act is not moral, even when it is in substantial agreement with the rule, if the consideration of consequences has determined it. Here, for the act to be everything it should be, for the rule to be obeyed as it ought to be, it is necessary for us to yield, not in order to avoid disagreeable results or some moral or material punishment, or to obtain a certain reward; but very simply because we must, regardless of the consequences our conduct may have for us. One must obey a moral precept out of respect for it and for this reason alone. The whole effect that it exerts upon our wills derives exclusively from the authority with which it is invested. Here authority operates alone; to the extent that any other element enters into conduct, to that extent it loses its moral character. We are saying, then, that while all rules command, a moral rule consists entirely in a commandment and in nothing else.

EM, pp. 32–5

For some authors, such as Hobbes and Rousseau, there is a break in continuity between the individual and society. Man is thus naturally refractory to social life; he can only resign himself to it when forced. Social ends are not simply the convergence of individual ends; they are, rather, contrary to them. Thus, to induce the individual to pursue them, it is necessary to constrain him; and the task of society consists above all in the institution and organisation of this constraint. Since, however, the individual is regarded as the sole reality of the human realm, this organisation, whose only object is to hinder and confine him, can only be conceived as artificial. It is not founded in nature, since it is designed to restrict it, by preventing it from producing antisocial consequences. It is a human creation, a mechanism constructed entirely by hand of man, which, like all products of this kind, is only what it is because men have willed it so. A decree of the will created it; another can transform it. Neither Hobbes nor Rousseau seems to have realised how contradictory it is to admit that the individual is himself the author of a machine which has for its essential role his domination and constraint; or at least, it seemed to them sufficient for this contradiction to disappear that it be disguised in the eyes of those who are its victims, by the clever artifice of the social contract.

The philosophers of natural law, the economists, and, more recently, Spencer, have taken their inspiration from a contrary notion. For them social life is essentially spontaneous and society is a natural phenomenon. But, if they give it this character, it is not because they recognise its specific properties, but merely because they find its basis in the nature of the individual. No more than the previous thinkers do they see it as a system of things with its own independent existence, by reason of causes specific to itself. But, whereas the former conceived of it only as a conventional arrangement which is not tied to reality and is left in mid-air, so to speak, Spencer and the economists give as its bases the fundamental instincts of human nature. Man is naturally inclined to political, domestic, and religious life, to commerce, etc.; and it is from these natural drives that social organisation is derived. Consequently, wherever it is normal, it has no need to impose itself. When it has recourse to constraint, it is because it is not what it ought to be or because the circumstances are abnormal. In principle, we have only to leave individual forces to develop freely for them to organise themselves socially.

Neither one of these doctrines is ours. To be sure, we do make constraint the characteristic of all social facts. But this constraint does not result from more or less effective machinery, designed to conceal from men the traps in which they have caught themselves. It is due simply to the fact that the individual finds himself in the presence of a force which is superior to him and before which he bows; but this force is a natural one. It does not derive from a conventional arrangement which human will has superimposed, fully formed, upon natural reality. It issues from innermost reality; it is the necessary product of given causes. Thus recourse to artifice is unnecessary to get the individual to submit to them of his entire free will; it is sufficient to make him become conscious of his state of natural dependence and inferiority, whether he forms a tangible and symbolic representation of it through religion, or whether he arrives at an adequate and definite notion of it through science. Since the superiority of society to him is not simply physical, but intellectual and moral, it has nothing to fear from a critical examination, provided it is applied accurately. By making man understand by how much the social being is richer, more complex, and more permanent than the individual being, reflected thought will simply reveal to him the intelligible reasons for the subordination demanded of him and for the sentiments of attachment and respect which habit has fixed in his heart.

Consequently it would be only an extremely superficial criticism to censure our conception of social constraints for reviving the theories of Hobbes and Machiavelli. But if, contrary to these philosophers, we say that social life is natural, our reason is not that we find its source in the nature of the individual. It is natural rather because it springs directly from the collective being which is, itself, of a *sui generis* nature, and because it results from special development which individual minds undergo in their association with each other, an association from which a new form of existence is evolved. If, then, we agree with the former that social reality appears to the individual under the aspect of constraint, we admit with the others that it is a spontaneous product of reality. The tie which binds together these two elements, which appear to be contradictory, is the fact that this reality from which it emanates surpasses the individual. That is to say, the words 'constraint' and 'spontaneity', have not in our terminology the meaning that Hobbes gives to the former and Spencer to the latter.

RMS, pp. 120–3

Society is not, then, as has often been believed, a stranger to the moral world, or something which has only secondary repercussions upon it; it is, on the contrary, the necessary condition of its existence. Society is not a simple aggregate of individuals who, when they enter it, bring their own intrinsic morality with them; rather, man is a moral being only because he lives in society, since morality consists in being solidary with a group and varies with this solidarity. Let all social life disappear, and moral life would disappear with it, since it would no longer have any objective. The state of nature of the philosophers of the eighteenth century, if not immoral, is, at least, *amoral*. Rousseau himself recognised this. This does not, however, lead us to a view of morality as a function of social interest. To be sure, society cannot exist if its parts are not solidary, but solidarity is only one of its conditions of existence. There are many others which are no less necessary and which are not moral. Moreover, it can happen that, in the system of ties which make up morality, there are some which are not useful in themselves or which have a force incommensurate with their degree of utility. The idea of utility thus does not enter as an essential element in our definition.

As for what is called individual morality, if we understand by that a body of obligations of which the individual would, at the same time, be subject and object, which would refer only to himself, and which would, consequently, exist even if he were alone – this is an abstract conception which has no relation to reality. Morality, in all its forms, is never met with except in society, and only varies in relation to social conditions. To ask what it would be if societies did not exist is thus to depart from facts and to enter the domain of gratuitous hypotheses and unverifiable flights of the imagination. The duties of the individual towards himself are, in reality, duties towards society. They correspond to certain collective sentiments which he may not offend, whether the offended and the offender are one and the same person, or whether they are distinct. Today, for example, there is in all healthy minds a very pronounced sense of respect for human dignity, to which we are supposed to conform as much in relation to ourselves as in relation to others, and this constitutes the essential quality of what is called individual morality. Every act which contravenes this is censured, even when the agent and the sufferer are the same person. That is why, according to the Kantian formula, we must respect human personality wherever we find it, which is to say, in ourselves as in those like us. The sentiment of which it is the object is not less offended in one case than in the other.

DTS, pp. 394–5

THE 'NORMAL' AND THE 'PATHOLOGICAL'

Instead of claiming to determine at the outset the relations of the normal and the morbid to vital forces, let us simply seek some external, immediately perceptible, but objective characteristic which will enable us to distinguish these two orders of facts.

Every sociological phenomenon (as well as every biological phenomenon) can assume a different form in different circumstances while still conserving its essential characteristics. We can distinguish two such forms. Some are distributed in the entire range of the type; they are to be found, if not in all individuals, at least in the majority of them. If they are not identical in all the cases where they occur, but vary from one individual to another, these variations occur within narrow limits. There are others, by contrast, which are exceptional: not only do we find them in only a minority of cases, but, where they do occur, they most often do not persist throughout the life of the individual.

They are an exception both in time and in space. Here are, then, two distinct varieties of phenomena which should be designated by different terms. We shall call 'normal' these social conditions that are most general in form, and the others 'morbid' or 'pathological'. If we call the 'average type' that hypothetical being that is constructed by assembling in the same category the most frequent forms, in a sort of abstract individuality, one may say that the normal type merges with the average type, and that every deviation from this standard of health is a morbid phenomenon. It is true that the average type cannot be determined with the same degree of clarity as an individual type, since its constituent attributes are not absolutely fixed but are likely to vary. But the possibility of its constitution is beyond doubt, since, merging as it does with the generic type, it is the immediate subject-matter of science. It is the functions of the average organism that the physiologist studies, and the sociologist does the same. Once we know how to distinguish the various social types from one-another – a problem which will be treated below – it is always possible to find the most general form of a phenomenon in a given species.

It is clear that a phenomenon can be defined as pathological only in relation to a given type. The conditions of health and illness cannot be defined *in abstracto* and in an absolute manner. This rule is not denied in biology; it has never occurred to anyone to assume that what is normal for a mollusc is normal also for a vertebrate. Each species has a health of its own, because it has an average type of its own, and there exists a state of health for the lowest species as well as for the highest. The same principle applies to sociology, although it is often misunderstood here. We must abandon the still too common habit of judging an institution, a practice, or moral standard, as if it were good or bad in and by itself, for all social types indiscriminately.

Since the point of reference for judging health or morbidity varies with the species, it can also vary for a single species, if this species itself changes. Thus, from the purely biological point of view, what is normal for the savage is not always normal for the civilised man, and vice versa. There are, especially, the variations depending on age, which are important because they occur regularly in all types. The health of the aged person is not that of the adult and, similarly, the health of the latter is not that of the child; the same is true of societies. A social fact can, then, be called normal for a given social species only in relation to an equally specific phase of its development; consequently, to know if it should be termed thus, it is not enough to observe the form it takes in the generality of societies belonging to this type; we must also take care to examine them at the corresponding phase of their development. . .

Since generality, which is the external characteristic of normal phenomena, is itself an explicable phenomenon, after it has been definitely established by observation it should be explained. Although we may be assured in advance, of course, that it is produced by a definite cause, it is preferable that we know exactly what this cause is. The normality of the phenomenon will, indeed, be indisputable if it is demonstrated that the external sign, which had at first revealed it, is not purely fortuitous but grounded in the nature of things; if, in a word, one can show this normality of fact to be a normality governed by necessity. Furthermore, this demonstration will not always consist in showing that the trait is useful to the organism, although this is most frequently the case, for reasons which have just been stated; but it can also happen, as we have also remarked above, that a situation is normal without being at all useful, simply because it is necessarily implied in the nature of the being. Thus, it would perhaps be desirable if childbirth did not occasion such violent disturbances in the female organism, but this is impossible. Consequently, the normality of the phenomenon is to be explained by the fact alone that it is bound up with the conditions of existence of the species under consideration, either as a mechanically necessary effect of these conditions, or as a means permitting the organisms to adapt themselves to them.

This proof is not simply useful as a check. It must not be forgotten that, if there is any usefulness in distinguishing the normal from the abnormal, it is primarily in clarifying our practice. Now, to act with full knowledge of the facts, we need to know not only the proper procedure but also the reasons for it. Scientific propositions concerning the normal state will be more immediately applicable to individual cases when accompanied by their reasons, for then we shall be better able to recognise in which cases, and in which direction, they should be modified in their application.

There are circumstances in which this verification is absolutely necessary, since the first method, if used alone, can lead to error. This is the case with periods of transition, when the entire type is in process of evolution, without having yet become stabilised in its new form. The only normal type that is given in these circumstances is the type from the previous stage, and yet it no longer corresponds to the new conditions of existence. A phenomenon can thus persist throughout the entire range of a type although no longer adapted to the requirements of the situation. It is then normal only in appearance; for its universality is now illusory, since its persistence, due only to the blind force of habit, can no longer be accepted as an index of a close connection with the general conditions of its collective existence.

The principal objective of every science of life, whether individual or social is, in brief, to define and explain the normal state and to distinguish it from its opposite. If, however, normality is not given in the things themselves but, on the contrary, is a characteristic we may or may not impute to them, this solid grounding disappears. The mind is then complacent in the face of a reality which has little to teach it; it is no longer restrained by the matter which it is analysing, since it is the mind, in some manner or other, that determines the matter. The various rules we have established up to the present are thus directly interdependent. In order that sociology may be a true science of things, the generality of phenomena must be taken as the criterion of their normality.

Our method has, moreover, the advantage of regulating action at the same time as thought. If the desirable is not subject to observation but can and must be determined by a sort of mental calculus, no limit, so to speak, can be set for the free inventions of the imagination in search of the good. For how may we assign to perfection a limit? It escapes all limitation, by definition. The goal of humanity then recedes into infinity, discouraging some by its very remoteness and, by contrast, arousing others who, in order to draw a little nearer to it, quicken the pace and plunge into revolutions. This practical dilemma may be escaped if the desirable is defined in the same way as is health, and if health is something that is defined as inherent in things. For then the object of our efforts is both given and desired at one stroke. It is no longer a matter of pursuing desperately an objective that retreats as one advances, but of working with steady perseverance to maintain the normal state, of re-establishing it if it is threatened, and of rediscovering its conditions if they have changed. The duty of the statesman is no longer to violently push society toward an ideal that seems attractive to him, but his role is that of the physician: he prevents the outbreak of illnesses by good hygiene, and he seeks to cure them when they have appeared.

RMS, pp. 55–7, 59–61 and 74–5

[Written in reply to criticism by Tarde of Durkheim's notions of
normality and pathology.]

...If I have said of crime that it was 'normal', it was through the
application of a general rule which I have tried to establish in
order to distinguish the normal from the abnormal. The discussion
of this rule should perhaps have formed the basis of this debate
for, once this has been set out, the rest follows. Tarde touches
upon this question only briefly. He raises two objections. 1. The
normal type, he states, must not be confused with the average
type; since, as everyone is ill in greater or lesser degree, illness
would then be normal. I reply to this: if everyone is ill, everyone
has his own particular illness; these individual characteristics thus
cancel each other out in respect of the generic type, which bears
no trace of them. Might it be said that, rather than for any particular illness, we should be looking, at least, for a propensity for
illness in general? This may be acceptable; but let us not be
satisfied with mere phrases. What does this propensity consist in?
Quite simply in the fact that the average individual, as with every
individual, has only limited powers of resistance, which consequently are constantly open to being overcome by greater,
opposing forces. What contradiction is there in saying that the
state of health implies only a limited vital energy? I see no more
than a truism in this. 2. In the second place, Tarde objects, a
society in which there were only average men, from the physical,
intellectual or moral point of view, would be at a lower level than
it could otherwise maintain. How, then, can we say that it is
healthy? What a strange confusion my ingenious opponent has
got himself into here! In the theory which I have formulated, a
society which was made up only of average individuals would be
essentially abnormal. For there is no society which does not
contain a profusion of individual anomalies, and such a universal
phenomenon cannot exist without reason. *It is therefore socially
normal that there should be psychologically abnormal individuals
in every society*; and the normality of crime is only a particular
case of this general proposition. As I expressly remarked in my
book [*The Rules of Sociological Method*], the conditions of individual health and those of social health may be very different,
and even contrary to one-another. This can be accepted without
difficulty, if one recognises, as I do, that there is a deep line of
demarcation between the social and the psychic. However, this
opposition can be directly proved in an empirical manner, without reference to any system. A society can only survive if it is

periodically renewed: that is to say, if the older generations cede place to new ones. Therefore it is necessary for the first to die. Thus the normal state of societies implies the illness of individuals; a certain rate of mortality, like a certain rate of criminality, is indispensable to collective health.

RP, 1895, pp. 522–3

4. Moral obligation, duty and freedom

REASON, ART AND MORAL OBLIGATION

Let us suppose that [a science of moral facts] has been perfected. Our ascendancy is culminated: we are masters of the moral order. It is no longer external to us, since from this point on we conceive of it in terms of a system of clear and distinct ideas whose relationships we understand. Now we are in a position to ascertain the extent to which the moral order is founded in the nature of things – that is, in the nature of society – which is to say to what extent it is what it ought to be. In the degree that we see it as such, we can freely consent to it. For to wish that it be other than is implied by the natural make-up of the reality that it expresses would be to talk nonsense under the pretext of free will. We can also see to what extent it is not based on the order of things, for it is always possible that it may involve abnormal elements. But then we should have available, thanks to the same science we are supposing to be established, the means of restoring it to a normal state. Thus, on condition of having adequate knowledge of moral precepts, of their causes and of their functions, we are in a position to conform to them, but consciously and knowing why. Conformity which has thus been assented to is no longer a constraint. No doubt we are still further from this ideal state in respect of our moral life than that relating to the physical world; for the science of morality has only recently developed, and its results are still imprecise. But that is not important. There remains, nonetheless, the means of liberating ourselves; and this is what lends substance to the aspiration for greater moral autonomy which is felt in the public consciousness. But, it will be said, from the moment that we understand the reason for the existence of moral rules, from the moment that we conform voluntarily to them, do they not immediately lose their imperative quality? And then are we not ourselves vulnerable to the criticism levelled at Kant, that is to say, of sacrificing one of the essential elements of morality to the principle of autonomy? Does not the idea of consent freely given exclude the notion of the imperative command, in spite of the fact that we have seen in the imperative quality of the rule one of its most distinctive traits? This, however, is not so. A thing does not lose its identity because we know why it exists. Because we know the nature and the laws of life, it does not at all follow that life loses even one of its specific characteristics. In the same way, because the science of moral facts teaches us the reason for the imperative quality inherent in moral rules, these latter do not thereby cease to be imperative. Because we know that there is something useful in that which is commanded, it follows not that we fail to obey but that we obey voluntarily. We can understand very well that it is in our nature to be limited by forces outside us; accordingly, we accept this limitation freely, because it is natural and good without being any the less real. But since it rests upon our informed consent it is no longer a humiliation and a bondage. Such autonomy, then, leaves to moral principles all their distinctive qualities, even those of which it seems to be – and in a sense is – the negation. The two contrary aspects are reconciled and rejoined. We are still limited, for we are finite beings; and, in a sense, we are still passive with respect to the rule that commands us. However, this passivity becomes at the same time activity, through the active part we take in deliberately willing it. We desire it because we know the reason for its existence. . .

Undoubtedly, if religious symbols were simply superimposed externally upon moral reality, it would simply be sufficient to erase them, thus leaving in a state of purity and isolation a self-sufficient rational morality. But, in fact, these two systems of beliefs and practices have been too inextricably bound together in history: for centuries they have been too interlaced for their connections possibly to be so external and superficial for the separation to be so easily made. We must not forget that only yesterday they were supported by the same keystone: God, the centre of religious life, was also the supreme guarantor of moral order. There is nothing surprising in this partial coalescence, if we remember that the duties of religion and those of morality are both duties, in other words, morally obligatory practices. It is hence completely natural that men should have been led to see in one and the same being the source of all obligation. But then one can easily foresee, by reason of this relationship and partial fusion, that certain elements of both systems approached each other to the point of merging and forming a single unity. Certain moral

ideas became united with certain religious ideas to such an extent
as to become indistinct from them: to such an extent that they
had, or seemed to have (which comes to the same thing) no
existence or reality apart from the latter. Consequently, if, in
rationalising morality in moral education, we confine ourselves to
eliminating from moral discipline everything that is religious
without replacing it, we almost inevitably run the danger of
eliminating at the same time all elements that are properly moral.
Under the name of rational morality, we would be then left only
with an impoverished and colourless morality. To avoid this
danger, we must therefore not be satisfied with a superficial
separation. We must seek, in the very heart of religious conceptions, those moral realities that are, as it were, lost and dispersed in it. We must separate them off, find out what they
consist in, determine their proper nature, and express them in
rational language. In a word, we must discover the rational substitutes for those religious notions that have, for so long, served
as the vehicle for the most essential moral ideas.

EM, pp. 133–5 and 9–10

. . .art, by definition, moves in the domain of the unreal, of the
imaginary. Even when the beings represented by the artist are
founded in reality, it is not this realism which gives them their
beauty. It is of small importance to me that the personage whom
the poet brings alive in his verses should ever have existed in
history; if I admire the creation, it is because it is beautiful, and
my admiration would be in no way diminished if it was entirely
invented by the imagination of the artist. Indeed, when the
illusion is too complete, and causes us to take the scene which is
portrayed for us as real, our pleasure in the beauty evaporates. We
feel it only when we are conscious that events which we witness
are not really capable of affecting human destiny, of making men
like ourselves suffer, either spiritually or physically; when we can
see the things which are described to us in quite another light
to that which they present in real life. In short, we can only
fully experience aesthetic feeling on condition of losing sight of
reality.

Morality, on the contrary, is the domain of action, and can only
be grasped in relation to real phenomena: otherwise, it is lost in
the void. To act morally is to do good to beings of flesh and blood,
to change something in reality. But in order to feel the need to
change, transform and improve reality, we cannot abstract ourselves from it. On the contrary, we have to embrace it and love it,

in spite of its ugliness, its pettiness and its meanness. We must not
turn away from it towards an imaginary world but, on the contrary, we must keep our eyes fixed upon it. This is why an exag-
geratedly aesthetic culture, by turning us away from the real
world, would relax the springs of moral action. Duty is not
learned through discovering how to combine ideas, or to harmonise phrases, sounds, or colours. And the more art is able to
hide from itself in its own shortcomings, the more harm it can
produce. For it can select morality itself as the subject of its
creations, and by placing before us idealised images of a lofty
morality, art makes us live an existence on the level of ideas
which, save that it is fictional and imaginary, has the external
characteristics of truly moral life. Now we readily take this simple
word-play seriously. We are quite prepared to believe ourselves
dutiful because we are capable of eloquently praising duty or
because we receive pleasure from hearing others offer such
eloquent praise; because we are able to discuss duty unam-
biguously, or because we participate in such discussions, we believe ourselves to be dutiful men. Is it necessary to point out that
this is only a false sentiment? For truth, in its essence, consists in
action, in accomplishment, in creating something of oneself outside of oneself – not in constructing beautiful images in the silence
of the mind, emotional images which are contemplated intro-
spectively.

EPF, pp. 240–1

DISCIPLINE AND FREEDOM

If we believe that discipline is useful, indeed necessary for the
individual, it is because it seems to us demanded by nature itself.
It is the way in which nature realises itself normally, not a way of
minimising or destroying nature. Like everything which exists,
man is a limited being: he is part of a whole. Physically, he is part
of the universe; morally, he is part of society. Therefore he cannot, without contradicting his nature, try to supersede the limits
imposed on every side. And, in fact, everything that is most
fundamental in him depends precisely upon this quality of
limitedness. To say that he is a person is to say that he is distinct
from everything which is not himself; this differentiation implies
limitation. If, then, from our point of view, discipline is good, it is
not because we regard the work of nature with a rebellious eye,
or that we see here a diabolical machination that must be foiled;
but that man's nature cannot be itself unless it is disciplined. If

we judge it essential that natural inclinations be held within certain bounds, it is not because they seem to us bad, or because we would deny the right to gratification; on the contrary, it is because otherwise such natural inclinations could have no hope of the satisfaction they deserve. Thus, there follows this first practical consequence: ascetism is not good in and of itself. . .

If discipline is a means through which man realises his nature, it must change as that nature changes through time. To the extent that we advance in history, and as a result of civilisation, human nature becomes richer, and has greater need of expression; this is why it is normal for the range of human activity to expand and for the boundaries of our intellectual, moral, and emotional horizons to constantly move back. Hence the arrogance of systems of thought, whether artistic, scientific, or in the realm of human welfare, which would prohibit us from going beyond the points reached by our fathers, or would wish us to return there. The normal limit is in a state of continual becoming, and any doctrine which, under the authority of absolute principles, would undertake to fix it once and for all, in an unchanging fashion must sooner or later come into conflict with the force of reality. Not only does the content of discipline change, but also the way it is and should be inculcated. Not only does man's sphere of action change, but the forces that set limits are not wholly the same at different historical periods. In the lower societies, since social organisation is very simple, morality has a uniform character; and consequently, it is neither necessary nor even possible that the nature of discipline be clearly understood. The very simplicity of moral practices makes it easy to transform such behaviour into habits, mechanically carried out; under these conditions such automatism poses no difficulties. For as social life is quite self-consistent, differing but little from one place to another, or from one moment in time to another, custom and unreflective tradition are quite adequate. Moreover, they have such prestige and authority as to leave no place for reasoning and questioning. On the other hand, the more societies become complex, the more difficult it is for morality to operate as a purely automatic mechanism. Circumstances are never the same, and as a consequence the rules of morality must be applied intelligently. Society is continually evolving; morality itself must be sufficiently flexible to change in proportion and to the degree to which this is necessary. But this requires that morality not be inculcated in such a way as to be beyond criticism or reflected thought, the primary agents of all change. Even while they conform, men must take account of what they are doing; and their conformity must not be pushed to the point where it completely subjugates the intellect. Thus, it does not follow from a belief in the need for discipline that it must be blind and slavish. Moral rules must be invested with the authority without which they would be ineffective. However, after a certain point in history it was no longer necessary to remove authority from the realm of discussion, converting it into icons to which man dare not, so to speak, lift his eyes. . .

Whenever society loses what it normally possesses – whenever the individual disassociates himself from collective goals in order to seek only his own interests. . .suicide increases. Man is the more vulnerable to self-destruction the more he is detached from any collectivity, that is to say, the more he lives as an egoist. Suicide is thus about three times more frequent among bachelors than among married people, twice as frequent in childless homes as in those with children; it even occurs in inverse ratio to the number of children. Thus, according to whether or not a person is a member of a family group, depending on whether the group is merely the married pair or has the stability conferred by children – to the extent that familial society is more or less cohesive, tightly-knit and strong – man is more or less strongly attached to life. He destroys himself less frequently to the degree to which he has things to concern him other than himself. Crises that activate collective sentiments produce the same results. For example, wars, in stimulating patriotism, silence preoccupation with the self. The image of the threatened fatherland occupies a place in men's minds that it does not have in peace-time; consequently, the ties between individual and society are strengthened, and, at the same time, the ties which attach him to life. Suicide decreases. Similarly, the greater the cohesiveness of religious communities, and the resultant strengthening of the bonds between members, the more they are protected against the thought of suicide. Members of religious minorities are always more tightly-knit groups because of the opposition to them, against which they have to struggle. Also, a given church will have fewer suicides in a country where it is in a minority than where it embraces a majority of the people. . .

Altruism, the attachment to other than oneself, has often been presented as a sort of mysterious, extraordinary, almost inexplicable faculty, by reason of which man does violence to his original nature and contradicts it. . .[in fact] nothing is less mysterious or more natural. And to dissipate this so-called mystery, it is not at all necessary to reduce altruism, as did La Rochefoucauld and the utilitarians, to a disguised form of selfishness. This amounts to denying altruism under the pretext of making it intelligible. In truth, altruism is as deeply rooted as is its contrary in the psychological nature of man. These two kinds of sentiment only express two different, but inseparable, aspects of every mental act. In so far as our activity is concentrated on ourselves, on that which comprises our individuality and differentiates us from beings and from things outside ourselves, there exists egoism. On the other hand, altruism exists where our activity pursues objects external to ourselves, objects that do not enter into the characteristics of our personality. But we cannot become attached to these external objects unless we represent them in some way; even if they are external they are elements of ourselves. They exist and live in us in the form of the representation expressing them. We are attached directly to the representation itself: it is this which is missing when the thing represented is no longer there or has changed. Consequently there is egoism in all altruism. Conversely, since the self is made up of elements that we have necessarily taken from the outside since the mind cannot feed exclusively on itself, since it cannot think in a vacuum, so there must necessarily be some substance that can only come from the outside world. There is in ourselves something other than ourselves: therefore, there is altruism in egoism itself. We have seen especially how egoism – active aggressive, and having as its objective the extension of our being – implies a certain expansion in external activity, a real tendency to extend our field of action. In short, by the very necessities of man's nature, consciousness is simultaneously oriented in two directions which are conventionally opposed to each other: the inward and the outward. It cannot be self-contained, and it cannot be entirely outside of itself. In either state, conscious life is suspended. In pure ecstasy, as in the self-absorption of the fakir, thinking stops simultaneously with activity. These are two forms of mental death. Although egoism and altruism are thus brought together to the point of interpenetration, they are still definitely distinct. The fact that they are no longer opposed to each other does not mean that they are indistinguishable. For there is always a difference between the objects to which we are attached in these two cases: although that difference is only one of degree, it is certainly real. It might be said that since altruistic drives, when they are satisfied, give us satisfaction, they are egoistic like any other drives. But there is always this major difference: that in the one case we find our satisfaction in the pursuit of objects specific to ourselves, whereas in the other case we find satisfaction in the pursuit of objects that, although they penetrate our consciousness symbolically, are nevertheless not distinctive elements of our personality.

EM, pp. 58–60; 77–8 and 255–7

. . .rights and liberties are not things inherent in the nature of the individual as such. If you analyse man's given constitution you will find no trace of this sacredness with which he is invested and which confers upon him these rights. This character has been added to him by society. Society has consecrated the individual and made him the primary object of respect. His progressive emancipation does not imply a weakening but a transformation of the social bonds. The individual does not separate himself from society but is joined to it in a new manner, and this is because society sees him in a new way, and wishes this change to take place.

The individual submits to society and this submission is the condition of his liberation. For man freedom consists in deliverance from blind, unthinking physical forces; he achieves this by opposing against them the great and intelligent force of society, under whose protection he shelters. By putting himself under the wing of society, he makes himself also, to a certain extent, dependent upon it. But this is a liberating dependence; there is no contradiction in this.

SP, p. 106

IN DEFENCE OF THE 'SCIENCE OF MORALITY'

[A discussion of works on ethical theory by Fouillée, Belot and Landry]

Ethics is the order of the day. For some time past we have seen the appearance of a large number of most varied essays concerned with the proper form of analysis of moral phenomena. Each of the authors whose names appear above offers his own personal solution: each attempts to *found* ethics in his own manner. We do not believe there is space here to describe and discuss in detail these different conceptions; for what they contain of a positive kind is of more interest to the philosopher than to the sociologist. These three authors, in fact, are philosophers and their objective is precisely to question that sociology has a role in the study of moral facts. But for this reason they are led to discuss the method which we follow, and the ideas which we have promoted. Thus their critiques, which, moreover, have an important place in their works, are of some interest to us. We will attempt to reproduce them as impartially as possible, and to reply to them.

First of all, it is of some significance to draw attention to their purely formal character. Each of these authors is concerned with the method that we practise, but in a completely abstract way, as if it were still nothing more than a scheme which had never been put into practice. However, if the science of moral facts, such as we conceive it, is still rudimentary, it has already begun, and it is something of an overstatement and an injustice to speak of it simply as a possibility which perhaps may be realised in the indefinite future. In our *Division of Labour in Society*, we have already set out what is described as 'above all an attempt to examine the facts of moral life according to the method of the positive sciences'. (Preface to the First Edition.) Our book on *Suicide*, all of the studies which we have published here [in the *Année sociologique*], and all of the reviews and discussions which we organise each year relating to books which concern moral sociology and the sociology of law, proceed from the same principles. Hence it would have been possible to criticise our method by showing how, in practice, it has given rise to errors; it is in terms of its application that a method must be evaluated. But, for reasons which we cannot enquire into, the controversy remains purely on the level of abstract argument. We do not even believe that our critics have on one single occasion felt the need to show how their objections may be applied, or are relevant to a specific problem. They talk only in generalities.

Landry is the only author for whom the controversy is not purely methodological – although it is still the case that he remains on a general and philosophical plane. He attributes to us 'an ethics' (we confess to having a poor understanding of what he means by that), and he discusses its positive content, without however connecting the criticisms relating to the basis of these ideas to the methodological criticisms which are contained in another part of his book. This doctrinal discussion is limited to one single point. Preoccupied with bringing within the framework of his thesis those conceptions which seem to deviate from it the most, Landry undertakes to demonstrate that the whole of our doctrine 'proceeds from a utilitarian principle', that all of our 'formulas are only of value so long as they can be deduced from the principle of general utility'; and he gives as proof of this that, according to our own admission, the majority of the most widespread forms of organisation would be inexplicable if, as a whole, they were not the most advantageous.

It is certainly true, in fact, that our conception quite naturally gives a certain place to the eudemonist and utilitarian principle. For we believe that moral institutions, precisely because they are social institutions, have useful ends and have a role to play in the totality of social life. But how much of an overstatement it is to consider us as a utilitarian is shown by the fact that it is even easier to find the opposite principle in our writings. One might even say that it occupies the primary place. In point of fact, we have not ceased to reiterate that for us the essential characteristic of a moral rule was obligation, in the Kantian sense of the word – that is to say, that distinctive property by virtue of which a rule of conduct seems to us to have to be obeyed, simply because it is a rule. And these principles, which at first might seem to be opposed, are not brought together in this way by a superficial eclecticism. The two can be reconciled without difficulty: for they simply express different aspects of moral reality. It is characteristic of the utilitarian, by contrast, that he only sees one of these aspects. He attempts to relate everything to one of these principles, and even to deduce everything from it. Now this archaic, one-sided, conception no longer seems to us worthy of persevering with today; for it is contradicted by everything that comparative history and ethnology teaches us about the moral life of man.

Let us now take up purely methodological questions. It is with a marked feeling of surprise that we read the pages that Fouillée has been kind enough to devote to us, because we found that they contain serious misinterpretations of our thought. Fouillée appears to hold a very peculiar, and quite inaccurate, notion of the method which we practise and the objective which we seek to attain. We are accused of declaring that, in questions of morality, human thought must not formulate any value-judgement or evaluation; it is held that we reduce examination of these questions to pure 'description'. What is the basis of this criticism? It derives from a point made by Lévy-Bruhl: that the respect which moral rules inspire in us is an obstacle to the formation of an objective science of morals (in Lévy-Bruhl: *La Morale et la science des moeurs*). We confess that we did not think that such an obvious truth could be disputed. Is it not clear, in fact, that not only the study of moral facts, but of social facts in general, is made much more difficult by this very thing: that, as we wrote already thirteen years ago, 'sentiment often plays a part'? In order that we should be able not merely to understand moral practices scientifically, but also to evaluate them objectively, it is necessary that we should succeed in considering them with an entirely open mind. Now this is naturally more difficult to obtain in relation to ideas or modes of behaviour which we hold in respect. The very fact of treating them scientifically is like a profanity. Does it follow from this state of affairs that we must forgo judging them? Not at all. But these ready-made judgements, the result of education and habit – in short, these unexamined prejudices – render more difficult the considered, clarified and methodical judgements which the science of moral facts, in our conception of it, should make possible. We wonder, in fact, how it could even have been believed that we refused to evaluate the morality of our contemporaries, since the first work of any importance which we published (*The Division of Labour in Society*) was explicitly directed at such an evaluation.

Moreover, in what respect could it be said that the method which we follow denies us the right of evaluation? To explain a moral rule is to show the cause of it, its function, what ideas and sentiments it results from, and what needs it answers. Once these needs are known, is it not legitimate to ask whether or not they are normal and justified? Once these ideas and sentiments have been determined, why should we be prevented from enquiring into whether they express the nature of things? (We leave on one side, for the moment, the question of discovering what 'the nature of things' refers to). And if the result of the research is that these are no more than survivals which no longer correspond to anything in reality, or that they are a product of transient and morbid disturbances, may we not legitimately conclude that the corresponding moral rule has no longer any basis for its existence; or that it must be modified, corrected, perfected or replaced? Should we not seek to discover, using parallels drawn inductively from historical evolution, in short, using all the information which science puts at our disposal, what sorts of corrections, modifications or changes are necessary? Certainly the explanation of a moral precept is not, *ipso facto*, a justification of it, but far from dispensing with it or making it impossible, explanation opens up the way for such justification. It might be objected to this that, if, as we claim, morality is a reality independent of the theories which justify it, any effort to criticise it rationally becomes futile. It would seem to be an altogether superfluous luxury. But while all the evidence indeed confirms the truth that morality has not waited for the theories of philosophers in order to become formed and to function, who would think of disputing that conscious deliberation cannot act to modify this automatic and unconscious functioning? Scientific thought and consciousness, which is simply the highest form of consciousness, are not ineffective epipheno-mena conjoined to reality; their very capacity for clarification places us in a position to change reality. If, therefore, we question the methods ordinarily followed by philosophers in their specula-tions about morality, this is not because they have attempted to make it the subject of conscious deliberation, and that we ad-judge these efforts to be of no practical utility; on the contrary, it is because they are only able to allow an inadequate role to free deliberation, since they do not take the steps necessary to liberate it from any kind of subjection to sentiment and prejudice. . .

The thesis advanced by Belot is not essentially different from that of Fouillée, at least in so far as it concerns us. While recognis-ing that sociology can offer considerable service to ethical analysis, he seems to us to practise a method which is not perceptibly different from that which is normally followed by moralists, particularly those of the utilitarian school. But his arguments are different in part. He is not unaware of the interest which a science of morals such as we are attempting to establish can have in itself; but, in so far as he believes it to be possible, he sees in it, nonetheless, only a purely scholarly enterprise, with no practi-cal implications. . .

The whole of Belot's argument, which seeks to demonstrate the impotence of our science, rests upon an arbitrary notion which corresponds to nothing in reality. No doubt it is perfectly true that a science is only possible when it has as its subject-matter a given field which the scholar focusses upon in a state of relative fixity, in order to be able to observe it. Anything which constantly vacillates escapes observation and, consequently, scientific study. But the procedure whereby this fixity is attained does not, how-ever, necessarily have the effect of changing its nature: of trans-forming it, for instance, from a living into a dead thing. In order to study a society we necessarily have to analyse it statistically; but although we study it in this way, it is true nonetheless that it changes and evolves constantly. Moreover, even the existing state which I attempt to stabilise in order to be able to describe and analyse it, is not made up solely of characteristics which are established, given, definite, finished and unchanging. Because it is always in movement, even at the moment at which, in order to study it, I immobilise it, it contains tendencies to movement, the germs of change. It contains aspirations to become something other than it is, ideals which are pressing for realisation; and it can very easily be the case that the real way in which a given society can remain true to itself is to accept one of these tendencies and to change. In order to be aware of what new developments have to be introduced in these circumstances, it is thus not at all futile to study present conditions, since new realities, not yet actualised, are as if foreshadowed in these conditions of the present. The future is already written there for him who knows how to read it; and this is the only way to predict it rationally. For there would be nothing gained in assigning to a society ends which would be in no way acceptable or known to it, and of which it felt no need. By taking the nature of this society as the point of reference, we can hope to choose between the different tendencies which are affecting it; and we can hardly but help clarifying the value, the real significance, of the needs which it is experiencing. It is argued that it is necessary sometimes to cut corners, to proceed by trial and error, and to take risks. This is completely true; but if we wish to act rationally, we must still have some reason to believe that such summary, precipitate and hazardous change is demanded by the nature of the situation. Thus, whatever we do, in order to do it we must always come back to the analysis of given reality.

AS, 1906(a), p. 352–6; 361–2; and 367–8

While the science of morality does not make us indifferent or passive observers of reality, at the same time it does teach us to treat it with extreme prudence, imparting to us a wisely conservative attitude. There has been good reason to question certain theories which are thought to be scientific, for being destructive and revolutionary: for they are scientific in name only. They construct, but they do not observe. They see in morality, not a collection of facts to study, but a sort of revocable law-making which each thinker establishes for himself. Morality as really practised by men is then considered only as a collection of habits or prejudices, valuable only if they conform to the doctrine proposed; and as this doctrine is derived from a principle which is not induced from observation of moral reality, but borrowed from other disciplines, it inevitably contradicts the existing moral order in various ways. But we are less exposed to this risk than others, for we regard morality as a system of substantive phenomena, bound up in the total world-system. Now, a fact cannot be modified by mere sleight of hand, even when this is desirable. Moreover, since it is bound up with other facts, it cannot be modified without the modification of these other facts, and it is often quite difficult to calculate in advance the final result of this series of repercussions; thus the boldest mind becomes cautious in the fact of such risks. Finally, and most important, no fact relating to life – and this applies to moral facts – can endure if it is not of some use, if it does not answer some need; until the opposite is proved true, such facts are entitled to our respect. No doubt there comes a time when everything is not as it should be, and that, consequently, will be the time to intervene, as we have just shown. But this intervention then is limited: it has for its object, not to make out of nothing an ethic completely different from the prevailing one, but to correct the latter, or partially to improve it.

Thus, the antithesis between science and ethics, that formidable argument with which the mystics of all times have wished to cloud human reason, disappears. To regulate our relations with men, it is not necessary to resort to any other means than those which we use to govern our relations with things; thought, methodically employed, is sufficient in both cases. What reconciles science and ethics is the science of ethics, for at the same time that it teaches us to respect moral reality, it gives us the means to improve it.

DTS, pp. xl–xli

It has been said that to see morality in this manner is to preclude all possibility of evaluating it. If morality is a collective product, it necessarily imposes itself upon the individual, who is in no position to question it whatever form it may take; he must accept it passively. We would thus be condemned to follow opinion without ever having the right to rebel against its dictates.

But here, as elsewhere, the science of reality puts us in a position to modify the real and to direct it. The science of moral opinion furnishes us with the means of judging it and of rectifying it. I will give a few examples of how this may be so, without listing them exhaustively.

First of all, it is possible that, as a result of some transient upheaval, some fundamental moral principle is hidden for a time from public awareness which, not feeling it, denies that it is there (theoretically and explicitly, or practically and in action; it does not matter). The science of morality can abstract from this temporarily troubled moral condition to that which pre-existed in what we may call a chronic condition. By contrasting the permanence in which this principle was held for so long, with the acute and temporary nature of the crisis during which it has been in abeyance, one can, in the name of science, awaken rational doubts as to the legitimacy of its negation. One can even by the same method do more, and show how this principle is related to given essential and ever-present conditions of our social organisation and collective mentality; how, in fact, one cannot ignore it without at the same time misunderstanding the conditions by which the collective, and hence the individual, exists. Let us suppose that at a given time the society as a whole tends to lose sight of the sacred rights of the individual. Could we not correct it with authority by reminding it that the rights of the individual are very closely bound to the structure of the great European societies and our whole mentality, and that to deny them, under the pretext of social interests, is to deny the most essential interests of society itself?

It is equally possible that, apart from the present existing order of morality, maintained by the forces of tradition, new tendencies, of a fairly self-conscious kind, are appearing. The science of morals allows us to take up a position between these two divergent moralities, the one now in existence and the one in the process of becoming. It teaches us, for example, that the first is related to an order which has disappeared or is disappearing, while the new ideas, by contrast, are related to recent changes in the conditions of collective existence, and are made necessary by these changes. Our science may help us to render these ideas more precise and to direct them, etc.

We are not then obliged to bow to the force of moral opinion. We are even in certain cases justified in rebelling against it. It may, in fact, happen that, for one of the reasons just indicated, we shall feel it our duty to combat moral ideas that we know to be out of date and nothing more than survivals. The best way of doing this will be to oppose these ideas not only theoretically, but also in action.

SP, pp. 86–8

5. Forms of social solidarity

The link of social solidarity to which repressive law corresponds is one whose break constitutes a crime; we give this name to every act which, in any degree whatever, evokes against its author the characteristic reaction which we term 'punishment'. To seek the nature of this link is thus to ask what is the cause of punishment, or, more precisely what crime essentially consists in...

... an act is criminal when it offends strong and defined states of the *conscience collective*. The statement of this proposition is rarely disputed, but it is ordinarily given a sense very different from that which it ought to have. We take it as if it expressed, not the essential property of crime, but one of its repercussions. We well know that crime violates very general and intense sentiments; but we believe that this generality and intensity derive from the criminal character of the act, which consequently remains to be defined. We do not deny that every delict is universally condemned, but we take as agreed that the condemnation to which it is subjected results from its delinquent character. Then, however, we are hard put to say in what its delinquent character consists. Is it to be found in an especially serious transgression? Perhaps so; but that is simply to restate the question by putting one word in place of another, for it is precisely the problem to understand what this transgression is, and particularly this specific transgression which society reproves by means of organised punishment and which constitutes criminality. It can evidently come only from one or several characteristics common to all criminological types. The only one which satisfies this condition is the very opposition between a crime, whatever it may be, and certain collective sentiments. It is, accordingly, this opposition which forms the crime, rather than being a derivation of crime. In other words, we must not say that an action shocks the *conscience collective* because it is criminal, but rather that it is criminal because it shocks the *conscience collective*. We do not condemn it because it is a crime, but it is a crime because we condemn it. As for the intrinsic nature of these sentiments, it is impossible to specify them; they have the most diverse objects and cannot be encompassed in a single formula. We cannot say that they relate to the vital interests of society, or to a minimum of justice: all such definitions are inadequate. By this alone can we recognise it: a sentiment, whatever its origin and end, is found in all minds with a certain degree of strength and clarity, and every action which violates it is a crime. . .

Punishment is, first and foremost, an emotional reaction. This character is especially apparent in less developed societies. Primitive peoples punish for the sake of punishing, making the guilty party suffer solely for the sake of making him suffer and without seeking any advantage for themselves from the suffering which they impose. The proof of this is that they seek neither to strike back justly nor to strike back usefully, but merely to strike back. Thus they punish animals which have committed a wrong-doing and even inanimate objects which were its passive instrument. When punishment is applied only to people, it often extends further than the guilty party and reaches the innocent, his wife, his children, his neighbours, etc. That is because the passion which is the spirit of punishment ceases only when it is exhausted. If, therefore, after it has destroyed the one who immediately called it forth, it still remains strong, it expands in a quite mechanical fashion. Even when it is fairly mild, and relates only to the guilty party, it makes its presence felt by the tendency to surpass in severity the action against which it is reacting. That is the origin of the refinements of suffering added to capital punishment. Even in Rome the thief not only had to return the stolen object, but also pay retribution of double and quadruple the amount. Moreover, is not the very common punishment of the *lex talionis* a mode of satisfying the passion for vengeance?

But today, it is said, punishment has changed its character; it is no longer to avenge itself that society punishes, it is to defend itself. The suffering which it inflicts is in its hands no longer anything but a methodical means of protection. It punishes, not because chastisement offers it any intrinsic satisfaction, but so that the fear of punishment may paralyse those who contemplate evil. It is no longer anger, but a well thought-out precaution which determines repression. The preceding observations could not then be generalised; they would refer only to the primitive form of punishment and would not extend to the modern form.

But to justify such a radical distinction between these two sorts of punishment, it is not enough to state that they are employed with different ends in view. The nature of a practice does not necessarily change because the conscious intentions of those who apply it are modified. It might, in fact, still play the same role as before, but without this being perceived. In this case, why should it only become changed in that we are more aware of the effects which it produces? It adapts itself to new conditions of existence without any essential changes. This is the case with punishment. In fact, it is a mistake to believe that vengeance is simply useless cruelty. It is very possible that, in itself, it consists of a mechanical and aimless reaction, an emotional and unthinking action, an irrational need to destroy; but, in reality, it does tend to destroy that which is a threat to us. It consists, then, in a true act of defence, although an instinctive and unreflective one. We avenge ourselves only upon what has harmed us, and what has harmed us is always a threat. The instinct of vengeance is, in sum, only the instinct of conservation heightened by peril. Thus, vengeance is far from having had the negative and sterile role in the history of mankind which is attributed to it. It is a defensive weapon which has a definite value, although it is a crude weapon. Since it is not informed with an awareness of the end it serves, but functions automatically, it cannot, consequently, regulate itself, but responds rather haphazardly to the blind causes which urge it on, without anything moderating its responses. Today, as we understand more clearly the end to be attained, we know better how to utilise the means at our disposal; we protect ourselves more systematically and, accordingly, more efficiently. But this result was also obtained previously, although in a rather imperfect manner. There is no radical division between the punishment of today and yesterday, and consequently it was not necessary for the latter to change its nature in order to accommodate itself to the role that it plays in our civilised societies. The whole difference derives from the fact that it now produces its effects with a heightened awareness of what it does. But, although the individual or social consciousness may not be without influence upon the reality that it clarifies, it has not the power to change its nature. The internal structure of the phenomenon remains the same, whether men be conscious of it or not. We may thus conclude that the essential elements of punishment are the same as of old.

And in fact, punishment has remained, at least in part, a work of vengeance. It is said that we do not make the guilty party suffer for the sake of suffering; it is nonetheless true that we find it right that he should suffer. Perhaps we are wrong, but that is not the question. We seek, at the moment, to define punishment as it is or has been, not as it ought to be. It is certain that this expression of public prosecution which finds its way again and again into the language of the courts is not a mere expression. In supposing that punishment can really serve to protect us in the future, we think that it must be above all an *expiation* of the past. This is shown by the minute precautions we take to allot punishment as exactly as possible in relation to the severity of the crime; this would be inexplicable if we did not believe that the guilty party ought to suffer because of his wrongdoing, and in the same degree. This gradation is not necessary if punishment is only a means of defence. No doubt, there would be danger for society if the most serious offences were treated as simple transgressions; but it would be greater, in the majority of cases, if the latter were treated in the same way as the former. Against an enemy, we cannot take too much precaution. Shall we say that the authors of the smallest misdeeds have less perverse natures, and that to neutralise their criminal instincts less stringent punishments will suffice? But if their inclinations are less vicious they are not on that account less intense. Robbers are as strongly inclined to rob as murderers are to murder; the resistance offered by the former is not less than that of the latter, and consequently, to control it, we would have recourse to the same means. If, as has been said, it was solely a question of putting down a noxious force by an opposing force, the intensity of the second would be measured solely by the intensity of the first, without the quality of the latter entering into the consideration. The penal scale would then encompass only a small number of gradations. Punishment would vary only as the criminal is more or less hardened, and not according to the nature of the criminal act. An incorrigible robber would be treated in the same way as an incorrigible murderer. But, in fact, if it were shown that a misdoer was completely incurable, we would still not feel bound to punish him excessively. This is proof that we are faithful to the talion principle, although we apply it in a more refined sense than previously. We no longer measure in so material and gross a manner either the extent of the deed or of the punishment; but we still think that there ought to be an equation between the two terms, whether or not we benefit from this balance. Punishment thus remains for us what it was for our forefathers. It is still an act of vengeance since it is an expiation. What we avenge, what the criminal expiates, is the outrage to morality...

As for the social character of this reaction, it comes from the social nature of the offended sentiments. Because they are found in the consciousness of every individual, the infraction which has been committed arouses the same indignation in those who witness it or who learn of its existence. Everybody is attacked; consequently, everybody opposes the attack. Not only is the reaction general, but it is collective, which is not the same thing. It is not produced in an isolated manner in each individual, but is a total, unified response, even if this varies according to the case. In fact, in the same way as contrary sentiments repel each other, similar sentiments attract each other, and they attract as strongly as they themselves are intense. As contradiction is a threat which stirs them, it adds to their force of attraction. Never do we feel the need of the company of our compatriots so greatly as when we are in a foreign country; never does the believer feel so strongly attracted to his fellow believers as during periods of persecution. Of course, we always love the company of those who feel and think as we do, but it is with passion, and no longer solely with pleasure, that we seek it immediately after discussions where our common beliefs have been directly attacked. Crime brings together honest men and concentrates them. We have only to notice what happens, particularly in a small town, when some moral scandal has just occurred. Men stop each other on the street, they visit each other, they seek to come together to talk of the event and to wax indignant in common. From all the similar impressions which are exchanged, and the anger that is expressed, there emerges a unique emotion, more or less determinate according to the circumstances, which emanates from no specific person, but from everyone. This is the public wrath.

Moreover, this is what gives it its functions: the sentiments in question derive all their force from the fact that they are common to everyone. They are strong because they are unquestioned. It is the fact that they are universally respected which gives them the specific respect which they are accorded. Now, crime is possible only if this respect is not truly universal; consequently, it implies that they are not absolutely collective, and thus damages this unanimity which is the source of their authority. If, then, when a crime takes place, the individuals whom it offends do not unite to manifest what they share in common, and to affirm that the case is anomalous, they would be permanently shaken. They must fortify themselves by the mutual assurance that they are still in unison. The only means for this is action in common. In short, since it is the *conscience collective* which is attacked, it must be that which resists, and accordingly the resistance must be collective...

Thus, the analysis of punishment has confirmed our definition of crime. We began by establishing inductively that crime consisted essentially in an act contrary to strong and defined states of the *conscience collective*. We have just seen that all the qualities of punishment ultimately derive from this nature of crime. That is because the rules that it sanctions express the most essential social likenesses.

Thus we see what type of solidarity penal law symbolises. It is well known, indeed, that there is a form of social cohesion whose cause lies in a certain conformity of all specific individuals to a common type which is none other than the mental type of the society. In these conditions, not only are all the members of the group individually attracted to one-another because they resemble one-another, but also because they are joined to that which is the condition of existence of this collective type: that is to say, to the society that they form by their union. Not only do citizens love each other and seek each other out in preference to strangers but they love their country. They want for it what they want for themselves, and wish it to prosper and endure, because without it, a great part of their psychological life would be hampered in its functioning. Conversely, society demands that they present these fundamental resemblances, because that is a condition of its cohesion. There are in us two forms of consciousness: one contains states which are personal to the character of each of us, while the states which comprise the other are common to the whole society. The first represent only our individual personality and constitute it; the second represent the collective type and, consequently, society, without which it would not exist. When it is one of the elements of this latter which determines our conduct, we do not act in our personal interest; we pursue collective ends. Although distinct, these two forms of consciousness are linked one to the other, since in the end they are only one, having one and the same organic substratum. They are thus interdependent. From this results a solidarity *sui generis*, based upon mutual resemblance, and directly linking individual to society.

DTS, pp. 35, 47–8, 52–6, 70–1 and 73–4

VARIATIONS IN THE CHARACTER OF PENAL SANCTIONS

The variations which punishment has undergone during the course of history are of two sorts: some quantitative, others qualitative. The laws which govern these are necessarily different. The *law of quantitative variation* can be formulated in the following way: '*The intensity of punishment is greater to the degree that a society belongs to a less developed type – and to the degree that the central power has a more absolute character.*'

Let us, to begin with, explain the meaning of these expressions. The first stands in no great need of definition. It is relatively easy to recognise whether one social type is more or less developed than another; we have only to distinguish how simply they are compounded and, if they are of parallel composition, the degree of organisation which they manifest. This hierarchy of social types does not imply, however, that the development of societies forms a single and linear sequence. On the contrary, it is certain that it should rather be portrayed as a tree having many branches which differ in greater or lesser degree. But societies are situated at varying heights on this tree, and at variable distances from the common trunk. On condition of treating them in this way, it is possible to speak of the general evolution of societies.

The second factor which we distinguished must be discussed at greater length. We call governmental power 'absolute' when no other social functions which it relates to are of a kind to balance and to limit it effectively. To be sure, the complete absence of any limitation is never found; one can even say that it is inconceivable. Tradition, and religious beliefs, serve as brakes upon even the strongest of governments. Moreover, there are always a certain number of secondary organs which are capable of resisting and maintaining their autonomy. The subordinate functions which are subject to the supreme regulatory function are never completely deprived of the whole of their individual energy. But it does happen that this limitation is not given by any legal obligation upon the government which experiences it; although it has a certain degree of influence over the exercise of governmental prerogatives, it is not given in written or customary law. In this case, the government wields power which one may call absolute. No doubt if it allows itself to go too far, the social forces which it encroaches upon can join together to react and to curtail it; in anticipation of this possible reaction, it may even curtail itself. But whether self-imposed, or physically imposed from outside, this curtailment is essentially contingent. It does not derive from the normal functioning of institutions. When it is due to governmental initiative, it is presented as a gracious concession, as a voluntary abandonment of legitimate rights; when it is the product of collective resistance, it has a frankly revolutionary character.

One can characterise absolute government in yet another way. Legal activity centres wholly around two poles: legal relationships are either unilateral, or otherwise, on the contrary, bilateral and reciprocal. These are, at least, two ideal types to which they approximate. The first is comprised exclusively of laws which specify the claims of one entity over another, without the second having any legal rights corresponding to his obligations. In the second, by contrast, the legal tie results from a perfect reciprocity between the rights conferred upon each of the two parties. Material rights, and more particularly property rights, represent the most defined example of the first type; the proprietor has rights over his possession, while it has none over him. Contract, and above all just contract – that is to say, where there is perfect equivalence in the social value of the things or benefits exchanged – is the prototype of reciprocal relations. Now the greater the degree to which the relations between the supreme power and the rest of society are of a unilateral character, or in other words, the more they resemble those which bind the person and his possession, the more absolute is the government. Conversely, the more completely bilateral its relations with other social functions are, the less absolute it is. Thus the most perfect model of absolute sovereignty is the *patria potestas* of the Romans, as it was defined in ancient law, since the son was put on the same level as a possession.

So what makes the central power more or less absolute is the extent to which there is a fundamental lack of any permanent counterweight which is organised with the object of moderating it. One can then foresee that what gives birth to a power of this kind is the more or less complete merging of all the directive functions of society in one and the same hand. In fact, because of their basic significance, they cannot be concentrated under one and the same person without giving him an exceptional dominance over the rest of society; and it is this dominance which constitutes absolutism. The wielder of such authority finds that he possesses a force which frees him from any collective constraint, and which, at least in certain measure, means that he is answerable only to himself, does what he chooses, and can impose his will completely. This hyper-centralisation brings into existence a social force *sui generis* which is so intense that it dominates all others and subordinates them. And this dominance is not exercised only in fact, but also in law. For he who is privileged to possess it is invested with such prestige that he seems to be superhuman in nature; thus it is even believed that he cannot be made subject to regular obligations as ordinary men are. . .

The law which we have just set up refers exclusively to the amount or quantity of punishment. That which we shall now turn to relates to its qualitative modalities. It can be expressed as follows: *Punishment involving deprivation of freedom, and of that alone, for periods of time which vary according to the gravity of the crime, tends increasingly to become the normal type of sanction. . .*

Having determined [in a part of the article not reproduced here] the mode in which punishment has varied over time, we shall seek to find the causes of these variations which we have documented – that is, we shall try to explain the two previously established laws. We shall begin with the second.

As we have already seen, imprisonment first appears in history only as a simple preventive measure. Later it assumes a repressive character, and eventually becomes the very typification of the penal system. In order to account for this evolution, we therefore have to discover what led to the emergence of the prison in its first form, and then, in turn, what determined the changes which it subsequently underwent.

It is easy to understand why the preventive prison is absent from the less developed societies: there is no need which it corresponds to. Responsibility, in fact, is collective; when a crime is committed, punishment or reparation is not simply owed by the guilty party, but also, either together with him or in his place if he defaults, the clan of which he is a member. Later, when the clan has lost its familial character, it is a circle – still a fairly extended one – of relatives. In these conditions, there is no reason to arrest and to hold under surveillance the presumed author of the act; since if, for one reason or another, he is missing, he leaves guarantors. Moreover, the moral and legal independence which such a family group possesses in these circumstances makes it impossible for it to be asked to deliver up in this way one of its members upon a simple suspicion. But to the extent that society becomes more concentrated, and these elementary groups lose their autonomy and become dissolved in the great mass, responsibility becomes an individual matter. From then on, measures are necessary to make sure that the individual concerned does not flee to escape sanction; and as at the same time they are less shocking to public morality, prisons appear. . .

As to the legal status of this new form of punishment from the time of its coming into existence, it can be adequately accounted for by combining the preceding considerations with the law relating to the progressive weakening of penal sanctions. Their weakening in effect occurs from top to bottom of the penal scale. In general, it is the harshest forms of punishment which are first affected by this backward movement: that is to say, which are the first to become weakened, and then to disappear. It is the worse types of capital punishment which are the first to become weakened, up to the time at which they are completely suppressed; cases in which capital punishment is applied become more and more restricted. Punishment by mutilation follows the same law. The consequence of this is that the lesser punishments become more important, since they must fill the gaps which this process of regression has left. To the degree that the archaic forms of repression disappear from the field of the penal system, the new forms invade the empty spaces which open up before them. Now these various modes of imprisonment comprise the later forms of punishment to emerge; by origin, they occupy a place right at the bottom of the penal scale, since in the beginning they were not even a type of punishment, properly speaking. They simply constituted the condition of true punishment, and for a long time retained a mixed and ambiguous character. For this very reason the future was reserved for them. They were the natural and necessary substitutes for other sorts of punishment which were disappearing. But, on the other hand, these themselves came to be subject to the same law of weakening intensity. This is why, while they were originally mixed with additional hardships, to which they were sometimes no more than ancillary, they shed these little by little, so as to become reduced to the most simple form, namely deprivation of liberty, not comprising any other gradations than those resulting from differences in the duration of this deprivation.

Thus the qualitative variations in punishment depend partly upon the quantitative changes which it has undergone at the same time. In other words, of the two laws which we have established, the first contributes to the explanation of the second. The time has now come to explain it in its turn. . . .

The collective sentiments which are transgressed and offended by the characteristic criminality of the less developed societies are collective, as it were, in two ways. Not only are they held by the collectivity and thus exist in the consciousness of the majority of individuals, but they also *relate to collective things*. By definition, these things are outside the field of our private interests.

The ends to which we are thus attached infinitely surpass the limited horizon which each of us possesses. It is not us personally whom they concern, but the collective entity. Consequently, the acts which we are obliged to carry out in order to attain them do not derive from the inclinations of our individual nature, but tend rather to violate them, as they consist in a whole variety of sacrifices and privations which man has to impose upon himself in order to please his god, either in order to satisfy custom, or to obey authority. We have no inclination to fast, to subject ourselves to self-mortification, to abstain from such and such meats, to sacrifice our favourite animals upon the altar, to suffer discomfort out of respect for custom, etc. Thus in the same way as sensations come from the external world, such feelings are in, but not of, us; indeed, in a certain degree they are there in spite of ourselves, and they have this character because of the constraint which they exert over us. Hence we are compelled to alienate them, to relate them to some external cause, as we do with sensation. Moreover, we are forced to conceive of it as a power which is not only separate, but also superior to us, since it commands us and we obey. This voice which speaks to us in such an imperative tone, which enjoins us to change our own nature, can only derive from a being which is distinct from ourselves, and which also dominates us. In whatever specific form men have portrayed it (god, ancestors, all kinds of exalted beings), it always possesses, in relation to them, a transcendent or superhuman quality. This is why this aspect of morality is permeated with religiosity. It is because the duties which are prescribed to us call upon us to obey a personality which is infinitely superior to our own; this is the collective personality, such as we conceive of it in purely abstract form, or, as is most commonly the case, with the aid of wholly religious symbols.

But the crimes which violate these sentiments, and which consist in failures to carry out specific obligations, cannot help but appear to us to be directed against transcendent beings, since in reality they do relate to them. It follows from this that they seem to us to be exceptionally offensive; for a transgression is correspondingly more shocking if the offended being is superior in nature and dignity to the transgressor. The more something is held in respect, the more abhorrent is a lack of respect. The same act which, directed against an equal, is merely reprehensible, becomes impure when it concerns a being superior to us; the horror which it inspires can only be assuaged by violent repression. The faithful must normally submit to numerous hardships, simply in order to please their gods and to keep in regular contact with them. What hardships, then, will they have to undergo when they have angered them! Even when there is a strong feeling of pity for the guilty party, it does not outweigh the indignation aroused by the act of sacrilege. Nor, consequently, does it perceptibly modify the punishment; for the two sentiments are too unequal. The sympathy when men feel for one of their fellows, particularly when he has suffered a shameful lapse, cannot offset the reverential fear in which they hold the divinity. Compared to this power, which is so much higher than himself, the individual appears so small that his sufferings lose their relative significance and become a negligible quantity. What is the importance of individual suffering when there is a god who must be appeased?

It is different with collective sentiments whose object is the individual; for each of us is one. That which concerns man concerns all of us; for we are all men. Those sentiments relating to the protection of human dignity touch us personally. Of course, I do not want to say that we respect the life and property of our fellows only because of utilitarian calculation, in order to obtain a fair exchange from them. If we condemn acts which are deficient in this way, it is because they transgress feelings of sympathy which we hold for man in general, and these feelings are disinterested because they have a general object. This is the great difference which separates the moral individualism of Kant from that of the utilitarians. Both make the development of the individual, in a sense, the objective of moral conduct. But, for the latter, the 'individual' concerned here is the tangible, empirical individual, such as he is grasped in each specific mind; for Kant, on the other hand, it is the human being, humanity in general, in abstraction from the diverse concrete forms in which it manifests itself. Nevertheless, however universal it may be, such an objective is directly in line with that towards which our egoistic inclinations move us. Between man in general, and the man which each of us is, there is not the same difference as exists between a man and a god. The character of this ideal only differs from our own in a matter of degree; it is simply the model of which each of us is a different instance. The sentiments whereby we are attached to it are thus, in part, only an extension of those which attach us to ourselves. This is expressed in the popular saying: 'Do unto others as you would unto yourself.'

Since, therefore, as we develop, crime becomes progressively reduced to offences against persons alone, while religious forms of criminality decline, it is inevitable that the average strength of punishment should become weaker. This weakening does not stem from the fact that morals become less harsh, but from the fact that religiosity, which penal law and the sentiments underlying it were originally pervaded with, steadily declines. No doubt sentiments of human sympathy become stronger at the same time; but their increasing strength cannot explain this progressive reduction in punishment since, by itself, this would tend rather to make us more severe towards every crime in which a man is the victim, and would thus increase the punishment for such crimes. The true reason is that the compassion which is felt for the condemned man is no longer obviated by opposite sentiments which do not allow it to make itself felt.

AS, 1900, pp. 65–8, 77–8, 80–1, 84–5, 87–9 and 90–1

RESTITUTIVE SANCTIONS AND THE RELATIONSHIP
BETWEEN MECHANICAL AND ORGANIC SOLIDARITY

What distinguishes [the restitutive] sanction is that it is not expiatory but consists of a simple return in state. The person who violates or disregards the law is not made to suffer in relation to his wrongdoing; he is simply sentenced to comply. If certain things have already been done, the judge reinstates them as they should have been. He speaks of law; he says nothing of punishment. Damage payments have no penal character; they are only a means of reviewing the past in order to reinstate it, as far as possible, in its normal form. . .

Neglect of these rules is not even punished diffusely. The defendant who has lost in litigation is not disgraced, his honour is not smirched. We can even imagine these rules differing from how they are now without any feeling of distaste. The idea of tolerating murder makes us indignant, but we quite easily accept modification of the law of inheritance, and can even conceive of its possible abolition. It is at least a question which we do not refuse to discuss. In the same way, we readily accept that the law of easements or that of usufructs may be organised differently, that the obligations of vendor and purchaser may be determined in another way, or that administrative functions may be distributed according to different principles. As these prescriptions do not correspond to any sentiment in us, and as we generally do not know scientifically the reasons for their existence, since this science does not exist, they have no roots in the majority of us. Of course, there are exceptions. We do not tolerate the idea that a contract, contrary to custom or obtained either through force or fraud, can bind the contracting parties. Thus, when public opinion finds itself in the presence of a case of this sort, it shows itself less indifferent than we have previously said, and it increases the legal sanction by its censure. The different domains of moral life are not radically separated one from another; on the contrary, they are continuous, and accordingly they contain marginal regions where these different characteristics are found at the same time. However, the preceding proposition remains true in the great majority of cases. It is proof that rules with a restitutive sanction either do not at all derive from the *conscience collective*, or are only feeble states of it. Repressive law corresponds to the heart, the centre of the common conscience; purely moral rules are already a less central part; finally, restitutive law originates in very marginal regions, spreading well beyond. The more it becomes truly itself, the more removed it becomes.

This characteristic is, moreover, manifest in the manner of its functioning. While repressive law tends to remain diffuse within society, restitutive law creates organs which are increasingly specialised: commercial courts, councils of arbitration, administrative courts of many kinds. Even in its most general part, that which pertains to civil law, it is exercised only through particular functionaries: magistrates, lawyers, etc., who are able to fill this role in virtue of very specialised training.

But, although these rules are to some degree outside the *conscience collective*, they do not refer only to individuals. If this were so, restitutive law would have nothing in common with social solidarity, for the relations that it regulates would bind individuals to one-another without binding them to society. These would simply be happenings in private life, as friendly relations are. But it is necessarily the case that society is far from being absent in this sphere of legal life. It is true that, generally, it does not intervene directly and actively; it must be solicited by the interested parties. But in being called forth, its intervention is nonetheless the essential cog in the machine, since it alone makes it function. It propounds the law through the organ of its representatives.

It has been contended, however, that this role has nothing properly social about it, but reduces itself to that of a conciliator of private interests; that, consequently, any individual can fill it, and that, if society is in charge of it, it is only for reasons of convenience. But nothing is more incorrect than to consider society as a sort of third-party arbitrator. When it is led to intervene, it is not to rectify individual interests. It does not seek to discover what may be the most advantageous solution for the adversaries and does not propose a compromise for them. Rather it applies to the particular case which is submitted to its general and traditional rules of law. Now law is, above all, a social thing, the objective of which is something other than the interest of the litigants. The judge who examines a request for divorce is not concerned with knowing whether this separation is truly desirable for the married parties, but rather whether the causes which are adduced come under one of the categories embodied in the law. . .

Since rules with restitutive sanctions are foreign to the *conscience collective*, the ties that they determine are not those which relate indiscriminately to everyone. That is to say, they are established, not between the individual and society, but between restricted, specific parts of soicety, whom they link to one-another. But, on the other hand, since society is not absent, it must be more or less directly interested, and it must feel the repercussions. Thus, according to the force with which society feels them, it intervenes more or less directly and actively, through the intermediary of special organs charged with representing it. These relations are, then, quite different from those which repressive law regulates, for the latter attach the particular individual to the *conscience collective* directly and without mediation: that is, the individual to society. . .

To sum up: the relations governed by co-operative law with restitutive sanctions, and the solidarity which they express, result from the division of social labour. We have explained, moreover, that, in general, co-operative relations do not convey other sanctions. In fact, it is in the nature of specialised tasks to escape the action of the *conscience collective*, for, in order for a thing to be the object of common sentiments, it must necessarily be shared: that is to say, it must be present in all minds such that everyone can represent it in one and the same manner. To be sure, in so far as functions have a certain generality, everybody can have some idea of them. But the more specialised they are, the more restricted the number of individuals who know each of them; consequently, the more marginal they are to the *conscience collective*. The rules which determine them cannot have that dominating force and transcendent authority which, when offended, demands expiation. It is also from public opinion that their authority derives, as with penal rules, but from such opinion localised in restricted regions of society.

Moreover, even in the special circles where they apply and where, consequently, they are represented in man's minds, they do not correspond to very active sentiments, nor even very often to any type of emotional state. For, as they fix the manner in which the different functions ought to concur in diverse combinations of circumstances which can arise, the objects to which they are connected are not always present in consciousness. We are not constantly called upon to administer guardianship, trusteeship, or exercise the rights of creditor or buyer, etc., or, more important, to exercise them in such and such a situation. Now, states of consciousness are strong only in so far as they are permanent. The violation of these rules reaches neither the common spirit of society, nor even, generally speaking, that of special groups, and consequently it can stimulate only a very moderate reaction. All that is necessary is that the functions concur in a regular manner. If this regularity is disrupted, it is sufficient for us to re-establish it. Assuredly, this is not to say that the development of the division of labour cannot influence penal law. There are, as we already know, administrative and governmental functions in which certain relations are regulated by repressive law, because of the particular character of this agency of the *conscience collective* and everything connected with it. In still other cases, the links of solidarity which unite certain social functions can be such that their breach stimulates repercussions which are sufficiently extensive to provoke a penal reaction. But, for the reason we have given, these reactions are exceptional...[thus] we recognise only two kinds of positive solidarity, which are distinguishable by the following qualities:

1. The first ties the individual directly to society without any intermediary. In the second, he depends upon society, because he depends upon the parts which compose it.

2. Society is not seen in the same aspect in the two cases. In the first, what we call 'society' is a more or less closely organised totality of beliefs and sentiments common to all the members of the group: it is the collective type. By contrast, the society to which we are bound in the second instance is a system of differentiated and specialised functions which are united in definite relationships. These two societies really make up only one. They are two aspects of one and the same reality, but nonetheless they must be distinguished.

3. From this second difference there arises another which helps us to characterise and name the two kinds of solidarity.

The first can be strong only to the degree that the ideas and tendencies common to all the members of the society are greater in number and intensity than those which pertain to each individual member. Its strength is determined by the degree to which this is the case. But what makes our personality is how many particular characteristics we possess which distinguish us from others. This solidarity thus can grow only in inverse ratio to personality. There are in each of us, as we have said, two forms of consciousness: one which is common to our group as a whole, which, consequently, is not ourself, but society living and acting within us; the other, on the other hand, represents that in us which is personal and distinct, that which makes us an individual. Solidarity which comes from resemblance is at its *maximum* when the *conscience collective* completely envelops our whole consciousness and coincides in all points with it. But, at that moment, our individuality is nil. It can develop only if the community takes a lesser part of us. There are, here, two contrary forces, one centripetal, the other centrifugal, which cannot flourish at the same time. We cannot, at one and the same time, develop ourselves in two opposite senses. If we have a strong inclination to think and act for ourselves, we cannot be as strongly inclined to think and act as others do. If our ideal is to present a unique and personal appearance, we cannot resemble everybody else. Moreover, at the moment when this latter solidarity exercises its force, our personality vanishes, by definition, one might say, for we are no longer ourselves, but the collective being.

The social molecules which cohere in this way can act together only in so far as they have no action of their own, as with the molecules of inorganic bodies. That is why we propose to call this form of solidarity 'mechanical'. The term does not signify that it is produced by mechanical and artificial means. We call it that only by analogy to the cohesion which unites the elements of an inorganic body, as contrasted to that which forms a unity out of the elements of a living body. What finally justifies this term is that the link which thus unites the individual to society is wholly comparable to that which attaches a thing to a person. The individual consciousness, considered in this light, is a simple appendage of the collective type and follows all of its actions, as the possessed object follows those of its owner. In societies where this type of solidarity is highly developed, the individual is not his own master, as we shall see later; solidarity is, literally something which the society possesses. Thus, in these types of society, personal rights are not yet distinguished from real rights.

It is quite different with the solidarity which the division of labour produces. Whereas the previous type implies that individuals resemble each other, this latter presumes that they differ.

The former is possible only in so far as the individual personality is absorbed into the collective personality; the latter is possible only if each one has a sphere of action which is peculiar to him – that is, if he possesses a personality. It is necessary, then, that the *conscience collective* leave open a part of the individual consciousness in order that special functions may be established there, functions which it cannot regulate. The more this region is extended, the stronger is the cohesion which results from this solidarity. In fact, on the one hand, every individual depends more directly on society as labour becomes more divided; and, on the other, the activity of every individual becomes more personalised to the degree that it is more specialised. No doubt, as circumscribed as it is, it is never completely original; even in the exercise of our occupation, we conform to conventions and practices which are common to our whole occupational group. But, in this instance, the yoke that we submit to is much less heavy than when society completely controls us, and it leaves much more place open for the free play of our initiative. Here, then, the individuality of all grows at the same time as that of its parts. Society becomes more capable of collective action, at the same time that each of its elements has more freedom of action. This solidarity resembles that which we observe among the higher animals. Each organ, in effect, has its special character and autonomy; and yet the unity of the organism is as great as the individuation of the parts is more marked. Because of this analogy, we propose to call the solidarity which is due to the division of labour, 'organic'.

DTS, pp. 79, 80–2, 83, 96–101

6. The division of labour and social differentiation

Thus, it is an historical law that mechanical solidarity, which first stands alone, or nearly so, progressively loses ground, and that organic solidarity gradually becomes preponderant. But when the mode of solidarity becomes changed, the structure of societies cannot but change. The form of a body is necessarily transformed when the molecular relationships are no longer the same. Consequently, if the preceding proposition is correct, there must be two social types which correspond to these two types of solidarity.

If we try to construct hypothetically the ideal type of a society whose cohesion were exclusively the result of resemblance, we should have to conceive it as an absolutely homogeneous mass whose parts were not distinguished from one another, and which consequently had no structure. In short, it would be devoid of all definite form and all organisation. It would be the actual social protoplasm, the germ out of which all social types would develop. We propose to call the aggregate thus characterised, a *horde*.

It is true that we have not yet, in any completely authenticated fashion, observed societies which complied in all respects with this definition. What gives us the right to postulate their existence, however, is that the lower societies, those which are closest to this primitive stage, are formed by a simple repetition of aggregates of this kind. We find an almost perfectly pure example of this social organisation among the Indians of North America. Each Iroquois tribe, for example, is composed of a certain number of partial societies (the largest ones comprise eight) which present all the characteristics we have just mentioned. The adults of both sexes are equal to each other. The *sachems* and chiefs, who are at the head of each of these groups and by whose council the common affairs of the tribe are administered, do not enjoy any superiority. Kinship itself is not organised, for we cannot give this name to the distribution of the population in layers of generations. In the late epoch in which these peoples have been studied, there were, indeed, some special obligations which bound the child to its maternal relatives, but these are of little consequence, and are not perceptibly distinct from those which link the child to other members of society. . .

We give the name *clan* to the horde which has ceased to be independent by becoming an element in a more extensive group, and that of *segmental societies with a clan-base* to societies which are formed by an association of clans. We call societies 'segmental' in order to indicate that they are characterised by the repetition of similar groupings, rather like the rings of an earthworm, and we call this fundamental element a 'clan', because this word well expresses its mixed nature, at once familial and political. It is a family in the sense that all the members who compose it consider themselves relatives, and they are, in fact, for the most part consanguineous. The affinities that are created by these blood-ties are those which principally keep them united. In addition, they sustain relationships which we can term domestic, since we also find them in societies whose familial character is indisputable: I am referring to collective punishment, collective responsibility, and, as soon as private property makes its appearance, common inheritance. But, on the other hand, it is not a family in the proper sense of the word, for in order to belong to it, it is not necessary to have any definite relations of consanguinity with other members of the clan. It is enough to possess an external quality, which generally consists in having the same name. Although this sign is thought to denote a common origin, such a civil status really constitutes very inconclusive proof, and is very easy to copy. Thus, the clan contains a great many strangers, and this permits it to attain dimensions such as a family, properly speaking, never has. It often comprises several thousand persons. Moreover, it is the fundamental political unit; the heads of clans are the only social authorities.

We can thus label this organisation 'politico-familial'. Not only has the clan consanguinity as its basis, but different clans within the same society are often considered as kin to one-another. . .

This organisation, just like the horde, of which it is only an extension, evidently carries with it no other solidarity than that derived from resemblance, since the society is formed of similar segments and these in their turn enclose only homogeneous elements. No doubt, each clan has its own character and is thereby distinguished from others; but the solidarity is proportionally weaker as they are more heterogeneous, and vice versa. For segmental organisation to be possible, the segments must resemble one another: without that, they would not be united. And they must differ; without this, they would lose themselves in each other and be effaced. These two contrasting prerequisites are found in varying ratio in different societies, but the type of society remains the same...

The structure of societies where organic solidarity is preponderant is quite different.

These are formed, not by the repetition of similar, homogeneous segments, but by a system of different organs each of which has a special role, and which are themselves formed of differentiated parts. Not only are social elements not of the same nature, but they are not distributed in the same way. They are not juxtaposed in a linear fashion as the rings of an earthworm, nor entwined one with another, but co-ordinated and subordinated one to another around the same central organ which exercises a moderating action over the rest of the organism. This organ itself no longer has the same character as in the preceding case, for, if the others depend upon it, it, in its turn, depends upon them. No doubt, it still enjoys a special situation, a privileged position, but that is due to the nature of the role that it fills and not to some cause foreign to its functions, to some force communicated to it externally. Thus, there is no longer anything about it that is not temporal and human; between it and other organs, there is no longer anything but differences in degree. This is comparable to the way in which, in the animal, the dominance of the nervous system over other systems is reduced to the right, if one may speak thus, of obtaining the best food and of having its fill before the others. But it needs them, just as they have need of it.

This social type rests on principles so different from the preceding that it can develop only in proportion to the effacement of that type. In this type, individuals are no longer grouped according to their relations of lineage, but according to the particular nature of the social activity to which they devote themselves. Their natural and necessary milieu is no longer that given by birth, but that given by occupation. It is no longer real or fictitious blood-ties which mark the place of each one, but the function which he fills. No doubt, when this new form of organisation begins to appear, it tries to utilise and to take over the existing one. The way in which functions are divided thus follows, as faithfully as possible, the way in which society is already divided. The segments, or at least the groups of segments united by special affinities, become organs.

It is thus that the clans which together formed the tribe of the Levites appropriated priestly functions for themselves among the Hebrew people. In a general way, classes and castes probably derive their origin and their character in this way; they arise from the numerous occupational organisations which spring up within the pre-existing familial organisation. But this mixed arrangement cannot endure, for between the two conditions that it attempts to reconcile, there is an antagonism which necessarily ends in a break. It is only a very rudimentary division of labour which can adapt itself to those rigid, defined moulds which were not made for it. It can grow only by freeing itself from the framework which encloses it. As soon as it has passed a certain stage of development, there is no longer any connection either between the given number of segments and the steady growth of functions which are becoming specialised, or between the hereditarily fixed properties of the first and the new aptitudes that the second calls forth. The substance of social life must enter into entirely new combinations in order to organise itself upon completely different foundations. But the old structure, so far as it persists, is opposed to this. That is why it must disappear.

DTS, pp. 148–51, 152 and 157–9

THE DECLINE OF MECHANICAL SOLIDARITY
AND EMERGENCE OF MORAL INDIVIDUALISM

Not only, in a general way, does mechanical solidarity link men less strongly than organic solidarity, but also, as we advance in the scale of social evolution, it becomes increasingly weak.

The strength of the social ties which have this origin differ in relation to the three following conditions:

1. The relation between the volume of the *conscience collective* and that of the individual mind. The links are stronger the more the first completely envelops the second.

2. The average intensity of the states of the *conscience collective*. The relation between volumes being equal, it has as much power over the individual as it has vitality. If, on the other hand, it consists of only weak forces, it can move the individual only weakly in the collective direction. He will the more easily be able to pursue his own course, and solidarity will thus be less.

3. The greater or lesser the fixity of these same states the more defined are beliefs and practices which exist, and the less place they leave for individual differences. They are uniform moulds within which all our ideas and actions are formed. Consensus is

then as perfect as possible; all minds move in unison. Conversely, the more abstract and indeterminate the rules of conduct and thought, the more conscious direction must intervene to apply them to particular cases. But the latter cannot awaken without dissensions occurring, for as it varies from one man to another in quality and quantity, it inevitably leads to this result. Centrifugal tendencies thus multiply at the expense of social cohesion and the harmony of actions.

On the other hand, strong and defined states of the *conscience collective* are the basis of penal law. But we shall see that the number of these is less today than previously, and that it diminishes progressively as societies approach our social type. Thus it is the case that the average intensity and degree of fixity of collective states have themselves diminished. From this fact, it is true, we cannot conclude that the total extent of the *conscience collective* has narrowed, for it may be that the region to which penal law corresponds has contracted, and that the remainder, by contrast, has expanded. It may manifest fewer strong and defined states, but compensate with a greater number of others. But this growth, if it is real, is at most equivalent to that which is produced in the individual mind, for the latter has, at least, grown in the same proportions. If there are more things common to all, there are far more that are personal to each. There is, indeed, every reason to believe that the latter have increased more than the former, for the differences between men become more pronounced in so far as they are more educated. We have just seen that specialised activities have developed more than the *conscience collective*. It is, therefore, at least probable that, in each individual mind, the personal sphere has grown more than the other. In any case, the relation between them has at most remained the same. Consequently, from this point of view, mechanical solidarity has gained nothing, even if it has not lost anything. If therefore, from another aspect, we discover that the *conscience collective* has become weaker and more ill-defined, we can rest assured that there has been a weakening of this solidarity, since, in respect of the three conditions upon which its power of action rests, two, at least, are losing their intensity, while the third remains unchanged...

This is not to say, however, that the *conscience collective* is likely to disappear completely. Rather it increasingly comes to consist of very general and indeterminate ways of thought and sentiment, which leaves room open for a growing variety of individual differences. There is even a place where it is strengthened

and made precise: this is, in the way in which it regards the
individual. As all the other beliefs and all the other practices take
on a less and less religious character, the individual becomes the
object of a sort of religion. We have a cult of personal dignity
which, as with every strong cult, already has its superstitions. It is,
thus, we may say, a common faith but it is possible only by the
ruin of all others and, consequently, cannot produce the same
effects as this mass of extinguished beliefs. There is no compensa-
tion for these. Moreover, if it is common in so far as it is shared
by the community, it is individual in its object. If it turns all wills
towards the same end, this end is not social. It thus occupies a
completely exceptional place in the *conscience collective*. It is still
from society that it takes all its force, but it is not to society that it
attaches us; it is to ourselves. Hence, it does not constitute a true
social bond. That is why we have been justly able to criticise the
theorists who have made this sentiment the only fundamental
element in their moral doctrine with the ensuing dissolution of
society. We can then conclude by saying that all social links which
result from likeness progressively slacken.

DTS, 124–6 and 146–7

[Written in review of Tönnies' *Gemeinschaft und Gesellschaft*.]

Like the author I believe that there are two major types of society,
and the words which he uses to designate them indicate their
nature fairly well; it is a pity that they are untranslatable. I accept,
in common with him, that *Gemeinschaft* is the original phenomenon, and *Gesellschaft* the end result which derives from it.
Lastly I agree with the general lines of analysis and the description
of *Gemeinschaft* which he has given us.

The point over which I diverge from him, however, concerns
the theory of *Gesellschaft*. If I have properly understood his
thought, *Gesellschaft* is supposed to be characterised by a progressive development of individualism, the dispersive effects of
which can only be prevented for a time, and by artificial means,
by the action of the state. It is seen essentially as a mechanical
aggregate; what there is that remains of truly collective life is
presumed to result, not from an internal spontaneity, but from the
wholly external stimulus of the state. In short...it is society such
as Bentham conceived of it. Now I believe that the life of large
social agglomerations is just as natural as that of small groupings.
It is no less organic and no less internal. Outside of these purely
individual actions there is a collective activity in our contemporary

societies which is just as natural as that of the smaller societies of previous ages. It is certainly different; it constitutes a distinct type, but however different they may be, there is no difference in nature between these two varieties of the same genus. If in order to prove this, it would need a book; I can do no more than state the proposition. Is it likely, moreover, that the evolution of a single entity, society, begins by being organic only to subsequently become purely mechanical? There is such a chasm between these two modes of existence that it is impossible to see how they could form part of the same development. To reconcile the theory of Aristotle with that of Bentham in this way is simply to juxtapose opposites. We have to choose: if society is originally a natural phenomenon, it stays such until the end of its life.

But what does this collective life of *Gesellschaft* consist in? The procedure followed by the author does not allow an answer to this question, because it is completely ideological. In the second part of his work, Tönnies devotes more time to the systematic analysis of concepts than to the observation of facts. He proceeds by conceptual argument; we find in his writing the distinctions and symmetrical classifications which are so beloved of German logicians. The only way to avoid this would have been to proceed inductively, that is, to study *Gesellschaft* through the law and the mores which correspond to it, and which reveal its structure.

RP, 1889, pp. 421–2

The condemnation of individualism has been facilitated by its confusion with the narrow utilitarianism and utilitarian egoism of Spencer and the economists. But this is very facile. It is not hard, to be sure, to denounce as a shallow ideal that narrow commercialism which reduces society to nothing more than a vast apparatus of production and exchange; and it is perfectly clear that all social life would be impossible if there did not exist interests superior to the interests of individuals. It is wholly correct that such doctrines should be treated as anarchical, and we fully agree with this view. But what is unacceptable is that this individualism should be presented as the only one that there is, or even could be. Quite the contrary; it is becoming increasingly rare and exceptional. The practical philosophy of Spencer is of such moral poverty that it now has hardly any supporters. As for the economists, even if they once allowed themselves to be seduced by the simplicity of this theory, they have for a long time now felt the need to modify the severity of their primitive orthodoxy and to open their minds to more generous sentiments. M. de Molinari is almost alone, in France, in remaining intractable and I am not aware that he has exercised a significant influence on the ideas of our time. Indeed, if individualism had not other representatives, it would be quite pointless to move heaven and earth in this way to combat an enemy who is in the process of quietly dying a natural death.

However, there exists another individualism over which it is less easy to triumph. It has been upheld for a century by the great majority of thinkers: it is the individualism of Kant and Rousseau and the spiritualists, that which the Declaration of the Rights of Man sought, more or less successfully, to translate into formulae, which is now taught in our schools and which has become the basis of our moral catechism. It is true that it has been thought possible to attack this individualism by reference to the first type; but the two are fundamentally different, and the criticisms which apply to the one could not be appropriate to the other. It is so far from making personal interest the aim of human conduct that it sees personal motives as the very source of evil. According to Kant, I am only certain of acting properly if the motives that influence me relate, not to the particular circumstances in which I am placed, but to my equality as a man *in abstracto*. Conversely, my action is wrong when it cannot be justified logically except by reference to the situation I happen to be in and my social condition, class or caste interests, my emotions, etc. Hence immoral conduct is to be recognised by the sign that it is closely linked to the individuality of the agent and cannot be universalised without manifest absurdity. Similarly, if Rousseau sees the general will, which is the basis of the social contract, as infallible, as the authentic expression of perfect justice, this is because it is a resultant of the totality of particular wills; consequently it constitutes a kind of impersonal average from which all individual considerations have been eliminated, since, being distinct from and even antagonistic to one-another, they are neutralised and cancel each other out. Thus, for both these thinkers, the only modes of conduct that are moral are those which are applicable to all men equally: that is to say, which are implied in the notion of man in general.

This is indeed far removed from that apotheosis of pleasure and private interest, the egoistic cult of the self for which utilitarian individualism has validly been criticised. Quite the contrary: according to these moralists, duty consists in turning our attention from what concerns us personally, from all that relates to our empirical individuality, so as to pursue solely that which is demanded by our human condition, that which we hold in common with all our fellow men. This ideal goes so far beyond the limit of utilitarian ends that it appears to those who aspire to it as having a religious character. The human person, by reference to the definition of which good must be distinguished from evil, is considered as sacred, in what can be called the ritual sense of the word. It has something of that transcendental majesty which the churches of all times have accorded to their gods. It is conceived as being invested with that mysterious property which creates a vacuum about holy objects, which keeps them away from profane contacts and which separates them from ordinary life. And it is exactly this characteristic which confers the respect of which it is the object. Whoever makes an attempt on a man's life, on a man's liberty, on a man's honour, inspires us with a feeling of revulsion, in every way comparable to that which the believer experiences when he sees his idol profaned. Such a morality is therefore not simply a hygienic discipline or a wise principle of economy. It is a religion of which man is, at the same time, both believer and god.

But this religion is individualistic, since it has man as its object; man is, by definition, an individual. Indeed there is no system whose individualism is more uncompromising. Nowhere are the rights of man affirmed more energetically, since the individual is here placed on the level of sacrosanct objects; nowhere is he more jealously protected from external encroachments, whatever their source.

A verbal similarity has made possible the belief that *individualism* necessarily resulted from *individual*, and thus egoistic, sentiments. In reality, the religion of the individual is a social institution like all known religions. It is society which provides us with this ideal as the only common end which is today able to offer a focus for men's wills. To remove this ideal, without replacing it with any other, is therefore to plunge us into that very moral anarchy which it is sought to avoid.

Nonetheless we must not consider as perfect and definitive the formula with which the eighteenth century gave expression to individualism, a formula which we have made the mistake of maintaining in an almost unchanged form. Although it was adequate a century ago, it today needs to be enlarged and completed. It presented individualism only in its most negative aspect. Our forerunners were concerned solely with freeing the individual from the political shackles which hampered his development. Thus they regarded freedom of thought, freedom to write, and freedom to vote as the primary values that it was necessary to achieve – and this emancipation was indeed the precondition of all subsequent progress. However, carried away by the enthusiasm of the struggle, and concerned only with the objective they pursued, in the end they no longer saw beyond it, and made into something of an ultimate goal what was merely the next stage in their efforts. Now, political freedom is a means, not an end. It is worth no more than the manner in which it is put to use. If it does not serve something which exists beyond it, it is not merely fruitless, it becomes dangerous. If those who handle this weapon do not know how to use it in productive struggles, they will not be slow in turning it against themselves.

It is precisely for this reason that it has fallen today into a certain discredit. Men of my generation recall how great our enthusiasm was when, twenty years ago, we finally succeeded in toppling the last barriers which we impatiently confronted. But alas! disenchantment came quickly; for we soon had to admit that no one knew what use should be made of this freedom that had been so laboriously achieved. Those to whom we owed it only made use of it in internecine conflicts. And it was from that moment that one felt the growth in the country of this current of gloom and despondency, which became stronger with each day that passed, the ultimate result of which must inevitably be to break the spirit of those least able to resist.

Thus, we can no longer subscribe to this negative ideal. We must go beyond what has been achieved, if only to preserve it. Indeed, if we do not learn to put to use the means of action that we have in our hands, it is inevitable that they will become less effective. Let us therefore use our freedoms to discover what must be done and in order to do it. Let us use them in order to soften the functioning of the social machine, still so harsh to individuals, so as to put at their disposal all possible means for the free development of their faculties in order finally to progress towards making a reality of the famous precept: to each according to his works!

RB, 1898, pp. 7–8 and 12–13

THE CAUSES OF THE DEVELOPMENT OF
THE DIVISION OF LABOUR

We have seen that the organised structure, and thus the division of labour, develop correspondingly as the segmental structure disappears. Thus either this disappearance is the cause of the development, or the development is the cause of the disappearance, The latter hypothesis is unacceptable, for we know that the segmental arrangement is an unsurmountable obstacle to the division of labour, and must at least partially have become dissolved for the division of labour to emerge. The latter can only develop in so far as the former ceases to exist. To be sure, once the division of labour appears, it can contribute towards the hastening of the other's regression, but it only comes into being once this regression has begun. The effect reacts upon the cause, but never loses its quality of effect; its action, consequently, is secondary. The growth of the division of labour is thus brought about by the social segments losing their individuality, as the boundaries between them become less marked. In short, a merging takes place which makes it possible for social life to enter into new combinations.

But the disappearance of this type can have this consequence for only one reason. That is because it produces a coming together between individuals who were separated – or, at least, a closer relationship than existed previously. Consequently, there is an interchange of action between parts of the social mass which, until then, had no effect upon one another. The more pronounced the segmental system, the more are our relations enclosed within the limits of the segment to which we belong. There are, as it were, moral gaps between the different segments. By contrast, these gaps are filled in as the system becomes levelled out. Social life, instead of being concentrated in a large number of separate, small centres, each of which resembles the other, is generalised. Social relations – or more correctly, intra-social relations – consequently become more numerous, since they extend, on all sides, beyond their original limits. The division of labour develops, therefore, as there are more individuals sufficiently in contact to be able to act and react upon one-another. If we agree to call this coming together, and the active commerce resulting from it, 'dynamic' or 'formal' density, we can say that the progress of the division of labour is in direct ratio to the moral or dynamic density of society.

But this moral relationship can only produce its effect if the real distance between individuals has itself diminished in some way. Moral density cannot grow unless material density grows at the same time, and the latter can be used to measure the former. It is useless, moreover, to try to find out which has determined the other; it is enough to state that they are inseparable.

The progressive condensation of societies in the course of historical development is produced in three principal ways:

1. Whereas lower societies are spread over immense areas relative to the size of their populations, among more advanced peoples population tends to become more and more concentrated...The changes brought about in the industrial life of nations prove the universality of this transformation. The productive activity of nomads, hunters, or shepherds implies the absence of all concentration, dispersion over the largest possible surface. Agriculture, since it necessitates a life in a fixed territory, presupposes a certain tightening of the social tissues, but is still incomplete, for there are stretches of land between each family. In the city, although the condensation was greater, the houses were not contiguous, for joint property was no part of the Roman law. It grew up on our soil, and demonstrates that the social web has become tighter. On the other hand, from their origins, the European societies have witnessed a continuous growth in their density, short-lived regressions notwithstanding.

2. The formation of towns and their development is an even more characteristic symptom of the same phenomenon. The increase in average density may be due to the material increase of the birth-rate, and, consequently, can be reconciled with a very weak concentration, whereby the segmental type remains prevalent. But towns always result from the need of individuals to put themselves constantly in the closest possible contact with each other. There are so many points where the social mass is contracted more strongly than elsewhere. Thus when they multiply and expand the moral density must become raised. We shall see, moreover, that they receive a source of recruitment from immigration, something which is only possible when the fusion of social segments is advanced.

As long as social organisation is essentially segmental, towns do not exist. There are none in lower societies. They did not exist among the Iroquois, nor among the ancient Germans. It was the same with the primitive populations of Italy...But towns did not take long to appear. Athens and Rome are or become towns, and the same transformation occurred throughout Italy. In our Christian societies, the town is in evidence from the beginning, for those left by the Roman empire did not disappear with it. Since then, they have increased and multiplied. The tendency of the country to stream into the town, so general in the civilised world, is only a consequence of this movement. It is not of recent origin; from the seventeenth century, statesmen have been preoccupied with it.

Because societies generally begin with an agricultural period, there has sometimes been the temptation to regard the development of urban centres as a sign of old age and decadence. But we must not lose sight of the fact that the length of this agricultural phase is shorter the more advanced the society. Whereas in Germany, among the Indians of America, and with all primitive peoples, it lasts for the duration of their existence, in Rome and Athens, it ends fairly quickly; and, with us, we can say that it never existed in pure form. On the other hand, urban life begins earlier and consequently expands further. The constantly increasing acceleration of this development proves that, far from constituting a sort of pathological phenomenon, it comes from the very nature of higher social types. The supposition that this movement has attained alarming proportions in our societies today, which perhaps are no longer flexible enough to adapt themselves to it, will not prevent this movement from continuing either within our societies, or after them; and the social types which will be formed after ours will probably be distinguished by a still more complete and rapid contraction of rural life.

3. Finally, there are the number and rapidity of the means of communication and transportation. By suppressing or diminishing the gaps which separate social segments, they increase the density of society. It is not necessary, however, to prove that they become more numerous and perfected in societies of a more developed type.

Since this visible and measurable symbol reflects the variations of what we have called 'moral density' we can substitute it for this latter in the formula we have proposed. Moreover, we must repeat here what we said before. If society, in concentrating, determines the development of the division of labour, the latter, in its turn, increases the concentration of society. But this is not important, for the division of labour remains the derived fact, and, consequently, the advances which it has made are due to parallel advances of social density, whatever may be the causes of the latter. That is all we wished to prove...

If work becomes progressively divided as societies become more voluminous and dense, it is not because external circumstances are more varied, but because struggle for existence is more acute.

Darwin quite correctly observed that the struggle between two organisms is as active as they are similar. Having the same needs and pursuing the same aims, they are in rivalry everywhere. So long as they have more resources than they need, they can still live side by side, but if their number increases to such proportions that their needs can no longer all be adequately satisfied, war breaks out, and it is the more violent the more marked this scarcity; that is to say, as the number of participants increase. It is quite otherwise if the co-existing individuals are of different species or varieties. As they do not feed in the same manner, and do not lead the same kind of life, they do not disturb each other. What is advantageous to one is without value to the others. The occasions for conflict thus diminish with occasions of confrontation, and this happens increasingly as the species or varieties become more distant from one-another. . .

Men obey the same law. In the same city, different occupations can co-exist without being obliged mutually to destroy one another, for they pursue different objectives. The soldier seeks military glory, the priest moral authority, the statesman power, the businessman riches, and the scholar scientific renown. Each of them can attain his end without preventing the others from attaining theirs. It is still the same even when the functions are less separated from one another. The occulist does not compete with the psychiatrist, the shoemaker with the hatter, the mason with the cabinet maker, the physicist with the chemist, etc. Since they perform different services, they can perform them together.

The closer functions approach one-another, however, the more points of contact they have; the more, consequently, they are exposed to conflict. As in this case they satisfy similar needs by different means, they inevitably seek to curtail the other's development. The judge never is in competition with the businessman, but the brewer and the wine-grower, the clothier and the manufacturer of silks, the poet and the musician, often try to supplant each other. As for those who have exactly the same function, each can prosper only to the detriment of the others. If, then, these different functions are pictured as a series of branches issuing from a common trunk, the struggle is at its minimum between the extreme points, whereas it increases steadily as we approach the centre. It is so, not only inside each city, but in all society. Similar occupations located at different points are as competitive as they are alike, provided the difficulty of communication and transport does not restrict the circle of their action.

This having been said, it is easy to understand that any condensation of the social mass, especially if it is accompanied by an increase in population, necessarily stimulates an advance in the division of labour.

DTS, pp. 273–8, 239–41 and 248–50

7. Analysis of socialist doctrines

THE STUDY OF SOCIALISM

We can conceive of two very different ways of studying socialism. We can see it as a scientific doctrine on the nature and evolution of societies in general and, more specifically, of the most advanced contemporary societies. In this case, the analysis which we make does not differ from that to which scholars submit the theories and hypotheses of their respective sciences. It is considered abstractly, outside of time, space, and future history, not as a fact the origins of which we seek to discover, but as a system of propositions which express or are deemed to express reality; we then ask what is its truth or falsity, whether or not it corresponds to social reality, in what measure it is self-consistent, and conforms to things as they are. . .This will not be our point of view. The reason for this is that without diminishing in any way the importance of our interest in socialism, we cannot accord it a fully scientific character. In fact, 'research' only deserves to be called by that name if it has a definite and real subject-matter, which it simply aims to translate into intelligible language. Science is a study bearing on a delimited portion of reality which it aims at knowing and, if possible, understanding. To describe and explain what is and what has been – this is its sole task. Speculation about the future is not its concern, although it may ultimately seek to make this possible.

Socialism, on the contrary, is wholly oriented toward the future. It is above all a plan for the reconstruction of present-day society, a programme for a collective life which does not exist as yet, or only in dreams, and which is offered to men as a worthy object for their strivings. It is an ideal. It concerns itself much less with what is or was than with what ought to be. Undoubtedly, even in its most utopian forms it never disdained the support of facts, and has even in more recent times increasingly taken on a definitely scientific turn of phrase. It is undeniable that it has thus rendered social science more services than it received from it. For it has stimulated thought and scientific activity, it has instigated research, posed problems, so that in more than one way its history blends with the history of sociology itself. Yet, how can one fail to note the enormous disparity between the thin and meagre data it borrows from science and the extent of the practical conclusions that it draws – which are, nevertheless, the core of the system? It aspires to a complete remoulding of the social order. But in order to know what the family, property, political, moral, juridical, and economic organisation of the European peoples can and ought to be, even in the near future, we must necessarily have studied this host of institutions and practices in the past; we must have investigated the ways in which they have varied in history, and the principal conditions which have determined these variations. Only then will it be possible to ask oneself rationally what they ought to become now, given the present conditions of our collective existence. Now all these researches are still in their infancy. Several have hardly yet even been begun; the most advanced have not yet passed beyond a very rudimentary phase. Since each of these problems is a world in itself, the solution cannot be found in an instant, merely because the need is felt. The bases for a methodical prediction regarding the future, especially one of such breadth, are not established: they have to be worked out by the theorist. Socialism has not taken the time to do this; perhaps one could even say, it did not have the time.

That is why, to speak precisely, there cannot be a scientific socialism. Because, for such a socialism to be possible, sciences would be necessary that are not yet developed and which cannot be improvised. The only attitude that science permits in the face of these problems is reservation and circumspection, and socialism can hardly maintain this without deceiving itself. And, in fact, socialism has not maintained this position. Consider even the leading work – the most systematic, the richest in ideas – that this school has produced: Marx's *Capital*. What an abundance of statistical data, historical studies and comparisons would be required to solve any one of the vast numbers of questions that are covered there! Need we be reminded that an entire theory of value is established in a few lines? The truth is that the facts and observations assembled by the theorists anxious to document their affirmations are hardly there except to give form to the arguments. The researches they have carried out were undertaken to establish a doctrine that they had previously conceived, rather than the doctrine being a result of the research. Almost all such doctrines had become hardened before asking science for the help it could lend them. It is passion that has been the inspiration of all these systems; what gave them life and strength is a thirst for a more perfect justice, pity for the misery of the working classes, a general feeling for the distress of contemporary societies, etc. Socialism is not a science, a sociology in miniature – it is a cry of misery, sometimes of anger, uttered by men who feel most keenly our collective unease. Socialism is to the phenomena which produce it what the groans of a sick man are to the illness with which he is afflicted, to the needs that torment him. But what would one say of a doctor who accepted the replies or desires of his patient as scientific truths? The theories ordinarily invoked in opposition to socialism, however, are no different in nature and they no more merit the title we refuse the latter. When economists call for *laissez faire*, demanding that the influence of the state be reduced to nothing, that competition be freed of every limitation, they are not basing their claims on laws scientifically induced. The social sciences are still much too young to be able to serve as bases for such comprehensive and all-embracing practical doctrines. These latter are maintained by needs of another kind – a prizing of individual autonomy, a love of order, a fear of novelty, misoneism as it is called today. Individualism, like socialism, is above all an emotion which presses for recognition, although it may eventually ask reason for arguments with which to justify itself.

This being so, to study socialism as a system of abstract propositions, as a body of scientific theories and to discuss it formally, is to see and show a side of it which is of only moderate interest. Whosoever is aware of what social science must be, of the slowness of its processes, of the laborious investigations it implies to resolve even the most restricted questions, cannot accept these premature solutions, these vast systems so summarily sketched out. One is too aware of the distance that exists between the simplicity of its methods and the vast scope of its conclusions, and is consequently prompted to scorn the latter. But socialism can be examined from quite a different aspect. If it is not a scientific formulation of social facts, it is itself a social fact of the first importance. If it is not a scientific contribution, it is a subject for science. As such, we do not have to borrow from socialism such and such a proposition ready made; but we do have to know socialism, and to understand what it is, where it comes from, and where it is tending.

It is interesting to study socialism from this point of view, for two reasons. First, one can hope that it will aid us in understanding the social conditions which have given rise to it. For precisely because it derives from certain conditions, socialism manifests and expresses them in its own way, and thereby gives us another means of analysing them. It is certainly not that socialism reflects them accurately. Quite the contrary, for the reasons given above. We can be certain that it unknowingly distorts them and gives us only an unfaithful impression, just as a sick man faultily interprets the feelings that he experiences, and most often attributes them to a cause which is not the true one. But these feelings, such as they are, have an intrinsic interest, and the clinician notes them with care and takes great account of them. They are an element in diagnosis, and a very important element. For example, he is not indifferent as to where they are felt, when they began. In the same way, it is highly material to determine the epoch when socialism began to appear. It is a cry of collective distress, we might say. Well then, it is essential to fix the moment when this cry was uttered for the first time. For according to whether we see it as a recent phenomenon, related to entirely new social conditions, or, on the other hand, as a simple recurrence or variant of the lamentations that the wretched of all epochs and societies have made heard, the eternal claims of the poor against the rich, we will judge its tendencies manifest in socialism quite differently. In the second case, we will be led to believe that these can no more be abolished than human misery can end. They will be thought of as a kind of chronic human suffering which, from time to time in the course of history and under the influence of transient circumstances, seems to become more acute and pronounced, but which always ends by at last diminishing. In this case, we will strive only to discover some moderating factor to cause it again to abate. If, on the contrary, we find that it is of recent date, that it is related to a situation without parallel in history, we can no longer take for granted its chronic nature and we are less ready to take such a view. But it is not only to diagnose the nature of the evil that such a study of socialism promises to be instructive; it is, also, in order to find appropriate remedies. To be sure, we can be certain in advance that the remedies are not precisely those needed by the systems, just as the drink demanded by a man with fever is not necessarily what he requires. Nonetheless, the needs that he does feel do serve as some guide in the treatment. They are never without some cause, and sometimes it is best to satisfy them. In the same way, and for the same reason, it is important to know what social rearrangements, that is, what remedies, the suffering masses of society have spontaneously and instinctively conceived of, however unscientific their elaboration might have been. This is what socialist theories express. The material that one can gather on this subject will be especially useful if, instead of confining ourselves to one system, we make a comparative study of all these doctrines. For then we have greater opportunity to eliminate from all these aspirations what is necessarily individual, subjective, contingent, in order to extract and retain only their most general, most impersonal, and therefore their most objective characteristics.

Soc., pp. 3–9

EVALUATION OF MARXISM

[From a review of Labriola's exposition of historical materialism.]

We believe it to be a fruitful idea that social life should be explained, not in terms of the conception which its participants hold of it, but by reference to underlying causes which escape consciousness; and we also think that these causes have to be sought principally in the way in which associated individuals are grouped. It seems to us that it is indeed on this condition, and on this condition alone, that history can become a science and, in consequence, that sociology can exist. For in order for collective representations to be intelligible, it is certainly necessary that they should originate from something, and since they cannot form a circle closed upon itself, the source which they derive from must be outside them. Either the *conscience collective* floats in a void, a kind of indescribable absolute, or else it is connected to the rest of the world by a substratum upon which, consequently, it is dependent. Moreover, what can this substratum be made up of, if it is not the members of society, as they are combined socially? This proposition seems to us to be obvious. But we see no reason to link this, as the author does, to the socialist movement; it is totally independent of it. We ourselves arrived at it before knowing Marx, who has not influenced us in any way. The fact is that this conception is the logical end-result of all of the developments in history and psychology over these last fifty years. Historians have for a long time perceived that social evolution has causes which the authors of the historical events in question were not aware of. It is under the influence of these ideas that the role of great men tends either to be denied or to be limited, and that, in developments in literature, law, etc., there is a search to express collective thought which no definite individual embodies completely. At the same time, and above all, individual psychology has recently taught us that the consciousness of the individual is often no more than a reflection of the underlying state of the organism: that the course of our ideas is determined by causes which are not known to the subject. It was natural that, from there, this conception became extended to collective psychology. But it is impossible for us to see what part the unhappy conflict of classes which we witness today can have had in the elaboration or the development of this idea. No doubt this idea appeared at its given time and when the necessary conditions for its emergence were established. It was not always possible. But it is a question of knowing what these conditions are; and when Labriola asserts that it was called forth 'by the full, conscious and continuous development of modern technology, and by the inevitable suggestion of a new world which is in the process of being born', he states as evident a thesis for which there is no proof. Socialism has been able to make use of this idea to its own profit; but it has not created it and, most important, acceptance of it does not imply acceptance of socialism.

It is true that if this objective conception of history were necessarily bound to the doctrine of economic materialism, as our author asserts, one could accept that the former was established under the same influence and inspired by the same spirit, as the latter certainly has socialist origins. *But this assimilation is completely without foundation; and it is important to put an end to it.* These two theories are completely independent, and their scientific value is singularly different. Just as much as it seems to us to be that the causes of social phenomena must be sought outside of individual ideas, so it seems to us to be false that they derive ultimately from the state of industrial technology, and that the economic factor is the source of progress.

Even without opposing economic materialism by reference to any definite fact, how can one fail to notice the inadequacy of the evidence upon which it rests? Here is a law which is claimed to be the key to history! But in order to demonstrate it, an author is content to cite a few sparse and disjointed facts, which do not constitute a methodical range, and the interpretation of which is far from determined. Primitive communism, the struggles of the Patricians and the Plebeians, and of the third estate and nobility, are cited and explained in economic terms. Even though a few examples borrowed from the industrial history of England may be added to these rare documents, a generalisation of such magnitude will hardly be successfully substantiated in this way. On this point, Marxism is not in accord with its own principle. It begins by declaring that social life depends upon causes which escape awareness and conscious reasoning. But in order to discover these it must be necessary to make use of procedures which are at least as circuitous and complex as those employed by the natural sciences: many sorts of observations, experiments and laborious comparisons must be required in order to uncover even some of these factors separately, and without this there can be no question at present of obtaining a unitary formulation of them. And yet here, in an instant, all these mysteries are cleared up, and a single solution is given to problems which it seemed so difficult for the human intellect to penetrate! Could one perhaps reply to this that the objective conception, which we have just described briefly, has not been proved in any more adequate a manner? This is certainly the case. But this does not propose to do more than assign a definite origin to social phenomena: it is limited to the assertion that they have causes. For to say that collective representations have objective causes is to say nothing more than that their ultimate causes cannot be contained in themselves. This is therefore simply a postulate intended to guide research, and consequently always suspect: because it is experience which must decide, in the last resort. It is a methodological rule, not a law by reference to which we are authorised to deduce important consequences, whether they be theoretical or practical.

Not only is the Marxist hypothesis unproven, but it is contrary to facts which seem to be established. Sociologists and historians are tending increasingly to reach common agreement that religion is the most primitive of all social phenomena. All other manifestations of collective activity – law, morality, art, science, political formations, etc. – have emerged from it, by a series of transformations. In the beginning everything is religious. Now we know of no way of reducing religion to the economy, nor of any real attempt which has been made to effect this reduction. No-one has yet shown under what economic influences naturalism developed out of totemism, by what series of changes in technology it became in one place the abstract monotheism of Jahwe, and in another Graeco-Latin polytheism, and we strongly doubt that anyone could ever succeed in such an enterprise. More generally, it is indisputable that at the outset, the economic factor is rudimentary, while religious life is by contrast, luxuriant and all-pervading. Why could it not follow from this, and is it not probable, on the contrary, that the economy depends much more upon religion that the former does on the latter?

There would be no need, moreover, to push the preceding ideas to such an extreme that they lose all validity. Psycho-physiology, after having drawn attention to the foundation of psychic life in the organic substratum, often made the mistake of denying any reality to the latter. This was the source of the theory which reduces consciousness to nothing more than an epiphenomenon. The fact was lost sight of, that if ideas depend originally upon organic states, once they are formed they are, by that token, realities *sui generis*; they are autonomous, capable of being causes in their turn, and of producing new phenomena. Sociology must take care to avoid the same error. If the different forms of collective activity also have a substratum from which, in the last instance, they derive, they become in turn original sources of action, with their own specific effects, and they react upon the very causes which they stem from. We are thus far from holding that the economic factor is simply an epiphenomenon; once it exists, it has its own particular influence, and can partially modify the very substratum from which it results. But this is not reason to confuse it in any way with this substratum, in order to make of it something especially fundamental. Everything leads us to believe, on the contrary, that it is secondary and derived. From which it follows that the economic changes which have taken place during the course of this century, the substitution of large-scale for small-scale industry, in no way necessitate a disruption and radical reorganisation of the social order; and indeed that the malaise from which European societies may be suffering does not originate in these changes.

RP, 1887, pp. 648–51

DEFINITION OF SOCIALISM

After having discussed existing definitions and shown their inadequacy, we looked for the criteria by which one could recognise socialism and distinguish it from other phenomena; and by an objective comparison of the different doctrines concerned with social problems, we came to the following formula: we may call 'socialist' those theories which demand that economic functions, or certain of them, though diffused, become more or less completely connected with the conscious directive organs of society.

This definition calls for a few comments. . .[we say] 'connection' and not 'subordination', and one cannot too strongly stress this difference, which is essential. Socialists do not demand that the economic life be put into the hands of the state in order merely that the state should be in contact with the economy. On the contrary, they declare that it should react on the state at least as much as, if not more than, the latter acts on it. In their thinking, this interrelationship should have the effect, not of subordinating industrial and commercial interests to 'political' interests, but rather of elevating the former to the rank of the latter. For, once this constant communication is assured, economic interests would influence the functioning of the government organ much more profoundly than today, and would contribute in much larger measure to determining its operation. Far from relegating economic interests to second place, it would much rather be a question of calling upon them to play, in the whole of social life, a considerably more important role than is allowable today, when precisely because of their distance from the directing centres of society, they can activate the latter only weakly and in an intermittent way. Even according to the most celebrated theorists of socialism, it would be the state as we know it which would disappear and no longer be the central point of economic life, rather than economic life being absorbed by the state. For this reason, in our definition of socialism, we have not used this latter term, but the expression – expanded and somewhat figurative – 'the conscious, directive organs of society'. For in the doctrine of Marx, for example, the state itself – that is to say, in so far as it has a specific role, and represents interests which are superior, *sui generis*, to those of commerce and industry, historical traditions and common beliefs of a religious or other nature, etc. – would no longer exist. 'Political' functions, as such, which today are its special sphere, would no longer have a *raison d'être*, and it would have only economic functions. It would no longer be called by the same name, which is why we have had to resort to a more general term...

Comparing this definition with the conception generally held of socialism, we can now ascertain the differences. Thus, according to the terms of our formula, the theories which recommend, as a remedy for the evils suffered by contemporary societies, a greater development of either private or public charitable and provident institutions would not be called 'socialist', although very often one does call them this, either to attack or defend them. This is not because our definition is in error; it is that by referring to them in this way, one gives them an inappropriate name. For, however generous they may be, however useful it may be to put them into practice – which is not under discussion – they do not correspond at all to the needs and thoughts socialism has awakened and expresses. By giving them such a name, and placing them in a single category, we confuse very different things. To establish welfare projects by the side of economic life does not bind the latter to the public domain. The diffuse state in which industrial and commercial functions exist does not diminish because one creates welfare funds to soften the hardship of those who, temporarily or forever, have ceased to fulfil these functions. Socialism is essentially a movement to organise, but charity organises nothing. It maintains the *status quo*; it can only attenuate the individual suffering that this lack of organisation engenders. This example shows again how important it is to ascertain carefully the meaning of the word if one does not wish to be mistaken about the nature of the reality, or the significance of the practical measures taken or recommended.

Another important observation our definition gives rise to is that neither class war, nor preoccupations with rendering economic relations more equitable and even more favourable for workers, figures in it in any way. Not only are these characteristics far from being the whole of socialism; they do not even represent an essential element of it, nor are they *sui generis*, part of it. We are, it is true, so accustomed to an entirely different conception that at first such a statement is rather surprising and could arouse doubts as to the validity of our definition. Do not both proponents and critics constantly present socialism to us as the philosophy of the working classes? But now it is easy to see that this tendency is far from the only one which inspires it; it is actually only a specific, derived form of the more general tendency which we have defined. In reality, improvement of the workers' lot is only one of the consequences that socialism hopes to obtain from the economic organisation it demands, just as class war is only one of the means by which this reorganisation could result, one aspect of the historical development producing it.

What, in fact, according to socialists is it that causes the inferiority of the working classes and the injustice whose victims it declares them to be? It is that they are placed in direct dependence, not on society in general, but on a particular class powerful enough to impose its own wishes on them. That is, the 'capitalists'. The workers do not, in effect, interact directly with society; it is not society which directly remunerates them, it is the capitalist. But the latter is simply an individual who as such concerns himself, legitimately, not with social interests but with

his own. Thus, the services he buys he seeks to pay for not according to what they are worth socially, that is to say, according to the
exact degree of usefulness they have for society, but as cheaply
as possible. He possesses a weapon, however, that permits him to
constrain those who live only by their labour to sell him the
product for less than it is really worth. This is his capital. He can
live, if not indefinitely, at least for a long while, on his accumulated wealth, which he consumes instead of using to give work
to the labourers. Thus he purchases their help only if he wishes
and when he wishes; whereas they, on the contrary, cannot wait.
They must sell without delay the only thing they have to sell,
since, by definition, they have no other means of subsistence. So
they are obliged to yield in some degree to the orders of him
who pays them, to reduce their own demands below what they
would be if public interest alone served as the measure of value,
and consequently are forced to suffer deprivations. I do not have
to evaluate here whether this preponderance of capital is real or
if, as the orthodox economists say, the competition capitalists
create among themself reduces it to nil. It is enough to present
the socialist argument without judging it. These premises having been established, it is clear that the only means of at least
tempering this subjection and improving this state of affairs, is
to moderate the power of capital by another which, first, may be
of equal or superior strength but which, in addition, can make
its action felt in conformity with the general interests of society.
For it would be altogether useless to have another individual and
private force intervene in the economic mechanism. This would
be to replace with another kind, and not to suppress, the slavery
from which the proletariat suffers. Only the state thus is capable of
playing the role of moderator; but for that it is essential that the
economic agencies cease to operate outside of it, without the
state being aware of them. Rather, by means of a continuing
communication the state must know what is happening, and in
turn make its own action known. If one wishes to go still further,
if one intends not only to improve but to radically change this
situation, it is necessary to completely suppress the capitalist
intermediatry who, by interpolating himself between worker and
society, prevents labour from being properly appreciated and
rewarded according to its social value. Labour must be directly
evaluated and recompensed, if not by the collectivity, which is
practically impossible, then at least by the social agency which
normally represents it. This is to say that the capitalist class
under these conditions must disappear; the state must fulfil these

functions through being placed in direct relation with the working class, and in consequence, must become the centre of economic life. The improvement of the workers' lot is thus not a special objective; it is merely one of the consequences that the attachment of economic activities to the managing agents of society must produce.

Soc., pp. 27–33

THE RELATIONSHIP BETWEEN COMMUNISM AND SOCIALISM

Having thus defined socialism, it is necessary, in order to obtain a clear conception of it, to distinguish it from another group of theories with which it is often confused. These are the communist theories, which Plato first gave a systematic formula to in Antiquity, and which were again treated in modern times in Thomas More's *Utopia* and Campanella's *City of the Sun*, to cite only the most famous examples.

Is there really an identity or, at least, a close relation between these two kinds of systems? The question is very important, for, according to the answer one gives, socialism appears in an entirely different light. If it is merely a form of communism, or blends with it, one must see it as an old conception somewhat rejuvenated, which must be indeed like communist utopias of the past. If, on the other hand, it is distinct from it, it constitutes a manifestation *sui generis* which demands special study.

One primary fact which, without being proof, should put us on guard against the confusion, is that the word 'socialism' is quite new. It was coined in England in 1835. In that year a group which took the somewhat pompous name of 'Association of All Classes of All Nations' was founded under the auspices of Robert Owen, and the words 'socialist' and 'socialism' were used for the first time in the course of the discussions that took place on that occasion. In 1839, Reybaud used it in his book on *Réformateurs modernes*, in which the theories of Saint-Simon, Fourier, and Owen are studied. Reybaud even claims authorship of the word, which in any event is no older than fifty years. But let us pass on from the word to the thing.

A first difference, again purely external in character, but striking nonetheless, is that communist theories appear in history only sporadically. Their manifestations are usually isolated from each other by long periods of time. From Plato to Thomas More almost ten centuries elapsed, and the communist tendencies that one notes in certain Fathers of the Church are not enough to supply continuity. From *Utopia* (1518) to the *City of the Sun* (1623) there is a gap of over a century, and after Campanella one must wait until the eighteenth century to see communism reborn. In other words, expressions of communism are not abundant. The thinkers it inspires are isolated individuals who appear at long intervals but do not comprise a school. Their theories seem to express the personality of each theoretician rather than a general and constant state of society. They are dreams in which generous spirits take delight, which catch the attention and hold the interest because of this very generosity and dignity, but which, not answering the real needs felt by the social organism, exist only in the imagination and remain practically unproductive. Moreover, it is in this way that those who have conceived them, present them. They themselves see in them hardly more than attractive fictions which from time to time it is good to place before men's eyes, but which are not destined to become realities. . .

In addition, the very method of exposition followed by these authors very well indicates the character of their work. Almost all take for their framework a completely imaginary country, placed outside of every historical situation. This plainly shows that their systems resemble social reality only slightly and have little hope of changing it. The way in which socialism developed is quite different. Since the beginning of the century, theories which bear this name follow one-another without interruption. It is a continuous current which, in spite of a certain diminution towards 1850, becomes more and more intense. Moreover, not only do schools follow each other, but they appear simultaneously, apart from any borrowing or reciprocal influence, under a kind of pressure which is strong evidence that they respond to a collective need. Thus, at the same time, one sees the emergence of Saint-Simon and Fourier in France, and Owen in England – to recall only the most important names. The success they aspire to is never purely sentimental and artistic; it does not satisfy them to elevate the soul while lulling it with fine dreams; they expect to achieve practical results. There is not one among them who does not view his concepts as readily attainable; utopian as they may seem to us, they are not so to their authors. Their thought is not driven by their private feelings but by social objectives, which they demand to be effectively met; mere fictions could not suffice. Such a contrast in the manner in which these two kinds of doctrines manifest themselves can only derive from a difference in their nature.

And in fact, in certain essential ways they are polar opposites. Socialism, as we have said, consists of linking industrial activities to the state (we use this last word as a kind of abbreviation in spite of its lack of precision). Communism tends instead to put industrial life outside the state...

So to identify socialism and communism is to equate opposites. For the first, the economic organ must virtually become the directive agency of society; for the second, the one cannot be far enough removed from the other. Between these two manifestations of collective activity, the former see a close affinity, almost an identity in character; the latter on the contrary, perceive only antagonism and opposition. For communists, the state can fulfil its role only if it is completely separated from industrial life; for socialists, this role is essentially industrial and the connection could not be too complete. To the former, wealth is evil and must be put away from society; to the latter, on the contrary, it is bad only if it is not socialised. Without doubt – and this is deceptive – in both there is to be regulation, but it must be noticed that it operates in opposing ways. For the one, the aim is to moralise industry by binding it to the state; for the other, to moralise the state by excluding it from industry.

It is true that both systems allocate types of activity to the collective sphere which according to individualist concepts should belong in the private domain; and undoubtedly this has contributed most of all to the confusion. But here again they are sharply contrasted. According to socialism, strictly economic functions, that is to say, activities productive of services (commerce and industry), must be socially organised, but consumption is to remain private. There is, we have seen, no socialist doctrine which refuses the individual the right to possess and use in his own way what he has legitimately acquired.

Quite on the contrary, in communism, it is consumption that is communal and production which remains private. In *Utopia* each works in his own way, as he thinks proper, and is simply obliged not to be idle. He cultivates his garden, occupies himself with his trade, just as he would in the most individualistic society. There is no common rule which determines relationships among the different workers, or the manner in which all these diverse activities should co-operate for collective goals. As each one does the same thing, or almost the same, there is no co-operation to regulate. But what each has produced does not belong to him; he cannot dispose of it at will. He brings it to the community and consumes it only when society itself makes use of it collectively.

The difference between these two types of social arrangements is as great as that which separates the organisation of certain colonies of polyps from that of superior animals. In the first, each of the associated individuals hunts on his own account, in his own right; but what he catches is deposited in a common stomach, and he cannot have his share of the community wealth, that is to say he cannot eat, without all society eating at the same time. By contrast, among vertebrates each organ is obliged in its functioning to conform to rules designed to put it in harmony with the others; the nervous system assures this con- formity. But each organ, and in every organ each tissue, and in every tissue each cell, are fed separately and freely, without being dependent for this on the others. Each of the major parts of the organism even has its special food. The distance is no less con- siderable between the two social concepts which have been so frequently likened.

But it is not only in the conclusions they reach that these two schools contrast with one-another; it is also in their point of de- parture. . .socialism has as its basis observations – whether these are valid or not is irrelevant – which refer to the economic state of specific societies. For example, that in the most advanced societies of present-day Europe, production appears to be un- related to consumption needs; or that industrial centralisa- tion seems to have given birth to enterprises too large for society to be able to ignore; or that the incessant changes produced by technology, with the resultant social instability, rob the worker of all security and place him in a state of inferiority which prevents him from concluding equitable contracts; it is on this and other similar evidence that socialism bases its demands for reform of the contemporary order. In short, it is only countries with large- scale industry that it impugns; and in these countries it is ex- clusively the conditions of exchange and production of value that it attacks. All else is communist principle. The fundamental communist idea, which is almost everywhere the same, is that private property is the source of egoism and that from egoism springs immorality. But such a proposition does not strike at any social organisation in particular. It applies to all times and all countries; it fits equally the systems of large and of small industry. It does not relate to any economic fact, for the institution of property is a juridical and moral phenomenon which affects economic life without being part of it. In sum, communism is wholly bound to a shared conception of abstract morality which is of no one time nor of any one country. What it questions are the

moral consequences of private property in general and not, as does
socialism, the quality of a specific economic organisation appearing at a particular time in history. The two problems are entirely
different. One sets out to judge the moral value of wealth in the
abstract, and deny it; the other asks whether a given type of
commerce and industry accords with the conditions of existence
of the peoples practising it, and if it is normal or otherwise. Thus,
while communism concerns itself only secondarily with so-called
economic arrangements and modifies them only to the degree
necessary to place them in keeping with its principle, the abolition
of individual ownership, socialism touches private property only
indirectly, to the degree required to change it so that it may
harmonise with the economic arrangements which are the essential object of its attentions.

It is this, however, which explains the great difference we noted
in the way both systems manifest themselves historically. Theorists
of communism, we said, are isolated men who appear from time to
time and whose word seems only to awaken feeble echoes among
the masses surrounding them. They are in fact philosophers, who
deal with problems of general morality from the seclusion of the
study, rather than men of action whose thought has the sole object of easing the actual suffering felt around them. What are the
sources of egoism and immorality? This is what they ask, and the
question is eternal. . .

And yet we are aware that in spite of everything some relationship does exist between these two doctrines. What in fact happened was as follows. The sentiments that are at the root of
communism, being relevant to all times, are also relevant to ours.
It is true they do not express themselves in each epoch in doctrinal
form. But they do not disappear completely even though they are
not vigorous enough to give birth to a system which states them
methodically. Besides, it is clear that the times when such sentiments are most likely to manifest themselves are those when,
for whatever reasons, they particularly draw attention to the fate
of the deprived classes. Thus no century has ever been more
favourable than ours to the development of communist feelings.
Socialism, precisely because it has an altogether different goal,
could not satisfy these inclinations. Even if a socialist society
were as fully realised as possible, there still would be deprivations
and inequalities of every kind. The fact that no individual possesses capital will not eliminate inequality of talents, sickness or
invalidism. Since in such a view competition is not abolished, but
regulated, there will still be services of limited usefulness which,

even if regarded and recompensed according to their social value, will not suffice to give their performer a livelihood. There will always be inadequate individuals who despite themselves will be unable to earn an adequate living; and others who while earning strict necessities, will not succeed, any more than the worker today, in having more than a precarious and limited existence, hardly consistent with the effort expended. In short, in Marxist socialism, capital does not disappear; it is merely administered by society and not by particular individuals. The result is that the method it uses to compensate workers of all kinds no longer depends on individual interests, but only upon general interests. But merely because remuneration will be socially just, it does not necessarily follow that it will be sufficient for all. Just as with capitalists, society – if not motivated by other sentiments – will have an interest in paying the lowest possible price. There will always be, for ordinary, simple services, within everybody's reach, a widespread demand. Consequently, competition will be so sharp that society will oblige the mass to be satisfied with little; the pressure exerted on the lower strata would then emanate from the entire community and not from certain powerful individuals, but nevertheless it could still be very strong. Now the sentiments underlying communism are a protest against precisely this constraint, and its effects. Socialism thus by no means robs communism of the reason for its existence. Should the socialisation of economic forces be an accomplished fact tomorrow, communists would be opposed to the excessive inequalities which would obtain then as now. In a word, there is a place for communism in addition to socialism precisely because they are not oriented in the same direction. It happened, however, that communism, instead of remaining what it had been before the advent of socialism, an independent doctrine, was annexed by the latter once socialism was established. In fact, although conceived under entirely different conditions and answering entirely different needs, socialism, because it was led to take an interest in the working classes, found itself, very naturally, particularly susceptible to those feelings of pity and fraternity which could alleviate, without contradicting, what was still too harsh in its principle. For reasons that can be seen, but which we will have to examine more carefully later, it was consequently, for the most part, these same spirits who henceforth experienced both the new hopes that gave rise to socialism and the ancient aspirations that created the basis of communism. To give only one reason, how can one feel the need for economic functions to be integrated more closely, without at the same time having a general feeling of social solidarity and fraternity? Thus socialism was exposed to communism; it undertook to play a role in it at the same time as it pursued its own course. In this sense it was actually the heir of communism; and, without being derived from it, socialism absorbed it while remaining distinct.

Soc., pp. 38–9, 42, 47–9, 50–2 and 74–7

8. Anomie and the moral structure of industry

THE PROBLEM OF ANOMIE

The totality of moral rules truly forms about each person an imaginary wall, at the foot of which the flood of human passions simply dies without being able to go further. For the same reason – that they are contained – it becomes possible to satisfy them. But if it any point this barrier weakens, these previously restrained human forces pour tumultuously through the open breach; once loosed they find no limits where they can stop. They can only devote themselves, without hope of satisfaction, to the pursuit of an end that always eludes them. For example, if the rules of the conjugal morality lose their authority, and the mutual obligations of husband and wife become less respected, the emotions and appetites ruled by this sector of morality will become unrestricted and uncontained, and accentuated by this very release; powerless to fulfil themselves because they have been freed from all limitations, these emotions will produce a disillusionment which manifests itself visibly in the statistics of suicide. In the same way, should the morality governing economic life be shaken, and the search for gain become excited and inflamed beyond bounds, then one would observe a rise in the annual quota of suicides. One could multiply such examples. Furthermore, it is because morality has the function of limiting and containing that too much wealth so easily becomes a source of immorality. Through the power wealth confers on us, it actually diminishes the power of things to oppose us. Consequently, it lends strength to our desires and makes it harder to hold them in check. Under such conditions, moral equilibrium is unstable: it requires but a slight blow to disrupt it. Thus, we can understand the nature and source of this malady of infiniteness which torments our age. For man to see before him boundless, free, and open space, he must have lost sight of the moral barrier which under normal conditions would cut off his view. He no longer feels those moral forces that restrain him and limit his horizon. But if he no longer feels them it is because they no longer carry their normal degree of authority, because they are weakened and no longer as they should be. The notion of the infinite, then, appears only at those times when moral discipline has lost its ascendancy over wants; it is a sign of the attrition that occurs during periods when the moral system which has prevailed for centuries is shaken, and fails to respond to new conditions of human life, without any new system having yet been formed to replace that which has disappeared.

EM, 47–9

No living being can be happy, or even exist, unless his needs are adequately related to his means. In other words, if his needs require more than can be allocated to them, or even merely something of a different sort, they will be under continual friction and can only function painfully. Now an action which cannot be effected without suffering tends not to be reproduced. Unsatisfied tendencies atrophy, and as the impulse to live is merely the result of all other motivations, it is bound to weaken as the others lose their hold.

In the animal, at least in the normal state, this equilibrium is established with automatic spontaneity because the animal depends on purely material conditions. All the organism needs is that the supplies of substance and energy constantly employed in the process of living should be periodically renewed by equivalent quantities; that the replacement be equivalent to what is used up. When the gap created by the exigencies of life is filled, the animal, satisfied, asks nothing further. Its powers of thought are not sufficiently developed to imagine other ends than those implicit in its physical nature. Moreover, as the work demanded of each particular organ depends on the general state of vital energy and the needs of organic equilibrium, what is used up is in turn replaced and the balance is automatic. The limits of one are also those of the other; both are fundamental to the constitution of the existence in question, which cannot exceed them.

This is not the case with man, because most of his needs are not dependent on his body, or not to the same extent. Strictly speaking, we may consider that the quantity of material supplies necessary to the physical maintenance of a human life can be calculated, though this be less precise than in the preceding case, with a wider margin left for the free combinations of the will; for beyond the indispensable minimum which satisfies nature when instinctive, a more developed intelligence creates a wider range of conditions and desired ends demanding fulfilment. Such appetites, however, admittedly sooner or later reach a limit which they cannot pass. But how can we specify the quantity of well-being, comfort or luxury legitimately to be desired by a human being? Nothing appears in man's organic nor in his psychological constitution which sets a limit to such tendencies. The functioning of individual life does not require them to cease at one point rather than at another; this is shown by the fact that they have constantly increased since the beginnings of history, becoming satisfied more and more, without any weakening of average health. Above all, how can we establish their proper variation with different conditions of life, occupations, relative importance of services, etc.? In no society are they equally developed at the different levels of the social hierarchy. Yet human nature is substantially the same among all men, in its essential qualities. It is not human nature which can assign the variable limit necessary to our needs. These are thus unlimited so far as they depend on the individual alone. Irrespective of any external regulatory force, our capacity for feeling is in itself an insatiable and bottomless abyss.

But if nothing external can restrain this capacity, it can only be a source of torment to itself. Unlimited desires are insatiable by definition and insatiability is rightly considered a sign of morbidity. Being unlimited, they constantly and infinitely surpass the means at their command; they cannot be quenched. Inextinguishable thirst is constantly renewed torture. It has been claimed, it is true, that human activity naturally aspires beyond assignable limits and sets itself unattainable goals. But how can such an indeterminate state be any more reconciled with the conditions of mental life than with the demands of physical life? All man's pleasure in acting, moving and exerting himself implies the sense that his efforts are not in vain and that by walking he advances. However, one does not advance when one proceeds toward no goal, or – which is the same thing – when the goal is in infinity. Since the distance between us and it is always the same, whatever road we take, it is just as if we have not moved. Even our feeling of pride looking back at the distance covered can only give a deceptive satisfaction, since the remaining distance is not proportionately reduced. To pursue a goal which is by definition unattainable is to condemn oneself to a state of perpetual unhappiness. Of course, a man may hope contrary to all reason, and hope has its pleasures even when irrational. It may sustain him for a time; but it cannot indefinitely survive the repeated disappointments of experience. What more can the future offer him than the past, since he can never reach an acceptable position nor even approach the glimpsed ideal? Thus, the more one has, the more one wants, and satisfactions received only stimulate instead of filling needs. Shall action as such be considered pleasurable? First only on condition that we are blind to its uselessness. Secondly, for this pleasure to be felt and to temper and partly veil the disquiet and distress which goes with it, such unending motion must at least always be easy and unhampered. If it is frustrated, only restlessness is left, with the unhappiness which it brings in tow. Now it would be a miracle if no insurmountable obstacle were ever encountered. In this situation, one is held to life only by a very thin thread, which can be broken at any moment.

To achieve any other result, the passions first must be limited. Only then can they be harmonised with capacities and satisfied. But since the individual has no way of limiting them, this must necessarily be accomplished by some force outside him. A regulative force must play the same role for moral needs which the organism plays for physical needs. This means that the force can only be moral.

Su, pp. 272–5

To [socialists] it appears that the way to realise social peace is to free economic appetites of all restraint on the one hand, and on the other to satisfy them by fulfilling them. But such an undertaking is contradictory. For these appetites cannot be appeased unless they are limited, and they cannot be limited except by something other than themselves. They cannot be regarded as the only purpose of society since they must be subordinated to some end which surpasses them, and it is only on this condition that they are capable of being really satisfied. Imagine the most productive economic organisation possible, and a distribution of wealth which assures abundance even for the most humble: perhaps such a transformation, at the very moment it was effected, would produce a measure of gratification. But this gratification could be no more than transitory. For although they may be temporarily assuaged, these demands will quickly make themselves felt again. Unless it is admitted that each individual should be equally compensated – and such levelling, if it conforms to the communist ideal, is completely opposed to the Saint-Simon doctrine, as to every socialist theory – there will always be some workers who will receive more and others less. So it is inevitable that at the end of a short time, the latter find their share inadequate compared with what others receive, and as a result new demands arise, at all levels of the social scale. Moreover, quite apart from any feelings of envy, desires will tend naturally to keep outstripping their goals, for the very reason that there will be nothing before them which stops them. Thus new satisfactions will be demanded, even more imperiously, since those already secured will have given them more strength and vitality. This is why those at the very top of the hierarchy, who consequently would have nothing above them to stimulate their ambition, could nevertheless not be held at the point they had reached, but would continue to be plagued by the same restlessness that torments them today. What is needed if social order is to reign is that the mass of men be content with their lot. But what is needed for them to be content, is not that they have more or less but that they be convinced they have no right to more. And for this, it is absolutely essential that there be an authority whose superiority they acknowledge and which tells them what is right. For an individual committed only to the pressure of his needs will never admit he has reached the extreme limits of his rightful portion. If he is not conscious of a force above him which he respects, which stops him and tells him authoritatively he has received his just due, then inevitably he will expect everything his needs demand. And since in our hypothesis these needs are limitless, their demands are necessarily without limit. For it to be otherwise, a moral power is required whose superiority he recognises, and which cries out 'you must go no further'.

This is precisely the role played in ancient society by the powers whose progressive dethronement Saint-Simon notes. Religion instructed the humble to be content with their situation, and, at the same time it taught them that the social order is providential: that it is God himself who has determined each one's share. Religion gave men a perception of a world beyond this earth where everything would be rectified; this prospect made inequalities less noticeable, it stopped men from feeling aggrieved. Secular power, too, precisely because it held economic functions under its domination, contained and limited them. But even *a priori* it is impossible to suppose that, while for centuries it was in the nature of economic interests to be subordinated, in the future the roles will become completely reversed. This would be to admit that the nature of things could be completely transformed in the course of evolution. Undoubtedly one can be certain that this regulating function can no longer be fulfilled by the old forces, since nothing appears likely to stop their decline. Undoubtedly, too, this same function could not be exercised today in the same manner or spirit as formerly. Industry is now more highly developed and more essential to the social organism; thus it can no longer be contained within the same narrow bounds, subjected to a system as heavily repressive, and regulated to such a subordinate position. But it does not follow that it should be freed of all regulation, liberated from all limitations.

The problem is to know, under the present conditions of social life, what moderating functions are necessary and what forces are capable of executing them.

Soc., pp. 290–3

The preceding has removed one of the most serious charges which has been made against the division of labour.

It has often been accused of degrading the individual by reducing him to a mere machine. And if he does not know what the significance is of the operations he is called upon to perform, if he relates them to no end, he must indeed become wedded to routine. Every day he repeats the same movements with monotonous regularity, without being interested in them and without understanding them. He is no longer a living cell of a living organism which unceasingly interacts with neighbouring cells, which influences them, responds to their actions, and transforms itself in relation to changing circumstances and needs. He is no longer anything but an inert cog in the machinery, set in motion by an external force, and always moving in the same direction and in the same way. Obviously, no matter how one may represent the moral ideal, one cannot remain indifferent to such a debasement of human nature. If morality has individual perfection as its goal, it cannot permit such a degradation of the individual, and if it has society as its goal, it cannot let the very source of social life be drained; for the evil does not threaten only economic functions, but all social functions, however elevated they may be. . .

As a remedy, it has sometimes been proposed that in, addition to technical and specialised training, workers should be given a general education. But even if we can thus relieve some of the deleterious effects attributed to the division of labour, this is not a way of preventing them. The division of labour does not change its nature because it has been preceded by a general education. No doubt, it is good for the worker to be interested in art, literature, etc.; but it is still wrong that he should be treated as a machine all day long. Who cannot see, moreover, that two such

forms of existence are too opposed to be reconciled, and cannot
be followed by the same individual! If a man has become accustomed to vast horizons, total views, and fine abstractions, he cannot be confined within the strict limits of a specialised task without
becoming frustrated. Such a remedy would make specialisation
unobjectionable by making it intolerable and, consequently, more
or less impossible.

What solves the contradiction is that, contrary to what is often
said, the division of labour does not produce these consequences
because of a necessity of its own nature, but only in exceptional
and abnormal circumstances. In order for it to develop without
having such a disastrous influence on the human mind, it is not
necessary to temper it with its opposite. It is necessary and it is
sufficient for it to be itself, for nothing to come from without to
rob it of its specific character. For, normally, the role of each
special function does not require that the individual close himself
in, but that he keep himself in constant relations with neighbouring functions, take heed of their needs, of the changes which
these needs undergo, etc. The division of labour presumes that
the worker, far from being hemmed in by his task, does not lose
sight of his collaborators, that he acts upon them and reacts to
them. Then he is not a machine which repeats its actions without
knowing their meaning, but he knows that they tend, in some
way, towards an end that he can see fairly distinctly. He feels that
he is of some use. For that, he need not embrace vast portions
of the social horizon; it is sufficient that he perceive enough of it
to understand that his actions have an aim beyond themselves.
From that time on, as specialised and uniform as his activity may
be, it is that of an intelligent being, for it has direction, and he
knows it. The economists would not have allowed this intrinsic
characteristic of the division of labour to remain obscured and
consequently exposed to this unwarranted criticism, if they had
not reduced it to being merely a means of increasing social productivity: if they had seen that it is above all a source of
solidarity.

DTS, pp. 363 and 364–5

THE FORCED DIVISION OF LABOUR

It is not enough for there to be rules, however, for sometimes the
rules themselves are what is at fault. That is what occurs in class-
wars. The institution of classes or of castes constitutes an organisation of the division of labour, and it is a strictly regulated

organisation; but it is often a source of conflict. The lower classes not being, or no longer being, satisfied with the role which is theirs by custom or law, aspire to functions which are closed to them and seek to dispossess those who are exercising them. Thus civil wars arise which are due to the manner in which labour is distributed.

Nothing comparable to this can be observed in the organism. No doubt, during periods of crisis, the different tissues war against one another and nourish themselves at the expense of others. But a cell or organ never seeks to usurp a role different from the one which it possesses. The reason for this is that each anatomical element automatically executes its purpose. Its structure and its place in the organism determines its task; its function is a consequence of its nature. It can acquit itself poorly, but it cannot assume another's task unless the latter abandons it, as happens in rare cases of substitution. . .It is not so in societies. Here the possibility is greater: there is a wider gulf between the hereditary dispositions of the individual and the social functions he will fill. The first do not imply the second with such immediate necessity. The field which is thus open to striving and resolution is also subject to many factors which can make the individual nature deviate from its normal direction, and create a pathological condition. Because this organisation is more flexible, it is also more delicate and more open to change. No doubt we are not from birth predestined to some specific position; but we do have tastes and aptitudes which limit our choice. If no heed is given to them, and they are constantly contradicted by our daily occupation, we shall suffer and seek a way out of our suffering. Now there is no other way out than to change the established order and to set up a new one. For the division of labour to produce solidarity, it is not sufficient, then, for every individual to be given a task to perform; he has also to be suited to this task.

But this precondition is not realised in the example we are examining. If the institution of classes or castes sometimes gives rise to unfortunate frictions instead of producing solidarity, this is because the distribution of social functions on which it rests does not correspond, or rather no longer corresponds to the distribution of natural talents. . .For wants to spread from one class to another, the differences which originally separated these classes must have diminished or disappeared. As a consequence of changes produced in society, some must have become capable of functions which were at first beyond them, while others have lost their original superiority. When the Plebeians aimed to dispute the right to religious and administrative functions with the Patricians, it was not only in imitation of the latter, but because they had become more intelligent, richer, more numerous, and their tastes and ambitions had developed correspondingly. As a consequence of such changes, the correspondence between the aptitudes of individuals and the kind of activity assigned to them is broken in a whole large area of society; constraint alone, more or less violent and direct in character, ties them to their functions. Hence the solidarity which results is defective and strained.

This consequence is thus not a necessary characteristic of the division of labour. It comes about only under specific circumstances, that is, as the effect of external constraint. It is quite different when the division of labour is established in virtue of purely internal spontaneity, and where nothing hampers individual initiative. In this situation, harmony between individual natures and social functions is necessarily produced, at least in the majority of cases. For, if there is nothing which either unduly hinders or favours the chances of those competing for occupations, it is inevitable that only those who are most capable at each type of activity will move into it. The only factor which then determines the manner in which work is divided is the diversity of capacities; it comes about, inevitably, on the basis of aptitude, since this is the only determining element. Thus, the congruence between the constitution of each individual and his position is brought about of its own accord. It might be argued that this is still not enough to make men content, since there are some men whose aspirations outstrip their faculties. This is true, but these are exceptional and, one may say, morbid cases. Normally, man finds happiness in realising his nature; his needs are relative to his means. Thus, in the organism, each organ demands only as much food as it requires. The 'forced division of labour' is, then, the second abnormal type that we meet. But the meaning of the word 'forced' must not be misunderstood. Not every form of regulation is the same as constraint, since, as we have seen, the division of labour cannot operate without regulation. Even when functions are divided in accordance with pre-established rules, this is not necessarily the result of constraint. Such is the case even in a caste system, as long as it is founded in the nature of the society. This institution is never completely and wholly arbitrary. When it functions in a society in a regular way, and without opposition, it expresses, at least in a general way, the fixed manner in which occupation capacities are distributed. That is why, although tasks are, in certain measure, assigned by law, each organ executes its own function spontaneously. Constraint only begins when regulation, no longer corresponding to the real character of existence and, accordingly, no longer having any basis in customs, is only maintained by force.

Conversely, we may say that the division of labour produces solidarity only if, and in so far as, it is spontaneous. But by 'spontaneity' we should understand not simply the absence of all express and manifest violence, but also of everything that can even indirectly shackle the free unfolding of the social force that each carries in himself. It supposes, not only that individuals are not forcibly assigned to specific tasks, but also that no obstacle, of whatever nature, prevents them from occupying the place in the social framework which is compatible with their faculties. In short, labour is divided spontaneously only if society is constituted in such a way that social inequalities exactly express natural inequalities...

It is, moreover, easy to understand what makes this levelling process necessary. We have just seen that all external inequality compromises organic solidarity. There is nothing disturbing in this for less developed societies, where solidarity is determined primarily by common beliefs and sentiments. However strained the ties which come from the division of labour, since they are not the ones which most strongly attach the individual to society, social cohesion is not placed in jeopardy. The unhappiness which results from frustrated aspirations is not enough to turn men against the social order which creates them; they cling to this social order, not because they find it the necessary field for the development of their occupational activity, but because in their eyes it expresses the sum total of the beliefs and practices by which they live. They cling to it because their whole internal life is linked with it. All their convictions presuppose the existence of this order, because, serving as a basis for the moral and religious system, it appears to them as sacred. Personal, and temporal, frustrations are obviously too insignificant to upset states of consciousness which derive such an exceptional force from this origin. Moreover, since occupational life is not highly developed, these clashes occur only infrequently. For all these reasons, they have only a slight impact; they are accepted without difficulty. Men find these inequalities not only tolerable but even natural.

It is quite the opposite which occurs when organic solidarity becomes predominant: whatever undermines it attacks the social tie in its most essential form. In the first place, since in these conditions specialised activities are pursued almost continuously, they cannot be opposed without producing protracted discontent. Secondly, since the *conscience collective* is weaker, the frictions which are thus created can no longer be so completely nullified. Common sentiments no longer have the same capacity to keep the individual attached to the group under any circumstances. Subversive tendencies, no longer having the same counterweight, occur more frequently. Since it increasingly loses the transcendent character which placed it in a sphere above human interests, social organisation no longer has the same force of resistance, and at the same time becomes more subject to attack. As a purely human construction, it can no longer so directly oppose human demands. At the very moment at which the flood becomes more violent, the dam which holds it in is broken down; it thus becomes a greater threat. This is why, in organised societies, the division of labour must be increasingly placed in harmony with this ideal of spontaneity that we have just defined. If such societies direct, and must direct, their energies to abolishing external inequalities as far as possible, this is not only because enterprise is intrinsically worthwhile, but because their very existence is bound up with this problem. For these societies can survive only if there is solidarity between the elements of which they are composed; solidarity is possible only given this situation. Thus we may predict that this work of justice will become ever more complete, as the organised type develops. No matter how important the progress already made in this direction, in all probability it only gives a small idea of what will be achieved in the future.

DTS, pp. 367–70 and 373–4

THE SOCIAL AND POLITICAL ROLE OF THE OCCUPATIONAL GROUPS

The absence of corporative institutions thus creates in the organisation of a society like ours a void whose importance it is difficult to exaggerate. What is lacking is a complete system of agencies necessary to the functioning of social life. This structural defect is evidently not a localised failure, limited to one part of society; it is a malady *totius substantiae*, affecting the whole organism. Consequently, any attempt to put an end to it cannot fail to produce the most far-reaching consequences. It is the general health of the social body which is in question here.

That does not mean to say, however, that the corporation is a sort of panacea for everything. The crisis which we are experiencing is not to be traced to any one specific cause. In order to overcome it, it is not enough to establish some sort of regulation where it is needed. This regulation must be just. Now, as we shall say further on 'as long as there are rich and poor at birth, there cannot be just contract', nor an equitable distribution of social goods. But while corporative reform must be accompanied by other reforms, it is the primary condition for these others to be effective. Let us imagine that the primordial state of ideal justice were achieved; let us suppose that men enter life in a state of perfect economic equality, which is to say, that wealth has completely ceased to be hereditary. The problems with which we are now struggling with would not thereby be solved. Evidently there will always be an economic apparatus, and various agencies co-operating in its functioning. It will still be necessary to determine their rights and duties for each form of industry. In each occupation a body of rules will have to be established which fix the quantity of work expected, equitable rates of payment for different workers, their duties toward each other and toward the community, etc. We shall face a *tabula rasa*, just as now. Because wealth will not be inherited any longer, as it is today, it does not follow that the state of anarchy will disappear, for it is not a question of the ownership of wealth, but of the regulation of the activity to which this wealth gives rise. It will not regulate itself by magic, as soon as it is necessary, if the forces which can generate this regulation have not been previously aroused and organised...

Since a body of rules is the specific form which is assumed by spontaneously established relations between social functions in the course of time, we can say, *a priori*, that the state of *anomie* is impossible wherever interdependent organs are sufficiently in contact and sufficiently extensive. If they are close to each other, they are readily aware, in every situation, of the need which they have of one-another, and consequently they have an active and permanent feeling of mutual dependence. For the same reason that exchanges take place among them easily, they take place frequently; being habitual, they regularise themselves accordingly, and in time become consolidated. As the smallest reaction is transmitted from one part to another, the rules which are thus created express this directly: that is to say, they embody and fix, in detail, the conditions of equilibrium. But if, on the other hand, they are not clearly visible to each other, then only stimuli of a certain intensity can be communicated from one organ to another. The relationships being infrequent, they are not repeated often enough to become fixed; they must be established anew each time. The channels cut by the streams of movement cannot deepen because the streams themselves are too intermittent. If a few rules, at least, do come into existence, they are nevertheless too abstract and diffuse, for under these conditions it is only the most general outline of the phenomena that can become fixed. The same thing will be the case if the contiguity, although sufficient, is too recent or has not existed for long enough.

In a general way, this condition is realised in the nature of things. A function can be divided between two or several parts of an organism only if these parts are fairly close to each other. Moreover, once labour is divided, since these elements are dependent upon one-another, they naturally tend to lessen the distance separating them. That is why as one goes up the evolutionary scale, one sees organs coming together, and, as Spencer says, being introduced in the spaces between one another. But, in unusual circumstances, a different situation can be brought about.

This is what happens in the cases we are discussing. In so far as the segmental type is strongly marked, there are nearly as many economic markets as there are different segments. Consequently, each of them is very limited. Producers, being near consumers, can easily calculate the range of needs to be satisfied. Equilibrium is established without any difficulty and production regulates itself. On the other hand, as the organised type develops, the fusion of different segments draws the markets together into a single market which embraces almost all society. This even extends further, and tends to become universal, for the frontiers which separate peoples break down at the same time as those which separate the segments of each of them. The result is that each industry produces for consumers spread over the whole surface of the country or even of the entire world. Here the contact is broken; the producer can no longer take in the market at a glance, or even conceptualise it. He can no longer have an idea of its limits, since it is, so to speak, limitless. Accordingly, production becomes unchecked and unregulated. It can only operate haphazardly, and in the course of these gropings, it is inevitable that it will be out of proportion, either in one direction or the other. From this come the crises which periodically dislocate economic life. The growth of local, restricted crises – or business failures – is in all likelihood an effect of the same cause.

As the market extends, large-scale industry appears. This has the effect of changing the relations between employers and workers. An increasing fatigue of the nervous system joined to the contagious influence of large concentrations of population increase the needs of the workers. Machines replace men; manufacturing replaces hand-work. The worker is regimented, separated from his family throughout the day. He always lives apart from his employer, etc. These new conditions of industrial life naturally demand a new organisation, but as these changes have been accomplished with extreme rapidity, the interests in conflict have not yet had the time to become equilibrated...

An occupational activity can be effectively regulated only by a group close enough to it to know how it operates, what its needs are, and how it is likely to change. The only one that meets all these conditions is the one which might be formed by all the agents of the same industry united and organised into a single body. This is what we call the 'corporation' or 'occupational group'.

Now, in the economic order, the occupational group does not exist any more than occupational ethics. Since the eighteenth century suppressed the old corporations, *not without reason*, only fragmentary and inadequate attempts have been made to re-establish them upon new foundations. To be sure, individuals working at the same trade have contacts with one-another, because of their similar occupation. Their very competition puts them in relationship. But these relationships are not permanent; they depend upon chance meetings, and have, very often, an entirely personal aspect. A particular industrial worker is found in contact with a colleague; this does not result from the industrial body of this or that speciality united for common action. In rare cases, the members of the same occupation come together as a group to discuss some question of general interest, but these meetings are only temporary. They do not survive the particular circumstances which bring them into being, and consequently the collective life which they stimulate more or less disappears with them.

The only groups which have a certain permanence today are the unions, composed of either employers or workmen. Certainly there is here the beginning of occupational organisation, but still quite formless and rudimentary. For, first, a union is a private association, without legal authority, and consequently without any regulatory power. Moreover, the number of unions is theoretically limitless, even within the same industrial category; and as each of them is independent of the others, if they do not federate or unify there is nothing intrinsic in them expressing the unity of the occupation in its entirety. Finally, not only are the employers' unions and the employees' unions distinct from each other, which is *legitimate and necessary*, but there is no regular contact between them. There exists no common organisation which brings them together, where they can develop common forms of regulation which will determine the relationships between them in an authoritative fashion, without either of them losing their own autonomy. Consequently, it is always the rule of the strongest which setles conflicts, and the state of war is continuous. Save for those of their actions which are governed by common moral codes, employers and workers are, in relation to each other, in the same situation as two autonomous states, but of unequal power. They can form contracts, as nations do through the medium of their governments, but these contracts express only the respective state of their military forces. They sanction it as a condition of reality; they cannot make it legally valid.

In order to establish occupational morality and law in the different economic occupations, the corporation, instead of remaining a diffuse, disorganised aggregate, must become – or rather, must again become – a defined, organised group; in a word, a public institution. . .

What the experience of the past proves, above all, is that the framework of the occupational group must always be related to the framework of economic life: it is because of this dislocation that the corporative regime disappeared. Since the market, formerly localised in the town, has become national and international, the corporation must expand to the same degree. Instead of being limited only to the artisans within one town, it must grow in such a way as to include all the members of the occupation throughout the country, for in whatever area they are found, whether they live in the town or country, they are all interdependent, and participate in a common activity. Since this common activity is, in certain respects, independent of any territorial basis, the appropriate agency must be created that expresses and stabilises its operation. Because of the extensiveness of those dimensions, such an agency would necessarily be in direct contact with the central agency of collective life; for events which are important enough to interest a whole category of industrial enterprises in a country necessarily have very general implications, which the state cannot ignore. This leads it to intervene. Thus, it is not without reason that royal power tended instinctively not to allow large-scale industry to operate outside its control when it first appeared. It was impossible for it not to be concerned with a form of activity which, by its very nature, can always be capable of influencing the whole of society. But while this regulatory action is necessary, it must not degenerate into direct subordination, as happened in the seventeenth and eighteenth centuries. The two related agencies must remain distinct and autonomous; each of them has its function, which it alone can execute. While the function of formulating general principles of industrial legislation belongs to the governmental assemblies, they are not able to diversify them according to the different forms of industry. It is this diversification which is the proper task of the corporation. This unitary organisation, representing the whole country, in no way excludes the formation of secondary agencies, comprising workers of the same region or locality, whose role would be to further specify the occupational regulation demanded by local or regional conditions. Economic life would thus be regulated and determined without losing any of its diversity.

For that very reason, the corporative system would be preserved from the tendency towards stagnation that it has often been criticised for in the past, for this was a defect rooted in the narrowly communal character of the corporation. As long as it was limited to the town, it was inevitable that it become a prisoner of tradition, like the town itself. In so restricted a group the conditions of life are almost invariable, habit has complete control over people and things, and anything new comes to be feared. The traditionalism of the corporations was thus only an aspect of the traditionalism of the local community, and showed the same properties. Once it had become ingrained in the mores, it survived the factors which had produced and originally justified it. This is why, when the material and moral centralisation of the country, and large-scale industry which followed from it, had opened up new wants, awakened new deeds, introduced into tastes and fashions a changeability heretofore unknown, the corporation, which was obstinately attached to its established customs, was unable to satisfy these new demands. But national corporations, in virtue of their dimension and complexity, would not be exposed to this danger. Too many different men would be involved to lead to a situation of unchanging uniformity. In a group formed of numerous and varied elements, new combinations are always being produced. There would then be nothing rigid about such an organisation, and it would consequently be adopted to the changing equilibrium of needs and ideas.

DTS, pp. xxxiv–xxxv, 360–2, vi–viii and xxvii–xxx

9. Political sociology

An essential element that enters into any notion of a 'political' group is the opposition between governing and governed, between authority and those subject to it. It is quite possible that in the initial stages of social development this distinction may not have existed; such an hypothesis is all the more likely since we do find societies in which the distance between the two is barely perceptible. But in any case, the societies where it is found must not be confused with those where it does not occur. The former differ from the latter in type, and require different terms of description: we should keep the word 'political' for the first category. For if this expression has any meaning, it implies primarily the existence of some kind of organisation, however rudimentary; it implies an established power – which may be stable or fluctuating, weak or strong – to whose action individuals are subject, whatever it may be.

But a power of this type is not found solely in political societies. The family may have a head, with powers which are sometimes absolute in character, and sometimes restrained by those of a family council. The patriarchal family of the Romans has often been compared to a state in miniature. Although, as we shall see below, this expression is not justified, we could not object to it if the only distinguishing feature of the political society were the existence of a governmental structure. So we must look for some further characteristic.

This has sometimes been sought in the closeness of the ties which bind the political society to its territory. There is said to be a permanent connection between any nation and a given territory. . .But the family, at least in many countries, is no less bound to the land, i.e., to some defined area. The family, too, has its domain from which it is inseparable, since that domain is inalienable. We have seen that the patrimony of landed estate was sometimes the very core of the family; it is this which gave it its unity and continuity, and it was about this focus that domestic life revolved. Nowhere in political societies has territory had a more important role than this. We may add, moreover, that where prime importance attaches to national territory, it is of comparatively recent date. First, it seems rather arbitrary to deny any political character to the great nomad societies whose structure was sometimes very elaborate. Secondly, in the past it was the number of citizens and not the territory that was considered to be the primary element of the state. To annex a state was not to annex the country, but its inhabitants and to incorporate them within the conquering state. Conversely, a conquering people may settle down in the country which they have vanquished, without thereby losing their own cohesion or their political identity. During the whole early period of our history, the capital, that is, the territorial centre of gravity of the society, was extremely mobile. It is only recently that peoples became so identified with the territories they inhabit, that is, with what we should call the geographical expression of those peoples. Today, France is not only a mass of people consisting in the main of individuals speaking a certain language and who observe certain laws etc.; it is essentially a certain defined part of Europe. If indeed all the Alsatians had opted for French nationality in 1870, we might still be justified in considering France as mutilated or diminished, by the sole fact that she had abandoned a specific part of her soil to a foreign power. But this identification of the society with its territory has only occurred in the most advanced societies. This is undoubtedly the result of many factors: of the higher social value that the land has acquired, perhaps also of the relatively greater importance that the geographical bond has assumed since other social ties of a more moral kind have lost their force. We see the society of which we are members more as a defined territory because it is no longer perceived as essentially religious, or identified with its own unique set of traditions or with the support of a particular dynasty.

Leaving territory aside, perhaps we can find a criterion of the political society in the numerical size of the population. Certainly we should not ordinarily give this name to social groups comprising a very small number of individuals. Even so, a dividing line of this kind would be extremely ambiguous: when does a concentration of people become large enough to be classified as a political group? According to Rousseau, it entails at least ten thousand people; Bluntschli rates this as too low. Both estimates are equally arbitrary. A French *département* sometimes has more inhabitants than many of the city states of Greece and Italy. Any one of these, however, constitutes a state, whilst a *département* has no claim to such a name.

Nevertheless, we touch here upon a distinctive feature. To be sure, we cannot say that a political society differs from family groups or from professional groups because it is larger: for the numerical strength of families may in some instances be considerable, while the numerical strength of a state may be very small. But it must be recognised that there is no political society which does not comprise numerous different families or professional groups, or both at once. If it were confined to a domestic society or family, it would be identical with it and hence be a domestic society. But from the moment that it becomes composed of a number of domestic societies, the resulting combination is something more than each of its elements. It is something new, which has to be designated by a different term. Thus the political society should not be confused with professional groups, or with classes if these exist; but it is always an aggregate of various professions or classes as it is of different families. We may conclude that when a society is made up of a number of different forms of secondary group, without itself being a secondary group in relation to a larger society, then it constitutes a social entity of a specific type. We may then define a political society as one formed by the coming together of a fairly large number of secondary social groups, which is subject to the same one authority, where this is not itself subject to any other permanently constituted superior authority...

Now that we know the distinguishing features of a political society, let us see what the morals are that relate to it. From the very definition which has just been given, it follows that these consist essentially in rules which specify the relation of individuals to this sovereign authority, to whose control they are subject. Since we need a word to indicate the particular group of officials entrusted with representing this authority, it is convenient to reserve the term 'state' for this. It is true that very often we apply the word not to the instrument of government but to the political society as a whole, or to the people governed and its government taken as one, and we ourselves have often used the term in this sense. It is in this way that we speak of the 'European states' or that we call France a 'state'. But since it is as well to have separate terms for phenomena as different as the society, and one of its organs, we apply the term 'state' more specifically to the agents of the sovereign authority, and 'political society' to the complex group of which the state is the highest organ. . .

The state may thus be defined as a group of officials *sui generis*, within which ideas and policies involving the collectivity are formulated, although they are not the product of collectivity. It is not accurate to say that the state embodies the *conscience collective*, for the latter goes beyond the state at every point. It is primarily diffuse in character: there is always a vast number of different social sentiments and social conditions which escape the purview of the state. The state is the centre only of a particular kind of consciousness; one which is circumscribed, but which is higher, clearer and with a more vivid sense of itself. There is nothing more obscure and ambiguous than the collective representations that are diffused in every society – myths, religious or moral tales, etc. We do not know either where they originate or where they are tending; they are not the product of deliberated thought. The representations that derive from the state are always more self-conscious, aware of their causes and their aims; they are arrived at in a less obscure fashion. The collective agency which plans them is more fully aware of what it is attempting to do. This is not to say that there is not often obscurity here also. The state, like the individual, is often mistaken as to the motives underlying its decisions, but whether this is so or not, they are in some degree consciously motivated. There is always, or at least usually, some sort of deliberation, and an understanding of the circumstances as a whole that make the decision necessary; and it is precisely this inner organ, the state, that is called upon to conduct these debates. Thus we have the councils, assemblies, debates and rulings which control the pace at which ideas are formulated. We may say, in summary: the state is a specialised agency whose responsibility it is to work out certain ideas which apply to the collectivity. These ideas are distinguished from the other collective representations by their more conscious and deliberate character.

LS, pp. 52–5, 58–9 and 61–2

STATE POWER AND INDIVIDUAL LIBERTIES

. . .the place of the individual becomes greater. . .[as] the governmental power becomes *less absolute*. But there is no contradiction in the fact that the sphere of individual action grows at the same time as that of the state; or in the fact that functions which are not directly dependent upon the central regulative agency develop at the same time as the latter. Power can be at once absolute, and very elementary. The despotic government of a barbarian chief is very simple in structure: the functions he carries out are rudimentary and not very numerous. That is because the directive agency of social life can have absorbed all these in itself, without on that account being very highly developed, if social life itself is not very highly developed. This agency then holds exceptional power over the rest of society, because there is nothing to hold it in check or to neutralise it. But it is quite possible for it to expand at the same time as other agencies develop which form a counterweight to it. All that has to occur is for the total volume of the society to be increased. Undoubtedly the action that it exerts under these conditions is no longer of the same nature; the points at which it exercises its power have multiplied, and if it is less violent, it still imposes itself quite as strictly. Acts of disobedience to the commands of constituted authority are no longer treated as sacrilegious, or, consequently, repressed with the same severity. But they are not tolerated any more than before, although these commands are more numerous and govern a greater range of different conditions.

DTS, p. 199

...the degree of absolutism in government does not vary directly with the type of society. Since absolutism is found both in cases where collective life is extremely simple as well as in cases where it is very complex, it is not characteristic exclusively of less developed societies any more than it is of the others. One might consider, it is true, that the concentration of governmental powers always goes hand in hand with the concentration of the social mass, either because the first is a consequence of the latter, or because it contributes to forming it. But this is not the case. The Roman city, particularly after the fall of the Kings, was completely free from absolutism until the last century of the Republic: and the different segments or partial societies (*gentes*) of which it was composed reached a high degree of concentration and fusion precisely under the Republic. And in fact we find forms of government which deserve to be called absolute in the most different social types: in France in the seventeenth century, at the end of the Roman Empire, and in many primitive monarchies. Conversely, according to circumstances, the same society may pass from being an absolute government into a quite different form; but a single society can no more change its type during the course of its evolution than an animal can change its species during its individual existence. France of the seventeenth century and France of the nineteenth century belong to the same type, in spite of the fact that the regulative agency was transformed. It is impossible to hold that, from Napoleon I to Louis-Philippe, French society changed from one social type to another, only then to undergo the reverse transformation from Louis-Philippe to Napoleon III. Such transmutations are incompatible with the notion of social type.

This specific form of political organisation thus does not depend upon the basic constitution of society, but upon particular, transitory, and contingent circumstances...the nature of the social type and that of the governmental type must be carefully distinguished, since as they are independent, they act independently of one-another, and sometimes even in opposite ways.

AS, 1900, pp. 69–70

There is no doubt what was the real nature of the aims pursued by the state in many societies. To keep on expanding its power and to add lustre to its fame – this was the sole or the main object of public activity. Individual interests and needs did not come into the reckoning. The religious character which permeated the political system of these societies explains this indifference of the state for what concerns the individual. The destiny of a state was closely bound up with that of the gods worshipped at its altars. If a state suffered reverses, then the prestige of its gods declined in the same measure, and vice versa. Public religion and civic morals were fused: they were merely different aspects of a single reality. To bring glory to the city was the same as enhancing the glory of the city gods: the relation was reciprocal. Now, the characteristic of religious phenomena is that they are wholly unlike those of the human order. They belong to a world apart. The individual as such is part of the profane world, whilst the gods are the very core of the religious world; and between these two worlds there is a gulf. The gods are made of a different substance to men: they have different ideas, needs, and live an existence completely distinct from that of men. To say that the aims of the political system were religious and religious aims political, is to say that there was a cleavage between the aims of the state and the ends pursued by individuals as such. How was it, therefore, that the individual could thus occupy himself with the pursuit of aims which were to such a degree foreign to his own private concerns? The answer is this: his private concerns were relatively unimportant to him and his personality and everything dependent upon it had only a low moral value. His personal views, his private beliefs and various individual aspirations seemed insignificant factors. What were valued by everyone were the beliefs held in common, the collective aspirations, the popular traditions and the symbols that expressed them. In these circumstances, the individual yielded spontaneously and without resistance to the instrument by which aims were realised which did not relate directly to himself. Absorbed by society, he meekly followed its imperatives and subordinated his own lot to the destinies of collective existence without any sense of sacrifice. This is because his particular fate had in his own eyes nothing of the meaning and high importance that we attribute to it today. If things were so, this is because they had to be so; societies could only exist at that time by virtue of this dependence.

But the further one advances in history, the more one is aware of the process of change. The individual personality at first is lost in the depths of the social mass, and only later begins to emerge from it. At first limited in scope and of small regard, the circle of individual activity expands and becomes the primary object of moral respect. The individual comes to acquire ever wider rights over his own person and over the possessions to which he has title; he also comes to form ideas about the world that seem to him most fitting and to freely develop his own nature. War fetters his activity, diminishes his stature and so becomes the supreme evil. Because it inflicts undeserved suffering on him, he sees in it more and more the supreme form of moral offence. In these conditions it is quite contradictory to expect him to submit to the same subordination as before. One cannot make of him a god, a god above all others, and at the same time an instrument in the hands of the gods. One cannot make him the supreme end and reduce him to the role of means. If he is the moral reality, then it is he who must serve as the axis of public as well as private conduct. It should be the role of the state to help him to realise his nature. Some might argue that the cult of the individual is a superstition of which we ought to rid ourselves. But this would be to go against all the lessons of history: for the further we look, the more we find the human person tending to gain in dignity. There is no law more soundly established. Thus any attempt to base social institutions on an opposing principle is not feasible and could be convincing only for a moment. We cannot force things to be other than they are. We cannot stop the individual having become what he is – an autonomous centre of activity, an imposing system of personal forces whose energy can no more be destroyed than that of cosmic forces. It would be just as impossible to transform the physical atmosphere in the midst of which we breathe.

But then we seem to reach a contradiction that cannot be resolved. On the one hand we establish that the state goes on developing more and more: on the other, that the rights of the individual, which appear to be antagonistic to those of the state have a parallel development. The government organ takes on an even greater scale, because its function goes on growing in importance and because the aims that demand its intervention, increase in number; and yet we deny that it can pursue aims other than those that concern the individual. But these aims seems to belong to the individual alone. If, as is often supposed, the rights of the individual are given in the individual, the state does not have to intervene to establish them; they depend only upon the individual. But if this is so, and these rights are outside its sphere of action, how can this sphere of action go on expanding, if on the other hand it must avoid things which compromise the interests of the individual?

The only way of disposing of this difficulty is to reject the postulate that the rights of the individual are given in the individual, and to admit that the institution of these rights is in fact precisely the task of the state. Then, in fact, everything becomes clear. We can understand that the functions of the state may expand, without any diminishing of the individual. We can see too that the individual may develop without causing any decline of the state, since he would be in some respects himself the product of the state, and since the activity of the state would be essentially one of individual liberation.

LS, pp. 68–71

THE NATURE OF DEMOCRATIC GOVERNMENT

...the state is nothing if it is not an agency distinct from the rest of society. If the state is everywhere, it is nowhere. The state comes into existence by a process of concentration that detaches a certain group of individuals from the collective mass. In that group, social thought is subjected to elaboration of a special kind and reaches an exceptional degree of clarity. Where there is no such concentration and where social thought remains entirely diffuse, it also remains obscure and the distinctive feature of the political society will be lacking. However, contact between this special agency and other social organs may vary in its degree of

closeness and constancy. Certainly in this respect there can only
be differences of degree. There is no state with such absolute
power that those governing will sever all contact with the mass of
its subjects. But differences of degree can be important: these increase externally in relation to the presence or absence of definite
institutions designed to establish this contact, and how far they
are developed or merely rudimentary. These are institutions that
enable the people to follow the working of government (national
assembly, official journals, education intended to equip the citizen
to one day fulfil his functions, etc.), and also to communicate their
views to the organs of government, directly or indirectly (i.e.
electoral machinery). What we must reject above all is that conception which, by eliminating the state entirely, is a facile source
of criticism. 'Democracy' thus understood, only exists in the
early phases of the development of society. If everyone governs,
it means in fact that there is no government. Collective sentiments,
diffused, ambiguous and obscure as they may be, sway the people.
The life of such peoples is in no way guided by deliberate policies.
Societies of this description are like individuals whose actions are
directed solely by routine and prejudice. They cannot be looked
to as an example towards which we should progress: rather, they
are a starting point. If we agree to reserve the name 'democracy'
for political societies, it must not be applied to amorphous tribes
which do not possess a state, and which are not political societies.
The difference between this form and democracy, is thus very
wide, in spite of certain similarities. It is true that in both cases
– and this is what offers the resemblance – the whole society
participates in public life; but this occurs in very different ways.
The difference lies in the fact that in one case there is a state
and in the other this is lacking.

   This initial characteristic, the existence of a state, is only one of
the necessary features of democracy; there is a second one, related
to the first. In societies where the governmental consciousness is
restricted within narrow limits, it comprises only a limited range
of objectives. Since this clarified sector of the *conscience collective*
is limited to a small group of individuals, it does not possess much
range. There are all sorts of customs, traditions and conventions
which work automatically without the state itself being aware of
them, and which therefore are beyond its action. In a society such
as the monarchy of the seventeenth century the number of things
on which government deliberations had any bearing was very
small. The whole sphere of religion was outside its province,
and along with religion, every kind of collective prejudice: any

absolute power would soon have come to grief if it had attempted
to destroy them. Today, on the other hand, we do not admit there
is anything in the realm of public life which cannot become
subject to the action of the state. In principle, we hold that everything should be constantly open to question, that everything may
be discussed, and that in so far as decisions have to be taken,
we are not tied to the past. The state has really a far greater
sphere of influence today than in other times, because the sphere
of this clarified consciousness has widened. Those obscure sentiments which are diffuse in character, which are ingrained habits,
resist change precisely because they are obscure. What cannot be
seen is not easily modified. All such forms escape the grasp,
precisely because they are in the shadows. On the other hand, the
more the depths of social life become illuminated, the more can
changes be introduced. This is why the educated man, who is a
self-conscious being, can change more easily and radically than
the uneducated. The same is true of democratic societies. They are
more malleable and more flexible, and this advantage they owe to
the fact that the governmental consciousness has expanded in
such a way as to include a much broader range of objects. This
contrasts sharply with those societies that have been unorganised
from the start, the pseudo-democracies. They have wholly yielded
to the yoke of tradition. Switzerland, and the Scandinavian countries, too, are a good example of this.

To sum up, there is not, strictly speaking, a difference in nature
between the various forms of government; but they lie between
two contrasting poles. At one extreme, the governmental consciousness is almost completely isolated from the rest of the society,
and has a minimum range.

Aristocratic or monarchical societies, between which it is perhaps difficult to distinguish, fall into this category. The greater
the degree to which there is direct communication between the
governmental consciousness and the rest of society, the broader
the range and comprehensiveness of this consciousness, the more
democratic the society becomes. The concept of 'democracy' is
thus defined in terms of a maximal extension of this consciousness,
which determines this communication. . .

. . .[Thus] to arrive at a fairly definite idea of what a democracy
is, we must begin by getting away from a number of current
conceptions which simply confuse matters. The number of those
governing must be left out of account and, even more important,
their official titles. Neither must we believe that a democracy is
necessarily a society in which the power of the state is weak.

A state may be democratic and still have a strong organisation. The true characteristics of democracy are twofold: (1) a greater range of the governmental consciousness, and (2) closer communications between this consciousness and the mass of individuals. The confusions that have occurred can be understood to some extent by the fact that, in societies where government power is weak and limited, it is necessarily in quite close communication with the rest of society, because it is not distinct from it. It has no existence, so to speak, outside the mass of the people, and must therefore of necessity be in communication with that mass. In a small primitive tribe, the political leaders are only delegates, and always provisional, without any clearly defined functions. They live the same life as everyone else, and the decisions they make remain subject to the control of the whole collectivity. They do not form a separate and definite agency. Also we find here nothing resembling the second feature already mentioned – the plasticity deriving from the range of governmental consciousness, that is, from the formulation of clarified collective ideas. Societies such as these are the victims of traditional routine. The second feature is perhaps even more distinctive than the first. The first criterion can still be very useful providing it is employed with care: we must guard against identifying the diffuse situation in which the state is not yet detached from society, and separately organised, with the communications that may exist between a clearly defined state and the society it governs.

Seen from this standpoint, a democracy thus appears as the political system by which the society can achieve a consciousness of itself in its purest form.

LS, pp. 99–102 and 106–7

Every society is despotic, at least if nothing external intervenes to restrain its despotism. Still, I would not say that there is anything artificial in this despotism: it is natural because it is necessary, and also because, in certain conditions, societies cannot endure without it. Nor do I wish to argue that there is anything intolerable about it: on the contrary, the individual does not feel it any more than we feel the atmosphere that weighs on our shoulders. From the moment the individual has been raised in this way by the collectivity, he will naturally desire what it desires and accept without difficulty the state of subjection to which he finds himself reduced. If he is to be conscious of this and to resist it, individualist aspirations must develop, and they cannot develop in these conditions.

But for it to be otherwise, we may say, is it not enough for the society to be on a fairly large scale? There is no doubt that when society is small, when it surrounds every individual on all sides and at every moment, it does not allow him to develop in freedom. If it is always present and always operating, it leaves no room to his initiative. But it is no longer the same when society has reached sufficient dimensions. When it is made up of a vast number of individuals, a society cannot exercise over each one a control which is as close, vigilant or effective as when it is concerned only with a small number. A man is far more free in a crowd than in a small group. Hence it follows that individual diversities can develop more easily; collective tyranny declines and individualism establishes itself as a reality – and in time, the reality becomes a right. But this can only happen on one condition: that is, that within this society, there must be no secondary groups formed that enjoy enough autonomy for each to become a small society within the larger one. For in this situation each would act towards its members as if it stood alone, and everything would happen as if the total society did not exist. Each group, tightly enclosing its component individuals, would block their development; the collective will would impose itself on conditions applying to the individual. A society made up of juxtaposed clans, or of more or less independent towns or villages, or of numerous professional groups, each autonomous in relation to the others, would have the effect of being almost as completely repressive of individuality as if it were made up of a single clan or town or corporation. The formation of secondary groups of this kind is bound to occur, for in a large-scale society there are always particular local or professional interests which tend naturally to bring together the people concerned. Here we have the material for particular associations, corporations and groups of all kinds; and if there is nothing to offset or neutralise their activity, each of them will tend to absorb its members. In any case, there is always domestic society: we know how absorbing this is if left to itself – how it confines within its own circle and keeps in a state of dependence all who belong to it. (Even if secondary groups of this sort were not formed, a collective force would still establish itself at the head of the society to govern it. And if this collective force itself stands alone, if it has only individuals to deal with, the same necessary law will make those individuals fall under its domination.)

In order to prevent this happening, and to provide a sphere for individual development, it is not enough for a society to be large;

the individual must be able to move with some degree of freedom
over a broad field of action. He must not be curbed and dominated
by secondary groups, and these groups must not be able to acquire
a mastery over their members and mould them at will. There must
therefore exist above these local, domestic – in a word, secondary
– authorities, some overall authority which makes the law for them
all: this overall authority must remind each of them that it is but
a part, and not the whole, and that it must not monopolise what
rightly belongs to the whole. The only means of averting this
collective particularism, and the consequences which it implies
for the individual, is to have a specialised agency with the duty of
representing the overall collectivity, its rights and its interests, in
relation to these individual collectivities. These rights and these
interests merge with those of the individual. Thus the main
function of the state is to liberate individual personalities. Since it
holds its constituent societies in check, it prevents them from
exerting the repressive influences over the individual which they
would otherwise exert. So there is nothing inherently tyrannical
about state intervention in the different spheres of social life; on
the contrary, it has the objective and the effect of alleviating
tyrannies that do exist. But could it not be argued that the state in
turn might become despotic? This is undoubtedly the case, if
there is nothing to counter-balance it. In this situation, as the
only existing collective force, it produces the same effects upon
individuals as any other collective force not neutralised by a
counter-force. The state itself then becomes a levelling and repressive agency. And its repressive character is harder to endure
than that of small groups, because it is more artificial. The state
in our large-scale societies is so removed from individual interests
that it cannot take into account the special, local conditions etc., in
which they exist. Therefore when it attempts to control them, it
succeeds only at the cost of contravening and distorting them.
Moreover, it is too distant from the mass of the population to be
able to mould them inwardly so that they voluntarily accept its
influence. The individual eludes the state to some extent, since the
state can only be effective in the context of a large-scale society,
and individual diversity may not come to light. Hence, all kinds
of resistance and distressing conflicts arise. Small groups do not
have this disadvantage: they are close enough to the objects which
provide their reason for existence to be able to adapt their actions
as required; and they envelop the individuals fully enough to
shape them in their own image. The conclusion to be drawn from
this observation, however, is simply that if that collective force,

the state, is to be the liberator of the individual, it has itself need of some counter-balance. It must be restrained by other collective forces, that is, by the secondary groups. . .While it is not desirable for these groups to stand alone, their existence is necessary. And it is out of this conflict of social forces that individual freedoms are born. Here again we see the significance of these groups. Their usefulness is not merely to regulate and administer the interests under their supervision. They have a more general role; they form one of the conditions essential to the emancipation of the individual.

LS, pp. 74–8

10. The social bases of education

. . .every society sets up a certain ideal of man, of what he should be, as much from the intellectual point of view as the physical and moral. This ideal is, in some degree, the same for all members of society; but it also becomes differentiated beyond a certain point, according to the specific groupings that every society contains in its structure. It is this ideal, which is both integral and diverse, that is the focus of education. Its function, then, is to develop in the child: (1) a certain number of physical and mental states that the society to which he belongs considers should be possessed by all of its members; (2) certain physical and mental states that the particular social group (caste, class, family, profession) similarly considers ought to be possessed by all those who compose it. Thus both society as a whole and each particular social grouping determine the ideal that education realises. Society can survive only if there exists among its members a sufficient degree of homogeneity; education perpetuates and reinforces this homogeneity by fixing in the mind of the child, from the beginning, the essential similarities that social life demands. But on the other hand, without a certain diversity all co-operation would be impossible; education ensures the persistence of this necessary diversity by being itself diversified and specialised. If the society has reached a degree of development whereby the old divisions into castes and classes can no longer be maintained, it will prescribe an education more uniform at its base. If at the same time there is a more developed division of labour, it will arouse among children, on the basis of an underlying set of common ideas and sentiments, a richer diversity of occupational aptitudes. If it exists in a state of war with neighbouring societies, it tries to shape people according to a strongly nationalistic model; if international competition takes a more peaceful form, the type that it tries to form is more general and more humanistic. Education is thus simply the means by which society prepares, in its children, the essential conditions of its own existence. We shall see later how the individual himself has an interest in submitting to these requirements.

Thus we reach the following conclusion: *Education is the influence exercised by adult generations on those that are not yet ready for social life. Its object is to stimulate and develop in the child a certain number of physical, intellectual and moral states which are demanded of him by both the political society as a whole, and by the particular milieu for which he is specifically destined. . .*

Education has varied infinitely in time and place. In the cities of Greece and Rome, education trained the individual to subordinate himself blindly to the collectivity, to become the creature of society. Today, it is concerned with making the individual into an autonomous personality. In Athens, they sought to form cultivated souls, informed, subtle, enamoured of moderation and harmony, capable of enjoying beauty and the joys of pure speculation; in Rome, they wanted children to become primarily men of action, devoted to military glory, indifferent to letters and the arts. In the Middle Ages, education was above all Christian; in the Renaissance, it took on a more secular and literary character; today science tends to assume the place in education formerly occupied by the arts. Should we say, however, that reality is not the ideal: that if education has varied, it is because men have misunderstood the form it should take? But if Roman education had been infused with an individualism comparable to ours, the Roman state could not have continued in existence; Latin civilisation would not have developed, nor, furthermore, our modern civilisation, which is in part descended from it. The Christian societies of the Middle Ages would not have been able to survive if they had given to free enquiry the place that we give to today. There are thus inescapable necessities which we cannot deny. What point is there in imagining a kind of education that would be fatal for the society that put it into practice?. . .

. . .each society, considered at a given stage of development, has a system of education which exercises an influence upon individuals which is usually irresistible. It is idle to think that we can rear our children as we wish. There are customs to which we are bound to conform; if we flout them too severely, they take their vengeance on our children. The children, when they are adults, are unable to live in accord with their contemporaries. Whether they are raised under the influence of ideas that are absolute, or ones which are premature, does not matter; in the one case as in the other, they are not of their time, and therefore they are outside the conditions of normal life. Thus there is, at any point in time, a prevailing type of education from which we cannot deviate without encountering the strong resistance which counters the erratic impetus of disaffection.

Now, it is not we as individuals who have created the customs and ideas that determine this. These are the product of the life of the community, and they express its needs. They are, moreover, in large part the work of preceding generations. The entire human past has contributed to the formation of the set of principles that guide education today; our entire history has left its imprint upon it, and even the history of the peoples who went before. This is comparable to the way in which the higher animals carry in themselves the trace of the whole biological evolution of which they are the end-product. Historical investigation of the formation and development of systems of education reveals that they depend upon religion, political organisation, the degree of development of science, the state of industry, etc. If they are considered apart from these historical causes, they cannot be understood. How then can the individual claim to reconstruct, from within his own mind, something which is not a product of individual thought? He is not faced with a *tabula rasa* on which he can write what he wants, but with existing realities which he cannot create, or destroy, or transform, at will. He can act on them only to the extent that he has learned to understand them, to know their nature and the conditions on which they depend; and he can understand them only if he sets out to study and observe them, as the physicist observes inanimate matter and the biologist, living organisms.

ES, pp. 47–9, 39–40 and 41–3

THE DEVELOPMENT OF EDUCATIONAL SYSTEMS

All of the basic substance of our intellectual civilisation has come to us from Rome. One can thus infer that our pedagogy, the fundamental principles of our system of teaching, have come to us from the same source, since teaching is merely a shortened version of the intellectual culture of the adult. But in what way, and in what form, has this transmission taken place? The Germanic peoples – if not all of them, at least those who have given their name to our country – were barbarians who were indifferent to all the refinements of civilisation. Literature, the arts, and philosophy for them were without value; we know that even the monuments of Roman art inspired in them only hate and suspicion. Thus between them and the Romans there was a real moral discontinuity which would seem to have prevented any communication or assimilation between the two peoples. Since these two civilisations were alien to each other at this point, it would seem that they could only be mutually repellent. But happily there was one respect in which these societies, which were otherwise antagonistic and which only sustained relationships of mutual opposition and exclusion, were similar, which brought them together and allowed them to communicate. Although this did not come about immediately, it was not long delayed. Quite rapidly, one of the essential organs of the Roman Empire became extended into French society; it expanded and developed in the latter society without thereby changing its nature. This was the Church. And it was the Church which served as the mediator between the two heterogeneous peoples. It was the channel by which the intellectual life of Rome became transfused little by little into the new societies which were in the process of formation. And it was precisely through education that this transfusion was made. . .

In Antiquity, intellectual education had the objective of communicating to the child a certain number of defined talents. These were either considered as a sort of ornamentation, designed to elevate the aesthetic value of the individual, or else they were seen, as was the case in Rome, as instruments of action, as tools which an individual needed in order to play his role in life. In each case it was a matter of inculcating into the pupil certain habits and items of knowledge. Now these defined pieces of knowledge, these specific habits, could be acquired from different teachers without any difficulty. It was not a question of influencing the personality in terms of what makes for its fundamental unity, but in clothing it in a sort of external framework, the different parts of which could be created independently: so much so, that each workman could put his own hand to it separately. Christianity, by contrast, very early on acquired the conception that there is in each of us an underlying mode of being from which particular forms of intelligence and sensibility derive, and in which they find their unity; and that it is this underlying mode of being which has to be reached if one really wants to carry out the work of the educationalist and to produce a lasting effect. According to Christian belief, to shape a man is not to embellish his mind with certain ideas or to allow him to acquire certain specific habits, but to create in him a general attitude of the mind and the will which makes him see reality in general in a definite perspective.

And it is easy to understand how Christianity came to hold this view. It is because. . .in order to be a Christian, it is not enough to have learnt this or that particular item, to know how to discriminate between certain rites or pronounce certain formulas, or to know certain traditional beliefs. Christianity consists essentially in a certain attitude of the soul, in a certain *habitus* of our moral being. To foster this attitude in the child is thus the essential goal of education. This is what explains the appearance of an idea which was completely unknown to Antiquity, but which in Christianity, on the other hand, has played a considerable role: the idea of conversion. Conversion, as effectively understood in Christianity, is not the adhesion to certain particular conceptions, to certain specific articles of faith. True conversion is a profound transformation whereby the soul in its entirety, through turning in a completely new direction, changes its position or standpoint, and consequently alters its perspective upon the world. The acquisition of a certain number of truths is of such little importance that this change can occur instantaneously. It can happen that the soul, shaken to its roots by a sudden, powerful impulse, makes this act of conversion, that is to say, its perspective is changed in one immediate moment. This is what happens when, to use the religious terminology, the soul suddenly receives Divine grace. In these circumstances, by a sort of reversal, it finds itself, in an instant, facing totally new perspectives. Unsuspected realities and unknown worlds open up before it: things become known and perceived which a moment before went completely unrecognised. But this same transformation can take place more slowly, under a gradual and barely perceptible pressure: and this is what is achieved by education. But in order to act as powerfully upon the deep recesses of the soul, it is evidently necessary that the different influences to which the child is subject to should not be spread in diverse directions, but should, on the contrary, be energetically concentrated upon the same objective. This result can only be obtained by making children live in the same moral environment, the presence of which is always with them, which entirely surrounds them, and the actions of which, so to speak, they cannot escape. This is the explanation of the concentration of education, and even of the whole life of the child, with the emergence of the school as it has been organised under Christianity.

Now even today we understand intellectual education in the same way. For us too the principal object of education is not to provide the child with a greater or lesser degree of items of knowledge, but to create within him a deep-lying disposition, a kind of perspective of the soul which orients him in a definite direction, not only during childhood, but for life. No doubt this is not in order to make a Christian of him, since we have abandoned the pursuit of religious ends, but it is in order to make him a man. For in the same way as one must acquire a Christian mode of thought and feeling in order to become a Christian, so to become a man it is not sufficient to furnish the intellect with a certain number of ideas: it is necessary above all to acquire a truly human mode of thought and feeling. Our conception of the goal has become secularised; consequently the means employed themselves must change. But the abstract scheme of the educational process has not altered. It still is a matter of descending into depths of the soul which Antiquity was unconscious of.

This explains our present conception of the school; because, for us, the school should not be a sort of hostelry where different teachers, who are strangers to each other, come to instruct in a heterogeneous fashion pupils who have no connection with one-another and who are only temporarily assembled together. For us also, every level of school must form an integral moral environment, which closely envelops the child and acts upon his whole nature. We compare it to a society, we speak of the school society, and it is in fact a social group which has its own specific character and organisation, exactly like the adult society. This obviously presupposes that it is not simply composed, as it was in Antiquity, of an assembly of pupils physically gathered together in a single locale. This notion of the school as an organised moral environment has become so familiar to us that we are led to believe that it has always existed. We see, on the contrary, that it is relatively late in origin, that it only appeared and only could appear at a definite moment in history. It is bound up with definite conditions of civilisation, and we can see what these conditions are. It could only come into being when societies were formed for whom the true quality of human culture consists, not in the acquisition of certain practices or specific mental habits, but in a general orientation of the mind and will: that is, when these societies reached a high enough level of idealism. From then onwards, the object of education was inevitably to give the child the necessary momentum in the relevant direction, and it was essential that this should be organised in such a way as to produce the deep and lasting effect which was expected of it.

This observation leads to another, as a corollary. When one calls the Middle Ages the historical period which intervened between the fall of the Roman Empire and the Renaissance, one obviously conceives of it as an intermediate age whose role is presumed to be that of linking Antiquity and modern times, between the moment at which ancient civilisation came to an end and that at which it reawoke to begin a new life. It appears to to have no historical function save that of holding a place, of occupying the scene during an intermission. But nothing is more inaccurate than this conception of the Middle Ages and nothing, in consequence, is more unwarranted than the word by which this epoch is labelled. Far from having been simply a period of transition, a period of no originality between two brilliant and original civilisations, it was, on the contrary, the time at which there emerged the fertile seeds of an entirely new civilisation. . .

Since the men of the Renaissance gave themselves the task of dissolving and reorganising the work of their forerunners from top to bottom, it is worth again emphasising what there was of value in the latter: only on this condition will it be possible to understand and to judge that of their successors.

What must, at the outset, be admitted without reserve of the period just mentioned is its admirable fruitfulness in matters of educational organisation. It was at this time, in fact, that the most powerful and complete educational system ever known in history was formed, almost out of nothing. In place of the cathedral and abbey schools, which could never house more than a modest number of pupils, and which were not connected with each other, there came into being, at a definite point on the European continent, a vast anonymous and impersonal – and consequently, permanent – teaching body, comprising hundreds of teachers and thousands of students. This body was organised in such a way that, as far as possible, it represented all the human disciplines. Secondary organs were created within the system which, under the name of faculties, corresponded to different specialisations of knowledge. Around the schools, there were founded hostels, modes of teaching, and colleges, which provided a moral refuge for the young students. Grades were instituted, which divided up and marked the stages of school life; and examinations were introduced which governed access to these grades. Finally curricula were established which fixed for the student the knowledge which he must acquire during each of these phases, and for the teacher, the subject-matter which he must teach. These major innovations appeared within the space of two or three centuries.

Each of this series of creations was the original and singular product of the Middle Ages. . .Neither Antiquity, nor the Carolingian age, provided anything which could serve as a model for it.

And although all of these institutions originally stemmed directly from conditions specific to mediaeval life, they became so firmly hardened at that time that they have continued up to our day. Certainly we do not regard them in the same way as our forbears: we have infused them with a different spirit. But their structure has hardly changed. If a student from the Middle Ages were to come back among us, and heard us speak of universities, faculties and colleges, of the *baccalauréat*, degree, doctorate, curriculum, *leçons ordinaires* and *leçons extraordinaires*, he might believe that nothing has changed, except that French words had taken the place of the Latin words of previous times. It would only be when he went into our lecture-rooms and classes that he would notice the changes which have occurred. Then he would see that educational life has been transformed. But it continues to flow in the channels which were created by the Middle Ages. . .

The mental attitude of a people only becomes modified when basic conditions of social life themselves are modified. One may thus be assured in advance that the Renaissance is not to be treated, as is often done, as the result of the accidental un-earthing at that period of certain particular Ancient writings, but derives from profound changes in the organisation of the European societies. Without pretending to offer here a complete and de-tailed picture of these changes, I would like at least to indicate the most important ones, in order to be able to discover the social roots of the pedagogic movement which we are subsequently going to describe.

In the first place, there was a whole group of transformations in the economic order. The latter was at last emerging from the mediocrity of the Middle Ages, in which the general insecurity of relationships paralysed the spirit of enterprise, where the narrow-ness of the markets stifled any larger aspirations, and where the extreme simplicity of tastes and needs allowed men no other choice but to accommodate themselves to their environment. Little by little, order became established; a more effectively organised police and administration served to restore confidence. Towns multiplied and became more populous. Finally, and most important of all, the discovery of America and the route to the Indies, by opening up new worlds to economic activity, had something of a galvanic effect. As a result, there was a rise in material well-being; great fortunes were accumulated, and there awoke and developed the taste for an easy, elegant and luxurious life. Already under Louis XII, thanks to the internal peace, this development was sufficiently defined to strike the eyes of observers. . .

If, however, this transformation had remained limited to the world of the nobility alone, it would probably not have had very extensive social consequences. But at the same time, as a result of the accumulating wealth, there occurred a drawing together of all classes. Previously the bourgeoisie had not dared even to raise their eyes to the nobility, and felt themselves separated from the latter by a complete gulf; and they found it quite natural to lead a separate existence. But as the bourgeoisie became richer, and consequently more powerful, they also became more ambitious, and sought to reduce the distance between themselves and the nobility. Their needs having grown with their resources, the life which they previously led appeared intolerable. Thus they were no longer afraid to cast their eyes upwards, and sought themselves to live the life of the lords, to imitate their style, manners and luxury...One may surmise without much difficulty the consequences which such a change in the mode of life must have had in the mode of education. Teaching designed to produce a good bachelor of arts, initiated into all the secrets of syllogism and debate, could not serve to create the elegant gentleman – eloquent, able to take his place in the salon, and expert in all the social graces.

But besides this transformation, a no less important one took place directly in the realm of ideas.

The great European nations were, in large part, formed by the sixteenth century. While in the Middle Ages there was only one Europe, a single, homogeneous Christian world, by this date there exist great collective entities which have their own separate intellectual and moral identity. England became conscious of itself and its unity with the Tudors, Spain with Ferdinand de Castille and his successors, Germany with the Habsburgs (although with less clarity), France above all with the Capetians. The old Christian unity was thus definitely broken. Whatever the respect which continued to be professed for the basic dogmas, which still seemed to be unchangeable, each of these groups which were thus formed had its specific way of thought and sentiment; each had its own temperament which necessarily tended to put its mark upon the system of ideas hitherto accepted by the great majority of believers. And since the great moral personalities who then emerged could not develop their individual nature, since they could think and believe in their own way only if the right to depart from previously established beliefs was accorded them, they demanded it, and in demanding it, proclaimed it. That is to say, they did not claim it in an absolute way (there could be no question of this yet), but within certain limits – the right of schism, the right of free examination. This was the basic cause of the Reformation, the other aspect of the Renaissance; it was the natural consequence of the movement towards individualisation and differentiation which took place at that date within the homogeneous European mass...

...two great educational currents...appeared in the sixteenth century. The first is that represented by Rabelais, and which is characterised by a need to expand human nature in all senses, but above all by an intemperate taste for erudition, by a thirst for knowledge which nothing can slake. The second current, personified by Erasmus, did not possess this extensiveness, and did not manifest such lofty ambitions: on the contrary, it reduced the main elements of human culture to literary culture alone, and it made the study of classical Antiquity almost the sole instrument of this culture. The art of writing and speaking occupied here the place taken by knowledge in Rabelaisian pedagogy. The essential objective of education was to allow the child to sample the masterpieces of Greece and Rome, and to be able to imitate them intelligently. Thus educational formalism, from which we seemed to have been on the brink of being freed with Rabelais and the great scholars of the sixteenth century, was revived in new guise with Erasmus. A new type of formalism now succeeded the grammatical formalism of the Carolingian epoch and the conceptual formalism of the scholastics: this was literary formalism.

Having described this second current, we must seek to explain it. The question is made more important by the fact that there are obvious connections between these pedagogic conceptions and those – apparently so far distant – which are still at the basis of classical education today. It is thus of great interest to know where they derive from, and what needs they respond to.

Now at the same moment at which this new pedagogic influence became manifest, there occurred a change in the mores whose importance can hardly be exaggerated: this was the formation of polite society. Undoubtedly, as we have already noted, the world of the nobility and the chateaux had always constituted a specific milieu in which, under the dominant influence of women, manners and customs were permeated by an elegance and courtesy which was unknown elsewhere. But in the sixteenth century, this need for politeness and refinement, this taste for the most delicate pleasures of society, became both intensified and more widespread. One can see, in the book by Bourciez: *Polite Manners and Courtly Literature under Henry II* how, at this time, the cliques and salons, in which the woman played the predominant role, multiplied, together with the tournaments, the great calvacades, and the long hunts at which, in time of peace, the knights amused themselves.

The strength of this need is shown, moreover, by the fact that, when the normal means of satisfying it were lacking, various other artifices were invented. Educated men, scattered over the whole face of Europe, being unable to discuss verbally, replaced the pleasures of conversation by those of correspondence. Not being able to converse, they wrote. Letter-writing thus assumed a quite exceptional literary importance and development. Petrarch tells us that he devoted a substantial part of his life to writing letters. These letters were not simply intimate messages such as we write today, whose object is to inform someone who is away about what we are doing and what has become of us. They were pieces of literature, treating some subject of general interest, some moral problem, or certain literary questions, as one would have been able to do in a salon. Moreover, they were not addressed to a single correspondent, but passed from hand to hand, or were circulated, at least in copied form. The learned men of Europe thus formed, as a whole, a society of great minds which, while being dispersed at all points on the continent, from Naples to Rotterdam, Paris to Leipzig, possessed its own unity, such was the care which its members took to maintain connections and to communicate, in spite of the distance.

Now it is very clear that Scholasticism had nothing of what was needed to satisfy these new tastes; on the contrary, it could only clash with them. . .

. . .if we leave aside the Carolingian age, which was a preliminary and introductory period, the path which we have followed since the beginning of this exposition comprises two main stages. There is first of all the Scholastic age, which goes from the twelfth to the fourteenth century, and then the humanist age, which lasts from the sixteenth to the end of the eighteenth century. To the first, we owe the whole of our educational organisation: universities, faculties, colleges, degrees, examinations – everything comes to us from that time. To the second, we owe the literary teaching which until recent times remained the basis of our intellectual education. On the eve of the Revolution, there begins finally a third phase, in the course of which there is an attempt to complement this literary education by an historical and scientific culture. This phase, which opened a century and a half ago, is still going on. We have not yet left it; it stretches up to our times. . .

It was in Protestant circles, and particularly in Germany, that this new pedagogical conception emerged for the first time; it is in the German countries, moreover, that it has remained most widespread.

One can say that, in principle, Lutheranism showed itself to be only moderately favourable to humanism. If Luther recommends that we should study the classical languages, it is in order that the preachers of the Reformed Church should seem up to their task; in order that, in a century in which a taste for eloquence began to spread, they should not appear as backward barbarians. But Luther himself felt no enthusiasm for classical learning comparable to that of Erasmus and of the great humanist of the Latin countries. Moreover, with the exception of Melanchthon, all his followers shared the same sentiments. The fact is that there was in Protestantism a sense of the lay society and its temporal interests which Catholicism did not, and would not, possess. If Luther demands schools it is, as he says himself, in order to 'maintain the outward state of temporal things, *den Weltlichen Stand,* so that men can govern the country effectively, so that women can bring up their children properly and care for their household'. He does not want the old system. 'It is not my view that schools should be organised as they have been up to now. It is now a different world, and things are changed.' And he asks that the young man should be prepared for his future function. So humanism has not had the same influence and authority in the Protestant countries of Germany as it has had among us. From the end of the sixteenth century, it lost its influence and its prestige.

The ground was thus prepared for the appearance of a new pedagogy which, contrary to humanism, set out to seek in things, in reality, the instrument of intellectual culture. And this pedagogy has been effectively in the process of being formed since the beginning of the seventeenth century. . .

France was, in this respect, a century behind Germany. . .It is only near the middle of the eighteenth century that this conception emerges among us, and it becomes more marked the closer we come to the Revolution. This is the moment at which French society becomes directly conscious of itself, learns to think of itself without reference to any religious symbolism. This is the time at which, in an entirely secular and self-sufficient way, it acquires a sufficient prestige in the eyes of men for its needs and interests, even purely temporal in character, to appear as sacred and eminently worthy of respect. Thus we see at this period the birth, and the remarkably rapid spread, of the new conception of

education which we referred to a short while earlier. All thought-
ful men of the time were in agreement that the essential objective
which must be assigned to it should be that of ensuring the proper
functioning of society. . .

In reality, the man whom the humanists educated, and still
continue to educate, was simply a fusion of the Christian ideal
with the Roman and Greek ideals. These were the three ideals
which served to shape it, because these were the three ideals
which were followed by the men who created it. This is what
explains its abstract and relatively universal character; it is the
product of a sort of spontaneous generalisation. In spite of this
generality, however, it is nonetheless a very specific and transient
ideal, which expresses the very distinctive conditions in which the
civilisation of the European peoples were formed – especially our
own. There is, therefore, no justification for presenting it as the
only human ideal, as the only one which expresses the nature of
man; on the contrary, it relates in a very definite way to a particular time and context. Thus if we wish to succeed in giving the
pupil some notion of what man is, objectively and in reality, and
not merely the way in which he has been conceived of ideally, or
at a given moment in history, we shall have to proceed otherwise.
We shall have to find a way of making him see not only what is
constant, but also what is irreducibly different in mankind. . .

Let us therefore continue the work of the humanists, but by
transforming it and infusing it with new ideas. Let us make use of
classical writings, not in order to allow the child to know that
abstract and general man which is the ideal type of the seventeenth century, but to show him man as he is, with his almost
endless variability, and with that extreme complexity of his
nature which allows it to assume the most diverse forms.

From EPF, pp. 26–7, 36–9, 188–9, 196–7, 198–9,
234–6, 317, 326–7, 330, 331, 374 and 381

RATIONALIST EDUCATION

. . .that a wholly rational moral education is possible is something
which is implied in the very postulate which is at the basis of
science. I refer to the rationalist postulate, which may be stated
as follows: there is nothing in reality that one is justified in considering as fundamentally beyond the scope of human reason.
When I call this principle a postulate, I am in fact using a very
improper expression. This principle had this character when the
human mind first undertook to master reality – if indeed one can

say that this first conquest of the world by the mind ever had a beginning. When science began to develop it necessarily had to postulate that it, itself, was possible: that is to say, that reality could be expressed in scientific language – or, in other words, rational language, for the two terms are synonymous. However, something that, at the time, was only an anticipation of the mind, a tentative conjecture, found itself progressively demonstrated by all the results of science. Science showed that facts should be connected with each other in accordance with rational relationships, by discovering the existence of such relationships. There are, of course, many things, even an infinite number of things, of which we are still ignorant. Nothing indicates that all of them will ever be discovered, that a moment will come when science will have finished its task and will have expressed adequately the totality of things. Rather, everything leads us to believe that scientific progress will never end.

But the rationalist principle does not imply that science can in fact exhaust the real. It only denies that one has the right to look at any part of reality or any category of facts as completely irreducible to scientific thought – in other words, as irrational in its essence. Rationalism does not at all suppose that science can ever reach the limits of given reality; only that there is not, in this reality, any limit that science can never go beyond. If it is understood in this way, we can say that it is demonstrated by the history of science itself. The manner in which science has progressed shows that it is impossible to mark a point beyond which scientific explanation will become impossible. All the limits within which men have tried to contain it have only served as challenges for science to surpass them. Whenever it was thought that science had reached its ultimate limit, it resumed, after varying periods of time, its forward march and penetrated regions thought to be outside its scope. Once physics and chemistry were established, it was thought that science had to stop there. The living world seemed to depend upon mysterious principles which escape the grasp of scientific thought. Yet the biological sciences eventually came into their own. Subsequently the founding of psychology demonstrated the applicability of reason to mental phenomena. We have no right, then, to suppose that it is different with moral phenomena. Such an exception, which would be unique, is contrary to every indication we have. There is no reason for supposing that this last barrier, which some still try to oppose to the progress of reason, is any more insurmountable than the others. In fact, a science has been founded, even if it is only in its beginnings, that undertakes to treat the phenomena of moral life as natural phenomena, that is, as rational phenomena. Now, if ethics is rational, if it comprises only ideas and sentiments deriving from reason, why should it be necessary, in order to instil it in the mind and character, to have recourse to methods beyond the scope of reason?

Not only does a purely rational education seem logically possible; it is demanded by our entire historical development. Certainly if education had suddenly taken on this character several years ago, we might well doubt whether so sudden a transformation were really implied in the nature of things. In reality, however, this is the result of a gradual development, whose origins go back, so to speak, to the very beginnings of history. The secularisation of education has been in progress for centuries...

Rationalism is only one of the aspects of individualism: it is its intellectual aspect. These are not two different states of mind, but two sides of the same coin. When one feels the need of liberating individual thought, it is because in a general way one feels the need of liberating the individual. Intellectual servitude is only one of the forms of servitude that individualism combats. The whole development of individualism has the effect of opening moral consciousness to new ideas and of making it more demanding. Since every advance that it makes results in a higher conception, a more refined awareness of the dignity of man, individualism cannot develop without making social relations which once seemed perfectly just now seem quite unjust. Moreover, the faith in rationalism also reacts back upon individualistic sentiment and stimulates it. For injustice is unreasonable and absurd, and, consequently, we are the more sensitive to it as we are more sensitive to the rights of reason. Consequently, an advance in moral education in the direction of greater rationality cannot occur without also bringing to light new moral tendencies, without inducing a greater thirst for justice, and stirring latent aspirations in public attitudes. The educator who undertakes to rationalise education, without foreseeing the development of new sentiments, without preparing that development, and directing it, will thus fail in one part of his task. This is why he cannot confine himself as has sometimes been suggested, to commenting upon the old morality of our forerunners. He must, in addition, help the younger generations to become conscious of the new ideal toward which they are moving confusedly. To orient them in that direction it is not enough for him to conserve the past; he must prepare the future.

Furthermore, it is on that condition alone that moral education fulfils its entire function. If we are satisfied with inculcating in children the body of conventional moral ideas which men have followed for centuries, we might in some degree protect the private morality of individuals. But this is only the minimum condition of morality, and a society cannot remain satisfied with it. For a great nation like ours to be in a true state of moral health it is not enough for most of its members to be sufficiently removed from the grossest transgressions – murder, theft, and the various kinds of fraud. A society in which there is peaceful transaction, and in which there is no conflict of any sort, but which has nothing more than that, would be quite mediocre in quality. It must, in addition, have before it an ideal toward which it reaches. It must have some good to achieve, an original contribution to bring to the moral heritage of mankind. Idleness is a bad counsellor for collectivities as well as individuals. When individual activity does not know where to aim at, it turns against itself. When the moral powers of society remain latent, when they are not engaged in accomplishing some end, they lose any sense of direction, and become employed in a morbid and harmful manner. Just as work is the more necessary to man as he is more civilised, similarly, the more advanced and complex the intellectual and moral organisation of societies, the more it is necessary that they provide new substance for their increased activity. A society like ours cannot, therefore, content itself with the complacent adherence to moral prescriptions that have been handed down to it. It must go on to new conquests; the teacher must prepare the children who are entrusted to him for those necessary advances. He must be on his guard against transmitting the moral gospel of their elders as a sort of closed book. On the contrary, he must excite in them a desire to add some lines of their own, and put them in a position to satisfy this legitimate ambition.

EM, pp. 4–6 and 13–15

11. Religion and ritual

[Written in review of Guyau's *L'irréligion de l'avenir*.]

For the author religion derives from a double source: firstly, the need to understand; and secondly, from sociability. We would say, at the outset, that these factors should be inverted, and that sociability should be made the determining cause of religious sentiment. Men did not begin by imagining gods; it is not because they conceived of them in a given fashion that they became bound to them by social feelings. They began by linking themselves to the things which they made use of, or which they suffered from, in the same way as they linked each of these to the other – without reflection, without the least kind of speculation. The theory only came later, in order to explain and make intelligible to these rudimentary minds the modes of behaviour which had thus been formed. Since these sentiments were quite similar to those which he observed in his relationships with his fellows, man conceived of these natural powers as beings comparable to himself; and since at the same time they differed amongst themselves, he attributed to these exceptional beings distinctive qualities which made them gods. Religious ideas thus result from the interpretation of pre-existing sentiments and, in order to study religion, we must penetrate to these sentiments, avoiding the ideas which are only the symbol and surface expression of these.

But there are two sorts of social sentiments. The first bind each individual to the person of his fellow-citizens: these are manifest within the community, in the day-to-day relationships of life. These include the sentiments of honour, respect, affection and fear which we may feel towards one another. The second are those which bind me to the social entity as a whole; these manifest themselves primarily in the relationships of the society with other societies, and could be called 'inter-social'. The first leave my autonomy and personality almost intact. No doubt they tie me to others, but without taking much of my independence from me. When I act under the influence of the second, by contrast, I am simply a part of a whole, whose actions I follow, and whose influence I am subject to. This is why the latter alone can give rise to the idea of obligation. Which of these two inclinations are those which have played a role in the genesis of religion? According to Guyau, it is the first. The relationships which unite man to the divinity are presumed to be analogous to those which link him with other members of the society: they are personal. Now the facts seem to prove the opposite. Among primitive peoples and even in later societies, gods are not the recognised protectors, or enemies, of the individual, but of the society (tribe, clan, family, city, etc.). The particular individual has no right to their assistance, nor cause to fear their hostility, except as a by-product of these. If he enters into relationship with the gods, it is not personally, but as a member of a society: it is the latter which is directly persecuted or favoured. This is because the natural forces which manifest some degree of exceptional power are again of less interest to the isolated individual than to the group as a whole. It is the whole tribe which is threatened by thunder, which benefits from rain, which a hail-storm damages, etc. Thus, among the cosmic forces, only those are accorded divinity which have a collective interest. In other words, it is inter-social factors which have given birth to the religious sentiment. Religious society is only human society stretched ideally to beyond the stars; the gods were not conceived of as members of the tribe, but formed one, or rather several societies located in specific, separate regions, some of which were friendly, others hostile, and with which men have entered into relationships of an international character. This hypothesis not only conforms more closely to the facts, it also allows us to explain why the superstitious natural philosophy of religion is obligatory, while that of the scholars is not. It is because everything which interests the collectivity in fact quickly becomes an imperative law; society does not allow its members to act with impunity in a way contrary to the social interest. This is also how the parallels, and the differences, between ethical commands and those of religion may be explained. Such is the second correction which we venture to make to Guyau's theory.

These intellectualist tendencies are naturally again to be found in the two concluding parts of Guyau's work, in which he describes how religions are in the process of disappearing, and what will survive of them. Thus he attributes a preponderant role to science and the critical spirit in bringing about this decomposition. If the only fault with religions was that they were out of accord with scientific truths, they would still be in good health. If, in spite of this conflict, society continued to have need of religious faith, they would not have been censured for contravening science; or rather religions would have been modified and adapted to the new ideas, since nothing indicates that the religious agency has reached the maximum flexibility and plasticity which it is capable of. In fact, if we consider one after the other the arguments which science can bring to bear against religion, we can see that, although they may be strong enough to fortify the sceptic in his opinion, there is not one which is of a kind to convert a believer. It is not with logic that one puts an end to faith. For logic can equally well serve to defend as to question; in order to validate religion, the theologian has recourse to reasoning which is as estimable as that which the free thinker advances to refute it. We might perhaps admit that, among highly cultivated minds, beliefs have become flexible enough in order to surrender to a single proof; but it will still be recognised that this is not the case with the vast majority. Since faith results from practical causes, it necessarily continues in existence for as long as these do, whatever is the state of science and philosophy. In order to show that religion has no future, it must be shown that the reasons which made its existence necessary have disappeared; and since these reasons are of a sociological order, we must discover what change has occurred in the nature of society which from now on makes religion futile and impossible.

In the same way, to be able to say that it will survive we have to know which of the social causes that have maintained it for such a long time will survive. We can then see that if something essential must remain of religion, it is not the metaphysical sentiment and the taste for grand syntheses. What, moreover, guarantees that metaphysics must be eternal? The great service which it rendered to science was to remind it constantly that it had limits, and that is why it has endured. But why should it not happen one day that this feeling of the limits of our science, confirmed by long experience, should not penetrate science itself, and become an integral element of the scientific spirit? Might one not even say that this development is in the process of being accomplished at the present time? From then on it would no longer be necessary to perpetually demonstrate a truth which no-one would dispute. It may be replied to this that the mind aspires to escape from its limits. It remains to be seen whether this aspiration is legitimate and reasonable, and if the constant reverses will not eventually discourage man from it. Is there not, in addition, something of a contradiction in declaring that knowledge is limited, and yet immediately trying to break out of these limits?

RP, 1887(a), pp. 308–11

It has often been said that religion was, at each moment of history, the totality of beliefs and sentiments of all sorts relative to the relations of man with a being or beings whose nature he regarded as superior to his own. But such a definition is manifestly inadequate. In point of fact, there is a vast number of rules, either of conduct or of thought, which are certainly religious, but which apply to relations of an entirely different sort. Religion forbids the Jews to eat certain meats and orders them to dress in a certain fixed way. It imposes such and such an option concerning the nature of man and things, or concerning the origin of the world. It often governs even juridical, moral, and economic relations. Its sphere of action extends, then, beyond the interaction of man with the divine. We know for certain, moreover, that a religion without a god exists (Buddhism). This alone should be sufficient to show that we should not continue to define religion in terms of the idea of god. Finally, if the extraordinary authority that the believer attributes to the divinity can account for the particular prestige of everything religious, it remains to be explained how men have been led to give such authority to a being who, so everyone avers, is in many cases, if not always, a product of the imagination. Nothing comes from nothing; this force must come to the individual from somewhere, and consequently, this formula does not get to the heart of the matter.

But this element aside, the only characteristic that all religious ideas and sentiments share equally seems to be that they are common to a certain number of people living together, and that they are also normally very intense. It is, indeed, a universal fact that, when a conviction of any strength is held by the same community of men, it inevitably takes on a religious character. It inspires in men's minds the same reverential respect as beliefs which are properly religious. It is, thus, very probable – this brief exposition, of course, is not rigorous proof – that religion corresponds to an equally very central area of the *conscience collective*.

DTS, pp. 142–3

Truly religious beliefs are always common to a specific group which professes to adhere to them and to practise the rites connected with them. They are not merely received individually by all the members of the group; they are what gives the group its unity. The individuals who compose the group feel themselves bound to each other by the very fact that they have a common faith. A society whose members are united by the fact that they represent the sacred world and its relations with the profane world in the same way, and by the fact that they translate these common ideas into common practices, is what we call a 'church'. In all history, we do not find a single religion without a church. Sometimes the church is strictly national, sometimes it cuts across frontiers; sometimes it covers an entire people (Rome, Athens, the Hebrews), sometimes only a part of them (the Christian societies since the advent of Protestantism); sometimes it is directed by a priesthood, sometimes it is almost completely devoid of any official directing body. But wherever we observe religious life, we find that it has a definite group as its foundation. Even the so-called 'private cults', such as the domestic cult or the corporative cult, satisfy this condition; for they are always celebrated by a group: the family or the corporation. Moreover, even these individual religions are ordinarily only special forms of a more general religion which embraces them all. These restricted churches are in reality only chapels of a vaster church which, by reason of this very extensiveness, merits this name still more.

It is quite another matter with magic. To be sure, magical beliefs always involve some degree of generality; they are very frequently diffused throughout large sectors of the population, and there are even societies where magic has as many adherents as religion as such. But it does not result in binding together those who adhere to it, nor in uniting them into a group leading a similar life. *There is no church of magic.* Between the magician and the individuals who consult him, as between these individuals themselves, there are no lasting bonds which make them members of the same moral community, comparable to that formed by the believers in the same god or the followers of the same cult. The magician has a clientele, not a church, and it is very possible that his clients have no relationships with one-another, or even do not know each other. Even the relationships which they do have with him are generally casual and transient; they are just like those of a sick man with his doctor. The official and public character which the magician is sometimes invested changes nothing in this situation: the fact that he works openly does not unite him more regularly or more permanently to those who have recourse to his services.

It is true that in certain cases magicians form societies among themselves. It happens that they come together in some sort of regular way to celebrate certain rites in common; it is well known what a place meetings of witches hold in European folk-lore. But it can be seen that these assemblies are in no way necessary to the working of magic; they are even rare and rather exceptional. The magician has no need of uniting himself to his fellows to practise his art. More frequently, he is a recluse; in general, far from seeking society, he flees from it. . .Religion, on the other hand, is inseparable from the idea of a church. From this aspect alone there is already an essential difference between magic and religion. But what is especially important, in addition, is that when these societies of magic are formed, they do not include all those who use the magic, but only the magicians; the 'laymen', if they may be so called – that is to say, those for whose benefit the rites are celebrated – in short, those who represent the worshippers in the regular cults, are excluded. Now the magician is for magic what the priest is for religion, but a college of priests is not a church, any more than a religious congregation which devotes itself to some particular saint in the shadow of a cloister, is a proper cult. A church is not simply a fraternity of priests, it is a moral community formed by all the believers in a single faith, laymen as well as priests. But magic normally lacks any such community. . .

Thus we arrive at the following definition: *A religion is a unified system of beliefs and practices relative to sacred things, that is to say, things set apart and forbidden – beliefs and practices which unite into a single moral community, called a 'church', all those who adhere to them.*

FE, pp. 60 and 65

THE GENESIS OF RELIGIOUS PHENOMENA

Ordinarily. . .[the clan] is regarded as simply a group of human beings. Being a mere subdivision of the tribe, it seems that, like the latter, it is made up of nothing but men. But in reasoning thus, we substitute our European ideas for those which the primitive has of the world and of society. For the Australian, things themselves, everything which is in the universe, are a part of the tribe; they are constituent elements of it and, so to speak, permanent members of it; thus, like men, they have a determined place in the framework of the society. . .

We have seen that totemism places the image or representation of the totem highest among those things it considers sacred; next come the animals or vegetables whose name the clan bears, and finally the members of the clan. Since all these things are sacred in the same way, although in differing degrees, their religious character cannot be due to any specific attributes distinguishing them from each other. If a certain type of animal or vegetable is the object of a reverential fear, this is not because of its special properties, for the human members of the clan enjoy this same privilege, though to a slightly lesser degree; and the mere image of this same plant or animal inspires an even more defined respect. The parallel sentiments inspired by these different sorts of things in the mind of the believer, which give them their sacred character, can evidently come only from some principle common to each: to the totemic emblems, the members of the clan and the species serving as the totem. In reality, it is to this common principle that the cult is addressed. In other words, totemism is the religion, not of such and such animals or men or images, but of an anonymous and impersonal force, found in each of these beings but not to be confused with any of them. No-one possesses it entirely and all share in it. It is so wholly independent of the particular subjects in whom it incarnates itself that it precedes them and survives them. Individuals die, generations pass away and are replaced by others; but this force always remains the same, real and vital. It inspires the generations of today as it did those of yesterday and as it will those of tomorrow. Using the word in a very broad sense, we may say that it is the god worshipped by each totemic cult. But it is an impersonal god, without name or history, immanent in the world and diffused in an endless diversity of things.

But this still gives us only an inadequate idea of the real ubiquity of this quasi-divine entity. It is not merely found in the whole totemic species, the whole clan and all the objects symbolising the totem: the circle of its action extends beyond that. In fact. . .in addition to these most holy things, all those attributed to the clan as dependent upon the principal totem have this same character to a certain degree. They also have something religious about them, for some are protected by interdictions, while others have determined functions in the ceremonies of the cult. Their religiosity does not differ in kind from that of the totem under which they are classified; it thus necessarily derives from the same source. It is because the totemic 'god' – to use again the metaphorical expression which we have just employed – is in them, just as it is in the species serving as totem and in the members of the clan. We can see that it is distinct from the beings in which it is present from the fact that it is the essence of so many different beings.

But the Australian does not represent this impersonal force in an abstract form. Under the influence of causes which we must examine, he has been led to conceive it under the form of an animal or vegetable species: in short as a visible object. This is what the totem really consists in: it is simply the material form in which the imagination represents this immaterial substance, this energy diffused through a variety of different things, which alone is the real object of the cult. We are now in a better situation to understand what a man means when he says that the men of the Crow phratry, for example, are crows. He does not exactly mean to say that they are crows in the everyday, empirical sense of the term, but that the same principle is found in all of them, which is their most essential characteristic, which they have in common with the animals of the same name and which is thought of under the external form of a crow. Thus the universe, as totemism conceives it, is pervaded and animated by a certain number of forces which the imagination represents in forms taken, with only a few exceptions, from the animal or vegetable kingdoms. There are as many of them as there are clans in the tribe, and each of them is also found in certain categories of things, of which it is the essence and vital principle.

When we say that these principles are forces, we do not use the word in a metaphorical sense; they act just like real forces. In one sense, they are even material forces which mechanically engender physical effects. If an individual comes in contact with them without having taken proper precautions, he receives a shock comparable to the effect of an electric discharge. Sometimes this is conceived of as a sort of fluid escaping through the extremities of the body. If they are introduced into an organism not made to receive them, they produce sickness and death by a wholly automatic action. Outside of man, they play the role of vital principle; it is by acting on them, we shall see, that the reproduction of the species is assured. It is upon them that the universal life rests.

But in addition to this physical aspect, they also have a moral character. When someone asks a native why he observes his rites, he replies that his ancestors always have observed them, and that he must follow their example. So if he acts in a certain way towards the totemic beings, it is not only because the forces resident in them are physically formidable, but because he feels himself morally obliged to act in this way; he feels that he is obeying an imperative, that he is fulfilling a duty. He does not just fear these sacred beings, he also respects them. Moreover, the totem is the source of the moral life of the clan. All the beings sharing the same totemic principle consider that owing to this very fact, they are morally bound to one-another; they have definite duties of assistance, vendetta, etc., towards each other; and it is these duties which constitute kinship. So while the totemic principle is a totemic force, it is also a moral power; and we shall see how it easily transforms itself into a divinity properly so-called.

Moreover, there is nothing here which is specific to totemism. Even in the most advanced religions, there is scarcely a god who has not kept something of this ambiguity and whose functions are not at once cosmic and moral. At the same time that it is a spiritual discipline, every religion is also a means enabling men to face the world with greater confidence. Even for the Christian, is not God the Father the guardian of the physical order as well as the legislator and the judge of human conduct? . . .

We are now better able to see why it has been impossible to define religion in terms of the idea of mythical personalities, gods or spirits; it is because this way of representing religious things is in no way inherent in their nature. What we find at the origin and basis of religious thought are not definite and distinct objects and beings possessing a sacred character of themselves; but abstract powers, anonymous forces, more or less numerous in different societies, and sometimes even reduced to a unity, whose impersonality is strictly comparable to that of the physical forces whose manifestations are studied by the natural sciences. As for particular sacred things, they are only individualised forms of this underlying principle. So it is not surprising that even in the religions where there are specific divinities, there are rites having an effective value in themselves, independently of all divine intervention. It is because this force may be attached to words that are pronounced or actions that are carried out just as well as to corporal substances; the voice or the actions may serve as its vehicle, and it may produce its effects through their mediation, without the aid of any god or spirit. Even should it happen to concentrate itself especially in a rite, this will become a creator of divinities by that very fact. That is why there is scarcely a divine personality who does not retain a quality of impersonality. Those who conceive it most clearly in a concrete and visible form, think of it both as an abstract power which cannot be defined except by its own efficacy and as a force spread out in space, which is contained, at least in part, in each of its effects. It is the power of producing rain or wind, crops or the light of day; Zeus is in each of the raindrops which falls, just as Ceres is in each of the

sheaves of the harvest. As a general rule, in fact, this efficacy is
so unclearly specified that the believer is able to form only a very
vague notion of it. Moreover, it is this lack of clarity which has
made possible the mergings and duplications in the course of
which gods are broken up, dismembered and confused in every
way. Perhaps there is not a single religion in which the original
mana, whether unique or multiform, has resolved entirely into a
clearly defined number of beings who are distinct and separate
from each other; each of them always retains an element of impersonality, as it were, which enables it to enter into new combinations, not as the result of a simple survival, but because it is
the nature of religious forces to be unable to individualise themselves completely.

FE, pp. 200–1, 268–72 and 285–7

When individual minds are not isolated, but enter into close relation with, and act upon, each other, from their synthesis arises
a new kind of psychic life. It is clearly distinct from that led by
the solitary individual because of its unusual intensity. Sentiments created and developed in the group have a greater energy
than purely individual sentiments. A man who experiences such
sentiments feels that he is dominated by forces which he does
not recognise as his own, and which he is not the master of, but
is led by; and everything in this situation in which he is sub-
merged seems to be shot through with forces of the same kind.
He feels himself in a world quite distinct from that of his own
private existence. This is a world not only more intense in
character, but also qualitatively different. Following the collectivity, the individual forgets himself for the common end and his
conduct is directed by reference to a standard outside himself. At
the same time, owing to their abstract nature, these forces are not
easily controlled, canalised and adjusted to clearly defined ends.
They necessarily overflow, for the sake of overflowing, as in play
without any specific objective, at one time in the form of stupid
destructive violence or, at another, of heroic folly. It is in a sense a
luxurious activity since it is extremely rich. For all these reasons
this activity is qualitatively different to the everyday life of the
individual, as is the superior to the inferior, the ideal to the
real.

It is, in fact, at such moments of collective ferment that are
born the great ideals upon which civilisations rest. These periods
of creation or renewal occur when men for various reasons are
led into a closer relationship with each other, when gatherings

and assemblies are more frequent, relationships closer and the exchange of ideas more active. Such was the great crisis of Christendom, the movement of collective enthusiasm which, in the twelfth and thirteenth centuries, bringing together in Paris the scholars of Europe, gave birth to Scholasticism. Such were the Reformation and Renaissance, the revolutionary epoch, and the socialist upheavals of the nineteenth century. At such moments this higher form of life is lived with such intensity and exclusiveness that it monopolises all minds to the more or less complete exclusion of egoism and the everyday. At such times the ideal tends to become one with the real, and for this reason men have the impression that the time is close when the ideal will in fact be realised and the Kingdom of God established on earth. This illusion can never last, because the exaltation cannot maintain itself at such a pitch; it is too exhausting. Once the critical moment has passed, social life relaxes again, intellectual and emotional intercourse is moderated, and individuals fall back to their ordinary level. Everything that was said, done and thought during this period of creative upheaval survives only as a memory, a memory no doubt as glorious as the reality it recalls, but with which it is no longer at one. It exists as an idea or rather as a totality of ideas. Between what is felt and perceived and what is thought of in the form of ideals there is now a clear distinction. Nevertheless these ideals could not survive if they were not periodically revived. This revival is the function of religious or secular feasts and ceremonies, public addresses in churches or schools, plays and exhibitions – in a word, whatever draws men together into an intellectual and moral communion. These are, as it were, minor versions of the great creative movement; but they have only a temporary effect. For a short time the ideal comes to life and approaches reality, but it soon becomes again differentiated from it.

SP, pp. 133–5

A god is not merely an authority upon whom we depend, but a force upon which our strength relies. The man who has obeyed his god and who for this reason believes the god is with him, approaches the world with confidence and with the feeling of increased energy. Similarly, social action does not confine itself to demanding sacrifices, privations and efforts from us. For the collective force is not entirely outside us, and does not act upon us wholly from without; but rather, since society cannot exist except in and through individual consciousness, this force must also penetrate us and organise itself within us. It thus becomes an integral part of our being and by that very fact this is elevated and magnified.

There are occasions when this strengthening and enlivening action of society is particularly manifest. In the midst of an assembly inspired by a shared emotion, we become capable of acts and sentiments which we are unable to pursue when reduced to our own forces; and when the gathering is dissolved and, finding ourselves alone again, we fall back to our ordinary level, we are then able to measure the height to which we have been raised above ourselves. History abounds in examples of this sort. It is enough to think of the night of the Fourth of August, 1789, when an assembly was suddenly led to an act of sacrifice and self-denial which each of its members had refused the day before, and at which they were all surprised the day after. This is why all forms of political, economic or religious groups are careful to have periodical reunions where their members may revive their common faith by manifesting it in common. To strengthen sentiments which, if left to themselves, would soon weaken, it is sufficient to bring those who hold them together and to put them into closer and more active relations with one-another. This is the explanation of the highly unusual attitude of a man speaking to a crowd, at least if he has succeeded in entering into communion with it. His language has a grandiloquence that would be ridiculous in ordinary circumstances; his gestures are rather domineering; his very thought is impatient of restriction and easily falls into all sorts of excesses. It is because he feels within him an unusual plethora of forces which overflow and emanate from him. Sometimes he actually has the feeling that he is dominated by a moral force which is greater than himself, for which he is merely the spokesman. This is the characteristic of what has often been called the 'demon' of oratorical inspiration. Now this extraordinary growth in power is something very real; it derives from the very group which he addresses. The sentiments provoked by his words come back to him, but enlarged and amplified, and to this degree they strengthen his own feeling. The passionate energies he arouses react within him and further his dynamic attitude. It is no longer merely an individual who speaks; it is a group incarnate and personified.

In addition to these temporary or transient occurrences, there are others which are more permanent, where this strengthening influence of society makes itself felt with more significant consequences and frequently with even greater impact. There are periods in history when, under the influence of some great social upheaval, social interaction becomes much more frequent and active. Men seek each other's company and assemble together more often. The general effervescence results which is characteristic of revolutionary or creative epochs. Now this greater activity results in a general stimulation of individual forces. Men see more and differently than in normal times. The changes which occur are not merely limited and small-scale: men become other than themselves. The emotions which move them are of such an intensity that they cannot be satisfied except by violent and unrestrained actions, actions of superhuman heroism or of bloody barbarism. This is what explains the Crusades for example, or many of the scenes, either sublime or savage, of the French Revolution. Under the influence of the general exaltation, we see the most mediocre and inoffensive bourgeois become either a hero or a butcher. And so clearly are all these mental processes the ones that are also at the root of religion that the individuals themselves have often pictured the pressure, in the face of which they thus gave way, in a distinctly religious form. The Crusaders believed that they felt God present in the midst of them, enjoining them to go to the conquest of the Holy Land; Joan of Arc believed that she obeyed celestial voices.

But it is not only in these extraordinary circumstances that this stimulating action of society makes itself felt; there is not, so to speak, a moment in our lives when some current of energy does not come to us from outside. The man who has carried out his duty finds, in the various expressions of the sympathy, esteem or affection which his fellows have for him, a feeling of comfort, of which he does not ordinarily take account, but which sustains him nonetheless. The feeling which society has for him enhances the feeling which he has for himself. Because he is in moral unison with his fellow men, he has more confidence, courage and boldness in action, just like the believer who thinks that he feels the regard of his god turned graciously towards him. It thus produces, as it were, a perpetual support for our moral nature. Since this fluctuates with a variety of external circumstances, in relation to the degree to which we are actively involved in the social groups which surround us, and to the differences between these groups themselves, we cannot fail to feel that this moral support depends upon an external cause; but we do not perceive what this is, or where it derives from. So we ordinarily conceive of it in the form of a moral power which, though immanent in us, represents within us something other than ourselves. This is the moral consciousness – which, moreover, men have never represented clearly except with the aid of religious symbols.

In addition to these freely-moving forces which are constantly helping to renew our own, there are others which are fixed in the methods and traditions which we employ. We speak a language that we did not make; we use instruments that we did not invent; we invoke rights that we did not found; a fund of knowledge is passed on to each generation which it did not accumulate for itself, etc. It is to society that we owe these varied benefits of civilisation, and if we do not ordinarily perceive the source from which we get them, we at least know that they are not our own creations. Now it is these which give man his special place among living beings. Man is human only because he is socialised. So he cannot escape the feeling that outside him there are active causes from which he acquires the characteristic attributes of his nature and which, as benevolent powers, assist him, protect him, and assure him of a privileged position. And he necessarily assigns to these powers a dignity corresponding to the high value of the good works he attributes to them.

Thus the environment in which we live seems to us to be peopled with forces that are at once imperious and helpful, august and gracious, and which relate to ourselves. Since they exercise over us a pressure which we are conscious of, we are forced to localise them outside ourselves, just as we do for the objective causes of our sensations. But the sentiments which they inspire in us are of a different nature to those which concern ordinary sensory objects. As long as these latter are perceived in terms of their empirical characteristics, as manifest in everyday experience, and as long as the religious imagination has not metamorphosed them, we hold them in no feeling of respect, and they contain within them nothing that is able to raise us above ourselves. Consequently the representations which express them appear to us to be very different from those aroused in us by collective influences. The two form two distinct and separate mental states in our consciousness, just as do the two forms of life to which they correspond. Thus we feel that we stand in relationship with two distinct sorts of reality, and that a sharply drawn line of demarcation separates them from each other: on the one hand is the world of profane things, on the other, that of sacred things.

FE, pp. 299–304

THE FUNCTIONS OF RITUAL

By definition, sacred beings are separate beings. Their principal characteristic is that there is a break in continuity between them and profane beings. Normally, the first are kept separate from the others. A whole group of rites has the object of ensuring that this state of separation, which is essential, is maintained. Since their function is to prevent illegitimate mixings, and to keep one of these two domains from encroaching upon the other, they impose only abstentions, that is, negative acts. For this reason, we propose to give the name 'negative cult' to the system formed by these special rites. They do not prescribe certain acts to the faithful, but confine themselves to forbidding certain modes of conduct; thus they all take the form of interdictions, or as is usually said in ethnography, *taboos*...

. . .owing to the barrier which separates the sacred from the profane, a man cannot enter into intimate relations with sacred things until he has rid himself of all that is profane in him. He cannot lead a religious lfe of any intensity unless he first withdraws more or less completely from temporal life. So the negative cult is in a sense a means to an end: it is a condition of access to the positive cult. It does not confine itself to protecting sacred things from contact with the everyday; it acts upon the worshipper himself and modifies his condition positively. The man who has submitted himself to its given prohibitions is not the same afterwards as he was before. Previously, he was an ordinary being who, for this reason, had to keep at a distance from religious forces. Afterwards, he is on a more equal footing with them; he has approached the sacred by the very act of leaving the profane. He has purified and sanctified himself by the very act of detaching himself from the impure and trivial characteristics that debased his nature. So negative rites confer effective powers just as much as positive rites; the first, like the second, can serve to elevate the religious tone of the individual. As has been very correctly observed, no-one can participate in a religious ceremony of any importance without first submitting himself to a sort of preliminary initiation which introduces him progressively into the sacred world. Unctions, lustrations, benedictions or any essentially positive operation may be used for this purpose; but the same result may be attained by means of fasts and vigils or retreat and silence, that is to say, by ritual abstinences, which are nothing more than definite prohibitions put into practice...

However important the negative cult may be, and though it may indirectly have positive effects, it does not contain its reason for existence in itself; it introduces men to religious activity, but it supposes this more than it constitutes it. If it orders the worshipper to flee from the profane world, it is to bring him nearer to the sacred world. Men have never believed that their obligations towards religious forces could be reduced simply to abstinence from all relationships; they have always considered that they upheld positive and bilateral relations with them, whose regulation and organisation is governed by a set of ritual practices. To this special system of rites we give the name of *'positive cult'*. . .

If sacred beings always manifested their powers in a perfectly homogeneous way, it would seem impossible that men should dream of offering them services, for there would be no need which they could have for them. But in fact, in so far as they are confused with things, and in so far as they are regarded as principles of cosmic life, they are themselves submitted to the rhythm of this life. Now this fluctuates in opposite ways, which succeed one another in a definite manner. Sometimes it is affirmed in all its glory; sometimes it weakens to such an extent that one may ask himself whether it is not going to fade away. Vegetation dies every year; will it be reborn? Animal species tend to become extinguished by the effect of natural and violent death; will they be renewed at such a time and in such a way as is required? Above all, the rain is capricious; there are long periods during which it seems to have disappeared for ever. These periodical variations of nature bear witness to the fact that at the corresponding periods, the sacred beings upon whom the plants, animals, rain, etc., depend are themselves passing through the same states of crisis; so they, too, have their periods of failure. But man cannot watch these occurrences as an indifferent spectator. If he is to live, the life of the universe must continue, and consequently the gods must not die. So he seeks to sustain and aid them; he puts at their service whatever forces he has at his disposition which he can muster for this purpose. The blood flowing in his veins has fertilising properties; he pours it forth. From the sacred rocks possessed by his clan he takes those germs of life which lie dormant there, and scatters them into space. In a word, he makes offerings.

These external and physical crises, moreover, duplicate internal and mental crises which tend toward the same result. Sacred beings exist only when they are represented as such in the mind. When we cease to believe in them, it is as though they did not exist. Even those which have a material form and are given in sensory experience depend in this way upon the thought of the worshippers who adore them; for the sacred character which makes them objects of the cult is not given by the natural consti-

tution, but is superimposed upon them by belief. The kangaroo
is only an animal like all others; yet, for the men of the Kangaroo,
it contains within it a principle which sets it apart from others,
and this principle exists only in the minds of those who believe in
it. If these sacred beings, once conceived, had no need of men to
continue, the representations expressing them would always remain the same. But this stability is impossible. In fact, it is in
group life that they are formed, and this is essentially intermittent.
So they necessarily share this same intermittency. They attain
their greatest intensity at the moment when men are assembled
together and are in immediate relations with one-another, when
they all share the same idea and the same sentiment. But when
the assembly has broken up and each man has returned to his own
particular life, they progressively lose their original energy. Being
overlain progressively by the rising flood of daily experiences, they
would soon fall into the unconscious, if we did not find some
means of recalling them into consciousness and revitalising them.
Now they cannot weaken without the sacred beings losing their
reality, since these beings only exist in and through them. If we
think of them less forcefully, they amount to less for us and we
count less upon them: they exist to a lesser degree. So here is
another way in which the services of men are necessary to them.
This second reason for their existence is even more important than
the first, for it is there permanently. The intermittent character
of physical life can affect religious beliefs only when religions
are not yet detached from their cosmic basis. The intermittency of
the social life, on the other hand, is inevitable: even the most
idealistic religions cannot escape it.

Moreover it is because of the fact that the existence of gods
depends upon human thought that men are able to believe in the
effectiveness of divine assistance. The only way of renewing the
collective representations which relate to sacred beings is to
retemper them in the very source of religious life, that is to say, in
assembled groups. Now the emotions aroused by these periodical
crises through which external reality passes induce the men who
witness them to assemble, to discover what should be done. But
by the very fact of uniting, they find mutual reassurance; they find
the answer because they seek it together. Common faith becomes
quite naturally revived in the heart of this reconstituted group;
it is reborn because it again meets the very conditions in which it
was created in the first place. After having been restored, it easily
triumphs over all the private doubts which may have arisen in
individual minds. The image of sacred things regains enough

strength to resist the internal or external causes which tended to weaken it. In spite of their apparent failure, men can no longer believe that the gods will die, because they feel them living in their own hearts. The means employed to support them, howsoever crude these may be, cannot appear vain, because everything proceeds as if they were really effective. Men are more confident because they feel themselves stronger; and they really are stronger, because forces which were languishing are now reawakened in consciousness...

However much they may differ from one another in the nature of the acts they imply, the positive rites which we have looked at have one common characteristic: they are all performed in a state of confidence, joy and even enthusiasm. Although the expectation of a future and contingent event is not without some uncertainty, still it is normal that the rain falls when the season for it comes, and that the animal and vegetable species reproduce regularly. Experience, repeated often, shows that rites generally do produce the effects which are expected of them and which are the reason for their existence. Men celebrate them with confidence, joyfully anticipating the happy event which they prepare and announce. The actions performed in these rites share in this state of mind: of course, they are characterised by the seriousness which always marks any religious ceremonial, but this excludes neither liveliness nor joy.

These are all joyful feasts. But there are sad celebrations as well, whose object is either to meet a calamity, or else quite simply to remember, and deplore it. These rites have a special character, which we must attempt to identify and explain. It is all the more necessary to study them separately since they will reveal to us a new aspect of religious life.

We propose to call the ceremonies of this sort 'piacular'. The term *piaculum* has the advantage that while it suggests the idea of expiation, it also had a much broader meaning. Every misfortune, everything of evil omen, everything that inspires sentiments of sorrow or fear, necessitates a *piaculum* and is therefore called *piacular*. So this word seems very suitable for designating the rites which are celebrated by those in a state of uneasiness or sadness...

...evil powers are the product of these rites and symbolise them. When a society is going through circumstances which sadden, worry or irritate it, it exercises a pressure upon its members to give evidence, by various significant actions, of their own sorrow, anxiety, or anger. It imposes upon them the duty of weeping, groaning or inflicting wounds upon themselves or others, for these collective manifestations, and the moral communion which they show and strengthen, restore to the group the energy which circumstances threaten to take away from it, and thus they enable it to become settled. It is this experience which men interpret when they imagine that outside them there are evil beings whose hostility, whether permanent or temporary, can be appeased only by human suffering. These beings are thus collective states objectified; they are society itself seen under one of its aspects. We know, moreover, that the beneficent powers are formed in the same way; they, too, result from the collective life and express it. They, too represent society, but seen under a very different aspect: that is, at the moment when it confidently affirms itself and ardently presses on towards the realisation of the ends which it pursues. Since these two sorts of forces have a common origin, it is not at all surprising that, although they are opposed, they have the same nature, that they are equally intense and contagious, and consequently forbidden and sacred.

On this basis, we are able to understand how they change into one-another. Since they reflect the affective mood of the group, it is enough that this mood change for their character to change. After the mourning is over, the domestic group is reassured by the mourning itself: it regains confidence. The anxious pressure which individuals felt exercised over them is relieved; they feel more at ease. Thus, it seems to them as though the spirit of the deceased had laid aside its hostile sentiments and become a benevolent protector...As we have already shown, the sanctity of a thing is due to the collective sentiment of which it is the object. If, in violation of the prohibitions which isolate it, it comes in contact with a profane person, then this same sentiment will spread contagiously to this latter and imprint a special character upon him. But in spreading, it comes into a very different state from the one it was in at first. Offended and irritated by the profanity implied in this abusive and unnatural extension, it becomes aggressive and inclined to destructive violence: it tends to avenge itself for the offence suffered. Therefore the infected subject seems to be filled with a massive and harmful force which threatens everything that approaches him; it is as though he were marked with a stain or blemish. Yet the cause of this blemish is the same psychic state which, in other circumstances, consecrates and sanctifies. But if the anger thus aroused is satisfied by an expiatory rite, it subsides, alleviated; the offended sentiment is conciliated and returns to its original state. So it acts once more as it acted in the beginning; instead of contaminating, it sanctifies. As it continues to pervade the object to which it is attached, this can never become profane and religiously neutral again. But the direction of the religious force with which it seems to be filled is inverted: from being impure, it has become pure and an instrument of purification.

FE, pp. 428, 441–2, 465, 491–4, 556–7 and 589–91

12. Secularisation and rationality

THE DEVELOPMENT OF CHRISTIANITY

The religions of Antiquity are, above all, systems of rites, the essential objective of which is to assure the regular working of the universe. For the wheat to spring up and yield an abundant harvest, the rivers to flow, and the stars to move in their appointed paths, the gods of the harvest, the gods of the rivers, and the gods of the stars must subsist, and it is the rites which allow them to do so. If they ceased to take place on the established days, and in the prescribed manner, the life of the universe would come to an end. It is understandable that the attention of the Greek should be entirely directed towards the outside, where, according to him, the principle of existence is to be found.

By contrast, Christian religion is centred in man himself, in the soul of man. An essentially idealistic religion, its god aspires to reign over the world of ideas, over the spiritual world, and not that of the body. To worship the gods of Antiquity was to maintain their material life with the help of offerings and sacrifices, since their life depended upon that of the world; the god of the Christians, on the other hand, wishes to be worshipped, as the phrase expresses it, in spirit and in truth. For him, to be, is to be believed, to be thought, to be loved. Everything thus inclines the Christian to turn his thought towards himself, because the source of life is to be found within himself: I mean true life, that which counts most in his eyes, the life of the spirit. The very specific characteristics of the practices of the creed makes this concentration upon himself necessary. The most common rite is prayer; and prayer is an internal meditation. Since for the Christian, virtue and piety do not consist in material acts, but in internal states of the soul, he is compelled to keep a perpetual surveillance over himself. Since he is obliged to perpetually examine his conscience, he must learn to question himself, to analyse himself and scrutinise his intentions: in short, to reflect upon himself. Thus, of the two possible poles of all thought, nature on the one hand, and man on the other, it is necessarily around the second that the thought of the Christian societies and consequently also their system of education, has come to gravitate.

In a word, with Christianity, the world lost the confused unity which it possessed formerly, and split into two parts, two halves of very unequal value: there is, on the one hand, the world of thought, consciousness, morality and religion, and on the other the world of inanimate matter, amoral and a-religious.

EPF, pp. 322–3

It has sometimes been said that primitive peoples had no morality. That was an historical error. There is no society without morality. However, the morality of undeveloped societies is distinct from ours. What characterises them is precisely that they are essentially religious. By that, I mean that the most numerous and important duties are not the duties of man toward other men, but of man toward his gods. The principal obligations are not to respect one's neighbour, to help him, to assist him; but to accomplish meticulously the prescribed rites, to give to the gods what is their due, and even, if need be, to sacrifice one's self to their glory. As for human morality, it is limited to a small number of principles, whose violation is repressed less severely. These peoples are only on the threshold of morality. Even in Greece, murder occupied a much lower place in the scale of crimes than serious acts of impiety. In these conditions, moral education could only be essentially religious, as was morality itself. Only religious ideas could serve as the basis for an education that, before everything, had as its chief aim to teach man the manner in which he ought to behave towards religious beings. But, gradually, things change. Gradually, human obligations become multiplied, more precise, and of primary importance; while others, on the contrary, tend to become diminished. One might say that Christianity itself has contributed most to hastening this result. It is an essentially human religion since its God dies for the salvation of humanity. Christianity teaches that the principal duty of man toward god is to love his neighbour. Although there are religious duties proper – rites addressed only to the divinity – the place they occupy and the importance attributed to them continually diminish. The primary vice is no longer sin: sin now tends to merge with moral transgression. No doubt God continues to play an important part in morality. It is he who assures respect for it and represses its violation. Offences against it are offences against him. But he is now reduced to the role of guardian. Moral discipline was not instituted for him, but for men. He only intervenes to make it effective. Thereafter our duties become independent, in large measure, of the religious notions that guarantee them, but do not form their foundation. With Protestantism, the autonomy of morality is still more accentuated by the fact that ritual itself diminishes. The moral functions of the divinity become his only *raison d'être*. This is the only argument brought forward to demonstrate his existence. Spiritualistic philosophy continues the work of Protestantism. But among the philosophers who believe today in the necessity of supernatural sanctions, there are none who do not admit that morality could be constructed quite independently of any theological conception. Thus, the bond that originally united and even merged the two systems has become looser and looser.

EM, pp. 6–7

Religion, the primary form of the *conscience collective*, originally absorbs all intellectual and practical functions. The former only become separated from the latter when philosophy appears. Now, this is possible only when religion has lost something of its hold. This new mode of representing things clashes with collective opinion, which resists it. It has sometimes been said that it is free enquiry which makes religious beliefs diminish; but this in turn presupposes a preliminary diminution of these very beliefs. It can only develop if the common faith permits.

The same antagonism breaks out each time a new science is founded. Christianity itself, although it rapidly gave individual thought a larger place than any other religion, could not escape this law. To be sure, the conflict was less acute as long as scholars limited their researches to the material world since this was in principle abandoned to the disputes of men. Yet, because this surrender was never complete, as the Christian god does not entirely ignore things of this world, it necessarily happened that, on more than one point, the natural sciences themselves found an obstacle in faith. But it was especially when man became the object of science that the resistance became fierce. The believer, indeed, cannot but find repugnant the idea that man may be studied as a natural being, in the same way as others, and moral facts as facts in nature. It is well known how these collective sentiments, under the different forms they have taken, have hindered the development of psychology and sociology.

DTS, pp. 269–70

The only essential difference between Catholicism and Protestantism is that the second permits free enquiry to a far greater extent than the first. Of course, by the very fact that it is an idealistic religion Catholicism concedes a far greater place to thought and deliberation than Graeco-Latin polytheism or Hebrew monotheism. It is not restricted to mechanical ceremonies, but seeks the control of the consciousness. So it appeals to conscience, and even when demanding blind submission of reason, does so by employing the language of reason. Nonetheless, the Catholic accepts his faith ready made, without scrutiny. He may not even submit it to historical examination since the original texts that serve as its basis are proscribed. A whole hierarchical system of authority is devised, with marvellous ingenuity, to render tradition invariable. All *variation* is abhorrent to Catholic thought. The Protestant is far more the author of his faith. The Bible is put in his hands and no interpretation is imposed upon him. The very structure of the reformed faith stresses this state of religious individualism. Nowhere except in England is the Protestant clergy a hierarchy; like the worshippers, the priest has no other source but himself and his conscience. He is a more educated guide than the majority of believers, but he has no special authority for fixing dogma. But what best proves that this freedom of enquiry proclaimed by the founders of the Reformation has not remained a Platonic affirmation is the increasing profusion of all kinds of sects, which forms such a striking contrast with the indivisible unity of Catholic Church. . .

Free enquiry is only the effect of another cause. When it appears – when men, after having long received their faith, ready-made by tradition, claim the right to shape it for themselves – this is not because of the intrinsic desirability of free inquiry, for the latter involves as much sorrow as happiness. It is because men henceforth need this liberty. This very need can have only one cause: the overthrow of traditional beliefs. If these still maintained the same hold, it would never occur to men to criticise them. If they still had the same authority, men would not demand the right to verify the source of this authority. Considered thought develops only if its development becomes imperative: that is, if certain ideas and instinctive sentiments which have hitherto adequately guided conduct are found to have lost their efficacy. Then conscious deliberation intervenes to fill the gap that has appeared, but which it has not created. Just as conscious thought appears to the extent that thought and action take the form of automatic habits, it awakes only when accepted habits become fragmented. It asserts its rights against collective beliefs only when the latter lose strength, that is, are no longer prevalent to the same extent. If these assertions occur not merely occasionally and as passing crises, but become chronic, if individuals constantly reaffirm their autonomy, it is because they are constantly subject to conflicting impulses, because a new standpoint has not been formed to replace the one no longer existing. If a new system of beliefs were established which seemed to everyone as irrefutable as those existing previously, no-one would think of discussing them any longer. Such discussion would no longer even be permitted; for ideas shared by an active society draw from this consensus an authority that makes them sacrosanct and raises them above dispute. For them to have become more flexible, they must first already have become the object of less general and complete assent and been weakened by preliminary controversy.

Thus, if it is correct to say that free enquiry, once proclaimed, multiplies schisms, it must be added that it presupposes them and derives from them, for it is claimed and instituted as a principle only in order to allow latent or half-declared schisms to develop more freely. So if Protestantism concedes a greater freedom to individual thought than Catholicism, it is because it has fewer common beliefs and practices. Now, a religious society cannot exist without a collective *credo* and the more extensive the *credo*, the more unified and strong is the society. For it does not unite men by an exchange and reciprocity of services, a temporal bond of union which permits and even presupposes differences. A religious society socialises them in proportion as this body of doctrine is extensive and firm. Thus the more numerous the modes of action and thought of a religious character which are removed from free enquiry, the more the idea of God presents itself in all aspects of existence, and makes individual wills converge to one identical goal. Conversely, the greater concessions a religious group makes to individual judgement, the less it dominates men's lives, and the less its cohesion and vitality.

Su, pp. 156–9

THE PERSISTENCE OF RELIGION

. . .there is something eternal in religion which is destined to survive all the particular symbols in which religious thought has successively enveloped itself. There can be no society which does not feel the need of upholding and reaffirming, at regular intervals, the collective sentiments and ideas which give it its unity and individuality. Now this moral reconstruction cannot be achieved except by means of reunions, assemblies and congregations, in which individuals, being brought together, reaffirm in common their common sentiments. From this source arise ceremonies which do not differ from properly religious ceremonies, either in their object, the results which they produce, or the processes employed to attain these results. What essential difference is there between an assembly of Christians celebrating the principal dates of the life of Christ, or Jews remembering the exodus from Egypt or the proclamation of the decalogue, and a gathering of citizens commemorating the institution of a new moral or legal system or some great event in national life?

If we find a little difficulty today in imagining what the feasts and ceremonies of the future could consist in, it is because we are going through a stage of transition and moral mediocrity. The great events of the past which filled our fathers with enthusiasm do not excite the same ardour in us, either because they have come into common usage to such an extent that we are unconscious of them, or else because they no longer answer to our present aspirations; but as yet there is nothing to replace them. We can no longer passionately devote ourselves to the principles in the name of which Christianity recommended that masters treat their slaves humanely; moreover, the idea which Christianity has formed of human equality and fraternity seems to us today to leave too much scope for unjust inequalities. Its pity for the humble seems to us too Platonic; we seek something else, of a more practical kind; but we cannot as yet clearly see what it should be or how it could be realised. In a word, the former gods are growing old or are already dead, and others are not yet born. This is what made Comte's attempt to organise a religion by artificially rejuvenating obsolete historical survivals impracticable: it is life itself, and not a dead past which can produce a living faith. But this state of uncertainty and confused agitation cannot last for ever. A day will come when our societies will again know those hours of creative ferment in the course of which new ideas and new formulas are found which will serve for a time as a guide to humanity; and when these hours have been once experienced, men will spontaneously feel the need of reliving them from time to time in thought, that is to say, of keeping alive their memory by means of celebrations which regularly reproduce their products. We have already seen how the French Revolution established a whole cycle of holidays to perpetually rejuvenate principles with which it was inspired. If this institution quickly lapsed, it was because the revolutionary faith lasted but a short while, and deceptions and discouragements rapidly succeeded the first moments of enthusiasm. But though the attempt may have miscarried, it enables us to imagine what might have happened in other conditions; and everything leads us to believe that it will be taken up again sooner or later. There are no gospels which are immortal, but neither is there any reason for believing that humanity is incapable of inventing new ones. As to the symbols with which this new faith will express itself, whether or not they will resemble those of the past, or be more adequate for the reality which they seek to represent, this is a question which goes beyond the human capacity to predict, and, moreover, is not the main problem.

FE, pp. 609–11

. . .If there is one truth that history teaches us beyond doubt, it is that religion tends to embrace a smaller and smaller sector of social life. Originally, it pervades everything; everything social is religious. The two words are synonymous. Then political, economic, scientific functions gradually free themselves from religious control, establish themselves separately and take on a more and more openly temporal character. God, if one may express the matter this way, was at first present in all human relations, but progressively withdraws from them; he abandons the world to men and their disputes. At least, if he continues to dominate it, it is from on high and at a distance, and the power which he exercises, becoming more general and abstract, leaves more place to the free play of human forces. The individual really feels himself less *acted upon*; he becomes more a source of spontaneous activity. In short, not only does the domain of religion not grow at the same time and in the same measure as temporal life, but it contracts more and more. This regression did not begin at some certain moment of history; we can follow its development from the early phases of social evolution. It is thus linked to the fundamental conditions of the development of societies, and this shows that there is a decreasing number of collective beliefs and sentiments which are both collective and strong enough to assume a religious character.

DTS, pp. 143–4

If it is only to conscious beings that we can be bound by duty, and if we eliminate the individual subject, there remains as the only other possible object of moral activity the *sui generis* collective subject formed by the plurality of individuals joined together in a group. The collective personality must be thought of as something other than the totality of individuals that compose it. If it were only an aggregate, it could have no greater moral value than its component parts, which in themselves have none. We thus arrive at the conclusion that if morality – or system of obligations and duties – exists, society is a moral being qualitatively different from the individuals it comprises, and from the aggregate from which it derives. The similarity between this argument and that of Kant in favour of the existence of God will be noted. Kant postulates God, since within this hypothesis morality is unintelligible. We postulate a society specifically distinct from individuals, since otherwise morality has no object and duty no roots. Let us add that this postulate is easily verified by experience. Although I have often treated this question in my books, it would be easy to give reasons other than those already advanced in defence of this conception.

This argument may be reduced to a number of very simple propositions. It hinges upon the fact that, as is generally accepted, morality begins with disinterestedness and devotion. Disinterestedness becomes meaningful only when its object has a higher moral value that we have as individuals. In the world of experience I know of only one being that possesses a richer and more complex moral reality than our own, and that is the collective being. I am mistaken; there is another being which could play the same part, and that is the divinity. Between God and society lies the choice. I shall not examine here the reasons that may be advanced in favour of either solution, both of which are coherent. I can only add that I myself am quite indifferent to this choice, since I see in the divinity only society transfigured and symbolically expressed.

SP, pp. 74–5

LÉVY-BRUHL AND 'THE ELEMENTARY FORMS'

[Written in review of both Durkheim's own work on religion and Lévy-Bruhl's *Les functions mentales dans les sociétés inférieures*.]

The objective of Lévy-Bruhl's book is to establish that human mentality does not manifest the invariability which certain philosophers, as well as the representatives of the anthropological school, have attributed to it. Beginning from the postulate that types of mentality must vary with types of society, he seeks to describe the mental type which characterises that – poorly defined – group of societies which are ordinary called the 'lower societies'. He is aware that, since very different societies are combined under this term, the corresponding logical type must share the same relative lack of clarity. One can only obtain in this way a very broad type which will include a large number of distinct forms. But, in the present state of research, it is only possible to undertake a general preliminary work; it has to be left to the future to make this more precise.

According to Lévy-Bruhl, primitive mentality is essentially religious or, as he says, mystical. Beings and objects are portrayed in men's minds as having properties that are very different from those revealed by sensory perception. The primitive sees occult powers everywhere, mysterious forces whose existence is in no way verified by experience, nor could it be so verified; they are objects of faith, and experience can no more serve to disconfirm this faith than it can validate it. Thus it is characteristic of this mentality to be refractory to any experimental proof.

In this respect already, the primitive mind is sharply distinct from ours. The way in which he connects his ideas together is no less specific: his logic differs from ours. What dominates the former is what Lévy-Bruhl calls the law of participation, which he expresses in the following way: 'In the collective representations of primitive mentality, in a way which is incomprehensible to us, objects, beings and phenomena can be, at the same time, themselves and other than themselves. In a way which is no less incomprehensible, they emit and imbibe forces, virtues, and qualities, mystical actions which are felt outside of themselves, without moving from where they are.' In short, primitive thought does not obey the principle of contradiction, and this is why Lévy-Bruhl calls it 'prelogical'.

After having thus defined this mentality, Lévy-Bruhl shows how this allows us to explain certain peculiarities of the language, notation, and of the institutions found in these sorts of societies.

The work which we published on *The Elementary Forms of the Religious Life* naturally led us to pose questions similar to or connected with the preceding ones; for we cannot understand the lower religions if we do not study the mentality of the peoples who practise them. Although we did not treat the problem directly, we could not avoid meeting with it in the course of our work, and we did not neglect the occasions which we had to confront it.

There is no need to state that there are fundamental principles which we share in common with Lévy-Bruhl. Like him, we believe that different types of mentality have succeeded each other in history. We also accept – and we have tried to establish this through factual analysis – that primitive mentality is essentially religious; that is to say, that the notions which dominate the movement of ideas are created in the very midst of religion. Moreover, since the main objective of the book is to show that the origins of religion are social, it follows that these notions and the corresponding logic have the same origin. This is what we strove to demonstrate in detail, through analysing the most important of these ideas. However, our point of view is somewhat different from that taken by Lévy-Bruhl. Since the latter is above all preoccupied with differentiating this mentality from ours, he has gone so far as to sometimes present these differences in the form of a real antithesis. Religious and primitive thought on the one hand, and scientific and modern thought on the other, are contrasted as two opposites. In one, the principle of identity and the sovereignty of experience are seen as unquestioned; in the other, there appears to hold sway an almost complete indifference to the lessons of experience and to contradiction. We consider, by contrast, that these two forms of human mentality, however different they may be, far from deriving from different sources, are created one by the other, and are two moments in the same evolution. We have shown, in point of fact, that the most essential ideas of the human mind – ideas of time, space, type and form, force and causality, and personality – those in short, to which philosophers have given the name of 'categories', and which dominate all logical activity, were elaborated within the very centre of religion. Science has borrowed them from religion. There is no gulf between these two stages in the intellectual life of mankind.

At the same time as we established the religious origins of the categories, we showed that they were impregnated with social elements, that they were, indeed, created in the image of social phenomena. Physical space was originally constructed on the model of social space, that is to say, the territory occupied by the society, such as it is represented by society; time expresses the rhythm of collective life; the idea of type was at first only another aspect of the idea of the human group; the collective force and its power over minds served as the prototype of the notion of force and causality, etc. It might appear, it is true, that, because of these origins, these fundamental representations necessarily lack all objective validity, and can only consist in artificial constructions which have no foundation in reality. For society is generally seen as an a-logical or illogical entity, which is in no way capable of satisfying conceptual needs. Thus it is not at first apparent how ideas which are the product of society, and which express it, could be qualified to play such a preponderant role in the history of thought and science. But we endeavoured to show that, contrary to how it may appear, logical life had its initial source in society. The distinguishing feature of the concept, as compared to a sensation or image, is its impersonality: it is a representation which, to the degree to which it preserves its identity, is common and communicable. It can pass from one mind to another; it is by means of concepts that intellects communicate. Now a representation can only be common to all the members of a single group if it was elaborated by them in common, if it is the work of the community. And if conceptual thought has a very special value for us, it is precisely because, being collective, it is replete with all the experience and science that has been accumulated by the community over the course of centuries. The intellectual capacity of society is infinitely greater than that of the individual, for the sole reason that it is the result of the convergence and collaboration of a vast number of intellects, and even of generations. As for those concepts *sui generis* which we call categories, if these are social not only by origin, but also in content, it is because these are the basic concepts: they dominate and envelop all others. 'Now for them to be able to fulfil such a task, they must be shaped by a reality of equal scope.' A conception of 'time' which includes all specific time intervals, of 'space' which comprises all particular extensions, and of overall 'type' which includes all known beings: these can only be the time, space, and the totality of things which is represented by the totality of particular individuals, and which is greater than them. It is society which taught man that there was another point of view than that of the individual, and which made him see things from the perspective of the whole.

Although therefore, human mentality has changed and evolved over the centuries in relation to society, the different types which it has successively manifested have each given rise to the other. The higher and more recent forms are not opposed to the lower and more primitive forms, but are created out of the latter. Indeed, certain of the contrasts which have been pointed out need to be toned down. We have shown, by the use of examples, that if the primitive mind tends towards confusion, it nonetheless recognises defined antitheses, and often applies the principle of contradiction in an extremely definite way. Conversely, the law of participation is not specific to primitive mentality: today as in other ages, our ideas share common characteristics. This is the very condition of all logical activity. The difference is above all in the way in which this participation takes place.

AS, 1912, pp. 33–7

13. Sociology of knowledge

THOUGHT AND REALITY

. . .even the most primitive religions are not, as is sometimes believed, merely phantasies that have no basis in reality. Certainly they do not express the things of the physical world as they are; they have little value as an explanation of reality. But they do interpret, in a symbolic form, social needs and collective interests. They represent the various connections maintained by society with the individuals who go to make it up as well as the things forming part of its substance. And these connections and interests are real. It is through religion that we are able to trace the structure of a society, the stage of unity it has reached and the degree of cohesion of its parts, besides the expanse of the area it inhabits, the nature of the cosmic forces that play a vital role in it, etc. Religions are the primitive way in which societies become conscious of themselves and their history. They are to the social order what sensation is to the individual. We might ask why it is these religions distort things as they do in their processes of imagery. But is it not true that sensation, equally, distorts the things it conveys to the individual? Sound, colour and temperature do not exist in the world any more than gods, demons or spirits do. By the fact alone that the representation presupposes a subject who thinks – (in one case, an individual, in the other, a collective subject) – the nature of this subject is a factor in the representation and distorts the thing represented. The individual, in picturing by means of sensation the relations he has with the world about him, puts into these images something that is not there, some qualities that come from himself. Society does the same in picturing its structure by means of religion. The distortion, however, is not the same in each case, because the subjects differ. It is the task of science to correct these illusions, although in the sphere of practice they are inevitable.

LS, pp. 189–90

[In discussion of pragmatism.]

If the objective of thought were simply to 'reproduce' reality, it would be the slave of things; it would be chained to reality. It would have no role except to 'copy' in a servile fashion the reality that it has before it. If thought is to be freed, it must become the creator of its own object; and the only way to attain this goal is to accord it a reality that it has to make or construct itself. Therefore, *thought has as its aim not the reproduction of a given reality, but the construction of a future reality*. It follows that the value of ideas can no longer be assessed by reference to objects but must be determined by the degree of their utility, their more or less 'advantageous' character.

In this we perceive the *scope of the propositions advanced by pragmatism*. If, in classical rationalism, thought has this character of 'rigidity', for which pragmatism criticises it, it is because in rationalism truth is conceived of as a simple thing, having almost a sacred quality, and which draws its whole value from itself. Since it is sufficient unto itself, it is necessarily placed above human life. It cannot be swayed by the demands of circumstances and differing temperaments. It is valid by itself and is good in an absolute sense. It does not exist for us, but for itself. Its role is to let itself be observed. It is almost deified; it becomes the object of religious worship. This is Plato's conception. This conception of the truth extends to the faculty by means of which we attain truth, that is, *reason*. Reason serves to explain things to us, but, in this conception, itself remains unexplained; it is placed outside scientific analysis.

To 'soften' truth is to take from it this absolute and almost sacrosanct character. It is to tear it away from this state of immobility that robs it of any sense of becoming or change and consequently eliminates the possibility of explaining it. We are asked to imagine that instead of being thus confined in a separate world, it is itself part of reality and life – not by a kind of fall or degradation that would disfigure and corrupt it, but because it is *naturally* part of reality and life. It is placed in changing reality, at the very core of things, having antecedents and consequences. It poses problems: we may legitimately ask ourselves where it originates, what good it does, and so on. It itself becomes an object of science. Here lies the interest of the pragmatist enterprise: it is an effort to *understand* truth and reason themselves, to restore to them their human interest, to make of them human creations that derive from temporal causes and engender temporal consequences. To 'soften' truth is to make it into something that can be analysed and explained.

It is here that we can establish a *parallel between pragmatism and sociology*. By applying the *historical* point of view to the human order of things, sociology is led to formulate the same problem. Man is a product of history and hence of a becoming; there is nothing in him that is either given or defined in advance. History begins at no specific instant, and has no end. Everything in man has been created by mankind in the course of time. Consequently, if truth is human, it is also a human product. Sociology applies the same conception to reason. All that constitutes reason, its principles and categories, is created in the course of history.

Everything is a product of certain causes. Phenomena must not be represented in closed series: then things have a 'circular' character, and analysis can be prolonged infinitely. This is why I cannot accept the statement of the idealists that *in the beginning there is thought*, nor that of the pragmatists that *in the beginning there is action*.

But if sociology poses the problem in the same sense as pragmatism, it is in a better position to solve it. Pragmatism, in effect, claims to explain truth psychologically and subjectively. However, the nature of the individual is too limited to explain by itself alone all things human. Hence if we consider individual elements alone, we are led to underestimate the breadth of the effects that we have to account for. How could reason, in particular, have developed in the course of the experiences undergone by a single individual? Sociology offers us a more adequate explanation. For sociology, truth, reason, and morality are the results of a becoming that covers the entire unfolding of human history.

Thus we see the advantage of the sociological over the pragmatist point of view. For the pragmatist philosophers, as we have said several times before, experience can take place *on one level only*. Reason is placed on the same plane as sensibility; truth, on the same plane as sensations and instincts. But men have always recognised in truth something that in certain respects imposes itself on us, something that is independent of the facts of sensibility and individual impulse. Such a universally held conception of truth must correspond to something real. It is one thing to question the correspondence between symbols and reality, but it is quite another to reject the thing symbolised along with the symbol. However, this pressure that truth admittedly exercises on minds is itself a symbol that must be interpreted, even if we refuse to make of truth something absolute and extra-human.

Pragmatism, which reduces everything to the same level, deprives itself of the means of making this interpretation by failing to recognise the *duality* that exists between the mentality which results from individual experiences, and that which results from collective experiences. By contrast, sociology reminds us that what is *social* always possesses a higher dignity than what is individual. We may assume that truth, like reason and morality, will always retain this character of having a higher value. This in no way prevents us from trying to explain it. The sociological point of view has the advantage of permitting us to analyse even the imposing phenomenon that is truth.

Up to now there has been no particular urgency in choosing between the points of view of sociology and pragmatism. In contrast to rationalism, pragmatism sees clearly that there is not error on one side and truth on the other, but that in reality truths and errors have often been moments in the evolution of truth. In the history of creation, there are unpredictable new phenomena. How, then, could truth be conceived of as something finished and definitive?

But the *reasons that pragmatism alleges* in support of this idea are subject to a great many objections. The fact that things change does not necessarily mean that truth changes at the same time. Truth, one could say, is *enriched*; but it does not actually *change*. It has certainly been enlarged and increased in the course of the development of history; but it is one thing to say that truth grows, and quite another to say that it varies in its very nature.

PS, pp. 141–4

The social realm is a natural realm which differs from the others only by reason of its greater complexity. Now it is impossible that nature should in different environments differ radically in its most essential qualities. The fundamental relations that exist between things – precisely that which it is the function of the categories to express – cannot be essentially dissimilar in the different realms. If, for reasons which we shall discuss later, they are more clearly delineated in the social world, it is nevertheless impossible that they should not be found elsewhere, though in less pronounced forms. Society makes them more manifest but it does not have a monopoly upon them. That is why ideas which have been elaborated on the model of social things can aid us in thinking of other realms of nature. If these ideas play the role of symbols, when they are thus turned aside from their original meaning, they are at least well-founded symbols. If they have a certain artificiality, which derives from the very fact that they are constructed concepts, it is an artificiality which follows nature very closely and which constantly approximates to it even more closely. From the fact that the ideas of 'time', 'space', 'class', 'cause', and 'personality' are constructed out of social elements, it is not necessary to conclude that they are devoid of all objective value. On the contrary, their social origin implies rather that they are not without foundation in the nature of things.

Thus transformed, the theory of knowledge seems able to unite the opposing merits of two rival theories, without incurring their defects. It conserves all the essential principles of the apriorists; but at the same time it is inspired by that positive spirit which the empiricists have striven to satisfy. It leaves the reason its specific power, but it accounts for it and does so without departing from the world of observable phenomena. It affirms the duality of our intellectual life, but it explains it, and in terms of natural causes. The categories are no longer considered as primary and unanalysable facts, yet they remain of a complexity which defies the simplistic analyses which the empiricists confine themselves to. They no longer appear as very simple notions which anyone can quite easily derive from his own personal observations and which popular thought has made needlessly complicated, but rather as effective instruments of thought which human groups have laboriously forged through the centuries, and in which they have pooled the best of their intellectual capital. A complete segment of the history of humanity is as if condensed within them. This is equivalent to saying that to succeed in understanding them and judging them, it is necessary to resort to other means than those which have been in use up to the present. To know the true substance of these conceptions, which we have not ourselves created, it does not suffice to depend upon introspection. We must look outside of ourselves, and it is history that we must observe. There is a whole science which must be formed, a complex science which can only advance slowly and by collective endeavour.

FE, pp. 25–8

Rationalists have been reproached for conceiving of truth as a sort of luxury provided by reality: as something finished and given, which is established solely in order to be gazed upon. Now such gazing, it has been said, is a sterile pleasure, an egoistic intellectual pleasure which yields no profit from the human point of view.

But the depiction of the real definitely has a useful function, which is accomplished by society – although one can also say just as well that this function itself derives from society. Certainly, when truth is represented as something which is complete, one is led to conceive of it in transcendental form. But if truth is a *social thing*, it is thereby human, and thus is drawn close to us, instead of becoming lost in the far reaches of an intelligible world or a divine understanding. No doubt it remains superior to individual minds. But even that which is intrinsically collective only exists through the medium of the consciousness of individuals: truth only becomes realised through individuals.

Let us add that, at the same time as it is social and human, truth is also living. It is intermingled with life, because it is itself a product of and a condition of that higher form of life which is social life. It is diverse, because social life manifests itself in many diverse forms. This diversification and similarly what pragmatism calls the 'dissection' of concepts, is in no way arbitrary: it is modelled upon reality, and especially the reality of social life.

Finally there is one last characteristic of truth, which I have previously insisted upon, but which I wish to re-emphasise in conclusion: this is its *obligatory* character. . .Pragmatism is a form of logical utilitarianism which cannot adequately explain the *authority* of truth – an authority which is easily understood, by contrast, if one sees that there is a social element in truth. This is why *truth is a norm for thought in the same way as the moral ideal is a norm for conduct.*

PS, pp. 196–7

THE RELIGIOUS ORIGINS OF KNOWLEDGE

The field of religious phenomena extends well beyond the limits within which, at first sight, it seems to be confined. It embraces not only the totemic animals and the human members of the clan; no known thing exists that is not classified in a clan and under a a totem, and hence there is nothing which does not in some degree possess something of a religious character. . .

We have shown how the clan, by the manner in which it acts upon its members, awakens within them the idea of external forces which dominate them and exalt them; but we still have to ask how it happens that these forces are thought of in the form of totemic species, that is to say, in the shape of an animal or plant.

It is because this animal or plant has given its name to the clan and serves it as emblem. In fact, it is a well-known law that the sentiments aroused in us by something spontaneously attach themselves to the symbol which represents it. For us, black is a sign of mourning; it also suggests sad feelings and ideas. This transference of sentiments comes simply from the fact that the idea of a thing and the idea of its symbol are closely linked in our minds; the result is that the emotions provoked by the one extend contagiously to the other. But this contagion, which always takes place in some degree, is much more extensive and marked when the symbol is something simple, definite and easy to represent, while the thing itself, owing to its dimensions, the number of its parts and the complexity of their arrangement, is difficult to conceive of. For we are unable to treat an abstract entity, which we can represent only with difficulty, and in a confused manner, as the source of strong sentiments which we feel. We cannot explain them to ourselves except by connecting them to some concrete object of whose reality we are vividly aware. If the thing itself does not fulfil this condition, it cannot serve as the accepted basis of these sentiments, even though it may be what really produced them. Then some sign takes its place; it is to this that we connect the emotions it stimulates. It is this which is loved, feared, respected; it is to this that we are grateful and for which we sacrifice ourselves. The soldier who dies for his flag, dies for his country; but in fact it is the flag which is in the forefront of his mind. It sometimes happens that this even directly determines action. Whether a flag remains in the hands of the enemy or not hardly determines the fate of the country, yet the soldier is prepared to risk death to regain it. He loses sight of the fact that the flag is only a symbol, and that it has no value in itself, but merely recalls the reality that it represents; it is treated as if it were this reality itself.

Now the totem is the flag of the clan. It is therefore natural that the impressions aroused by the clan in individual minds – impressions of dependence and of increased vitality – should attach themselves to the idea of the totem rather than that of the clan: for the clan is too complex a reality to be represented clearly in all its concrete unity by such rudimentary intellects. Moreover, the primitive does not even see that these impressions come to him from the collectivity. He does not realise that the coming together of a number of men associated in the same activity results in creating new energies which transform each of them. He only feels that he is raised above himself and that he sees a different life from the one he ordinarily leads. However, he must connect these sensations to some external object as their cause. Now what does he see around him? On every side what he perceives and what strike his imagination are the numerous images of the totem: the *waninga* and the *nurtunja,* which are symbols of the sacred being; the bull-roarers and *churinga,* upon which are generally carved combinations of lines having the same significance; and the decorations covering the different parts of his body, which are totemic marks. How could this image, repeated everywhere and in all sorts of forms, fail to stand out with exceptional relief in his mind? Placed thus in the centre of the scene, it becomes representative of these ideas and emotions. The sentiments which he feels become centred upon it, for it is the only concrete object to which they can attach themselves. It continues to bring them to mind and to evoke them even after the assembly has dissolved, for it survives the assembly, being carved upon the instruments of the cult, upon the sides of rocks, upon shields, etc. In this way, the emotions experienced are perpetually sustained and revived. Everything happens just as if the totemic image had inspired them directly. It is still more natural to attribute them to it because, as they are common to the group, they can be associated only with something that is equally common to all members. Now the totemic emblem is the only element satisfying this condition. By definition, it is common to all. During the ceremony, it is the focus of attention. While generations change, it remains the same; it is the permanent element of the social life. So it is from it that the mysterious forces seem to emanate with which men feel that they are in communication, and thus they are led to represent these forces in the form of the animate or inanimate being whose name the clan bears.

Having said this, we are in a position to understand all the essential properties of totemic beliefs.

Since the religious force is nothing other than the collective, anonymous force of the clan, and since this can be represented in the mind only in the form of the totem, the totemic emblem is like the visible body of the god. Therefore, it is from it that the beneficent or harmful actions seem to emanate which the cult seeks to provoke or to prevent; consequently, it is to it that the cult is addressed. This is the explanation of why the emblem of the totem holds the first place in the scale of sacred things.

But the clan, like every other sort of society, can live only in and through the consciousness of the individuals that compose it. So if the religious force, in so far as it is conceived as incorporated in the totemic emblem, appears to be outside of the individuals and to be endowed with a sort of transcendence over them, like the clan of which it is the symbol, it can be realised only in and through them. In this sense, it is immanent in them and they necessarily represent it as such. They feel it present and active within them, for it is this which raises them to a higher form of life. This is why men have believed that they contain within them a principle comparable to the one possessed by the totem, and consequently, why they have attributed a sacred character to themselves, but one less marked than that of the totemic emblem. The emblem is the primary source of religious life; man shares in it only indirectly, as he is well aware. He realises that the force which transports him into the world of sacred things is not inherent in him, but comes to him from the outside.

For a different reason the animals or plants of the totemic species possess the same character and to an even greater degree. If the totemic principle is nothing else than the clan, it is the clan conceived in the material form of the totemic emblem; now this form is also that of the concrete being whose name the clan bears. Because of this resemblance, they necessarily evoke sentiments similar to those aroused by the emblem itself. Since the latter is the object of religious respect, they too must inspire respect of the same sort, and appear as sacred. Having external forms so nearly identical, it would be impossible for the believer not to attribute to them forces of the same nature. This is why it is forbidden to kill or eat the totemic animal, and why its flesh is believed to have positive virtues, which the rites utilise; it is because it is like the emblem of the clan, that is to say, its own image. And since it necessarily resembles the emblem more than man does, it is placed on a higher level in the hierarchy of sacred things. There is undoubtedly a close relationship between these two beings, for they both share the same essence: both incarnate something of the totemic principle. However, since the principle itself is conceived in animal form, the animal seems to incarnate it more fully than man. Therefore, if men consider it, and treat it, as a brother, it is, at least as an elder brother.

But while, the totemic principle has its main basis in a specific species of animal or vegetable, it cannot remain localised there. The sacred quality is to a high degree contagious; it therefore spreads out from the totemic being to everything that is closely, or even remotely, connected with it. The religious sentiments inspired by the animal are communicated to the substances upon which it is nourished, and which serve to make or remake its flesh and blood, to the things that resemble it, and to the different beings with which it is constantly in contact. Thus, little by little, sub-totems are attached to the totems and form the cosmological systems expressed in primitive classifications. Finally, the whole world is divided up among the totemic principles of each tribe...

FE, pp. 219 and 314–18

SYSTEMS OF CLASSIFICATION

...these systematic classifications are the first we meet with in history, and they are modelled upon the social organisation, or rather, they have taken the framework of society as their own framework. The phratries have served as classes, and the clans as types. It is because men were organised that they have been able to organise things, for in classifying these latter, they limited themselves to giving them places in the groups of which they were members. And if these different classes of things have not been merely juxtaposed but arranged according to a unified plan, it is because the social groups with which they are inter-related are unified and, through their union, form an organic role, the tribe. The unity of these first logical systems simply reproduces the unity of the society. Thus we have an initial basis for verifying the proposition which we laid down at the commencement of this work, [i.e. *The Elementary Forms of the Religious Life*] that the fundamental ideas of the mind, the essential categories of thought, are the product of social factors. We now see in fact, that this is the case with the very notion of 'category' itself.

However, it is not our intention to deny that the individual mind, even when reduced to its intrinsic properties, is capable of perceiving resemblances between the different objects which it represents. Quite on the contrary, it is clear that even the most primitive and simple classifications presuppose this capacity. The Australian does not place things in the same clan or in different clans at random. For him as for us, similar images attract one-another, while opposed ones repel one-another, and it is on the basis of these affinities and oppositions that he classifies the cor-responding things one way or another.

There are also cases where we are able to perceive how this comes to be so. The two phratries [which comprise the tribe] were very probably the original and fundamental bases for these classifications, which were consequently at first dichotomous. Now, when a classification is composed of only two classes, these are almost necessarily conceived as antitheses; they are used primarily as a means of clearly separating things between which there is a very marked contrast. Some are set at the right, the others at the left. This is, in fact, characteristic of the Australian classifications. If the white cockatoo is in one phratry, the black one is in the other; if the sun is on one side, the moon and the stars of night are on the opposite side. Very often, the beings which serve as the totems of the two phratries have contrary colours. These oppositions are even met with outside Australia. Where one of the phratries is disposed to peace, the other is disposed to war, if one has water as its totem, the other has earth. This is undoubtedly the explanation of why the two phratries have frequently been thought of as naturally antagonistic to one another. It is accepted that there is a sort of rivalry or even a constitutional hostility between them. This opposition of things has extended itself to persons: the logical opposition has stimulated a sort of social conflict.

Moreover, within each phratry, the objects which seem to have the closest affinity with that which serves as the totem are placed within the same clan. For example, the moon is placed with the black cockatoo, and the sun, together with the atmosphere and the wind, with the white cockatoo. Or again, a totemic animal is classified with everything that serves him as food, as well as the animals with which he is most closely connected. Of course, we cannot always understand the obscure psychology which has governed many of these connections and distinctions, but the preceding examples are enough to show that a certain intuition of the way in which things resemble or differ from each other has played an important part in the genesis of these classifications.

But the feeling of resemblances is one thing and the idea of 'class' is another. The class is the external framework of which objects perceived to be similar form, in part, the contents. Now the content cannot comprise the framework into which it fits. It is made up of indefinite *and fluctuating* images, resulting from the superimposition and partial fusion of a *specific number of individual images*, which have common elements; the framework, on the other hand, is a *definite form*, with fixed outlines, and which may be applied to an indeterminate *number of things*, perceived or not, actual or possible. Every class, in fact, has possibilities of extension which go far beyond the circle of objects which we know, from direct experience, resemble each other. This is why every school of thinkers has refused, and not without good reason, to identify the idea of class with that sort of generic image. The generic image is only a blurred residue left in us by similar representations, when they are present in consciousness simultaneously; the class, however, is a logical symbol by means of which we conceptualise these similarities and other comparable ones in a distinct manner. Moreover, what shows most clearly the distance separating these two notions is that an animal is able to form generic images, but is incapable of thinking in classes and types.

The idea of 'class' is an instrument of thought which has manifestly been constructed by men. But in constructing it, we must have employed a model; for how could this idea ever have been born, if there had been nothing either in us or around us which was capable of suggesting it to us? To reply that it was given to us *a priori* is not to reply at all; this lazy man's solution is, as has been said, the death of analysis. Now the only place where we could have found this necessary model is in reference to collective life. A class, in point of fact, is a grouping of ideas which are connected internally, as in ties of kinship. Now the only groupings of this sort known from experience are those formed by men in mutual association. Material things may form collections of units, or aggregates, or mechanical assemblages with no internal unity, but not groupings in the sense we have given the word. A heap of sand or a pile of rock is in no way comparable to that definite and organised social form which constitutes a class. In all probability, we would never have thought of uniting the beings of the universe into homogeneous groupings, or classes, if we had not before our eyes the example of human societies; if we had not begun by making things themselves members of human society, such that human groups and logical groups were at first intermingled.

A classification, moreover, is a system whose parts are arranged according to a hierarchy. There are dominant elements and others which are subordinate to the first types; and their distinctive properties depend upon classes and the attributes which characterise them. Again, the different types within a single class are conceived as all placed on the same level in regard to each other. If these were to be arranged in terms of their degree of comprehensiveness, they would have to be ranked in the inverse order, with those types that are most specific and steeped in reality at the top, with the types that are most general at the bottom. But this would still have to be represented in a hierarchical form. And we must be careful not to suppose that the expression has only a metaphorical sense here: there really are relations of subordination and co-ordination, the establishment of which is the object of all classification, and men would never have thought of arranging their knowledge in this way if they had not known beforehand what a hierarchy was. But neither the observation of physical nature, nor the mechanism of mental associations, could furnish them with this knowledge. The hierarchy is exclusively a social thing. It is only in society that there are superiors, inferiors and equals. Consequently, even if the evidence was not conclusive on this point, the mere analysis of these ideas would reveal their origin. We have taken them from society, and projected them into our conceptions of the world. It is society that has provided the canvas upon which logical thought has worked.

FE, pp. 205–11

Primitive classifications are therefore not peculiar or exceptional, in no way comparable to those used by more advanced peoples; on the contrary, they appear as connected, without any break in continuity, to the first scientific classifications. However different they may be in certain respects from the latter, they nevertheless possess all the same essential characteristics. In the first place, like all sophisticated classifications, they are systems of ideas arranged in hierarchies. They do not set them out simply in the form of isolated groups; these groups stand in fixed relationships to each other, and together constitute a unitary whole. Moreover, these systems, like those of science, have a purely theoretical purpose. Their object is not to facilitate action, but to advance understanding, to make intelligible the relations which exist between things. Given certain concepts which are considered to be fundamental, the mind feels the need to connect to them the ideas which it forms about other things. Such classifications are thus intended, above all, to connect ideas, to unify knowledge; as such, they may be said, quite validly to be 'scientific', and constitute a preliminary philosophy of nature. The Australian does not divide up the universe between the totems of his tribe with a view to regulating his conduct, or even in order to justify his practice; he does so because, as the idea of the totem is fundamental for him, he necessarily has to order everything else that he knows in relation to it. We are thus justified in believing that the conditions which underlie these very ancient classifications may have played an important part in the genesis of the classificatory function in general.

Now our research shows that the nature of these conditions is social. Far from it being the case, as Frazer seems to think, that the social relations of men are based on logical relations between things, in reality it is the former which have provided the prototype for the latter. According to him, men were divided into clans by a pre-existing classification of things; but, quite on the contrary, they classified things because they were divided by clans.

We have seen, indeed, how these classifications were modelled on the most proximate and fundamental form of social organisation. This expression, however, is inadequate. Society was not simply a model which classificatory thought followed: its own divisions served as divisions for the system of classification. The first logical categories were social categories; the first classes of things were classes of men, into which these things were integrated. It was because men were grouped, and thought of themselves in the form of groups, that in their ideas they grouped other beings, and in the beginning the two modes of grouping were fused to the point of being indistinct. Phratries were the first classes; clans, the first types. Things were considered as integral parts of society, and their place in society determined their place in nature. We may even wonder whether the schematic manner in which classes are ordinarily conceived may not have depended in part on the same influences. It is a matter of common observation that the things which they comprise are generally thought of as situated in a sort of ideal sphere, with a more or less clearly delimited spatial circumscription. It is certainly not without cause that concepts and their interrelations have so often been represented by concentric and eccentric circles, superimposed upon one-another, etc. Might it not be that this tendency to imagine purely logical groupings in a form contrasting so much with their true nature derives from the fact that at first they were conceived in the form of social groups occupying, consequently, definite positions in space? And have we not, in fact, observed this spatial localisation of classes and types in a fairly large number of very different societies?

Not only the external form of classes, but also the relations uniting them to each other, are of social origin. It is because human groups fit one into another – the sub-clan into the clan, the clan into the phratry, the phratry into the tribe – that groupings of things are ordered in the same way. Their decreasing comprehensiveness, as we move from class to type, type to variety, etc., originates in the parallel diminution in social divisions as we move from the broadest and oldest forms to the more recent and derived ones. And if the totality of things is conceived as a single system, this is because society itself is conceived of in the same way. It is a whole, or rather it is *the unique whole* to which everything is related. Thus logical hierarchy is only another aspect of social hierarchy, and the unity of knowledge is nothing

else than the very unity of the collectivity, extended to the universe.
universe.   AS, 1902(a), pp. 66–8

CONCEPTUAL KNOWLEDGE AND SENSORY EXPERIENCE

At the root of all our judgements there are a certain number of
essential ideas which dominate all our intellectual life; they are
what philosophers since Aristotle have called the categories of
the understanding: ideas of time, space, class, number, cause, substance, personality, etc. They correspond to the most universal
properties of things. They are like a firm framework which encloses all thought; the latter does not seem to be able to detach
itself from them without destroying itself, for it seems impossible
for us to think of objects that are not in time and space, which
have no number, etc. Other ideas are contingent and changeable.
We can conceive of their being unknown to a man, a society or an
epoch; but these appear to be virtually inseparable from the
normal working of the intellect. They are like the backbone of
the intellect. Now when we systematically analyse primitive beliefs, inevitably the principal categories are found. They are born
in religion and of religion; they are a product of religious thought.
. . .So if the categories are of religious origin, they must share that
nature common to all religious facts; they too must be social things
and the product of collective thought. At least – for in the present
state of our knowledge of these matters, one should be careful to
avoid all radical and exclusive statements – it is legitimate to hold
that they are pervaded by social elements.

Even today, this can still be seen. For example, try to represent
what the notion of time would be without the processes by which
we divide it, measure it and express it with objective signs: a time
which is not a succession of years, months, weeks, days and hours!
This is something which is virtually unthinkable. We cannot
conceive of time, except on condition of distinguishing its different moments. Now what is the origin of this differentiation?
Undoubtedly, the states of consciousness which we have already
experienced can be reproduced in us in the same order in which
they occurred in the first place; thus portions of our past become
present again, while still being clearly distinguished from the present. But however important this distinction may be for our private experience, it is far from being enough to constitute the
notion or category of 'time'. This does not consist merely in a
residue, either partial or integral, of our past life. It is an abstract
and impersonal framework which surrounds, not only our individual existence, but that of all mankind. It is like an endless chart,

where all duration is spread out before the mind, and upon which all possible events can be located in relation to fixed and determined guide lines. It is not *my time* that is thus arranged; it is time in general, such as it is objectively thought of by everybody in a single civilisation. That alone is enough to give us a hint that such an arrangement must be collective. And observation proves, in fact, that these indispensable guide lines, in relation to which all things are temporarily located, are taken from social life. The divisions into days, weeks, months, years, etc., correspond to the periodical recurrence of rites, feasts, and public ceremonies. A calendar expresses the rhythm of the collective activities, while at the same time its function is to assure their regularity. . .

. . .the space which I know by my senses, of which I am the centre and where everything is located in relation to me, cannot be space in general; the latter comprises the totality of dimensions, and these are co-ordinated by impersonal guide lines which are common to everybody. In the same way, the concrete span of time which I feel passing within me and with me could not give me the idea of time in general: the first expresses only the rhythm of my individual life; the second must correspond to the rhythm of a life which is not that of any individual in particular, but which everyone shares. In the same way, finally, the regularities which I am able to perceive in the manner in which my sensations succeed one another may well have a value for me; they explain how it comes about that when I am given the first of two phenomena whose concurrence I have observed, I tend to expect the other. But this personal state of expectation should not be confused with the conception of a universal order of succession which imposes itself upon all minds and all events.

Since the world expressed by the system of concepts as a whole is that represented by society, society alone can furnish the most general notions in terms of which it can be conceived. Such an object can be embraced only by a subject which contains all individual subjects within it. Since the universe does not exist except in so far as it is conceived in thought, and since it is not thought of as a whole except by society, it is comprised within the latter; it becomes a part of society's interior life and this is the totality which embraces everything. The concept of totality is simply the abstract form of the concept of society: it is the whole which includes all things, the supreme class which embraces all other classes. Such is the final principle upon which repose all these primitive classifications, in which beings from every realm are placed and classified in social forms, exactly like men. If the world is inside society the space which this latter occupies becomes the same as space in its totality. In fact, we have seen how each thing has its assigned place in social space, and the degree to which this space in general differs from the concrete dimensions which we perceive with our senses is well shown by the fact that this localisation is wholly ideal, and in no way resembles what it would have been if it had been dictated to us by sensory experience alone. For the same reason, the rhythm of collective life dominates and embraces the varied rhythms of all the component lives from which it results; consequently the time which it expresses dominates and embraces all particular durations. It is time in general. For a long while the history of the world has been only another aspect of the history of society. The one commences with the other; the phases in the first are determined by those in the second. This impersonal and total duration is measured, and the guide lines in relation to which it is divided and organised are fixed by the movements of concentration or dispersion of society; or, more generally, by the periodical necessity for collective renewal. If these crucial occurrences are generally attached to some material phenomenon, such as the regular recurrence of such or such a star or the alternation of the seasons, it is because objective signs are necessary to make this essentially social organisation intelligible. In the same way, finally, the causal relation, from the moment when it is collectively stated by the group, becomes independent of every individual consciousness; it rises above all particular minds and events. It is an impersonal quality.

FE, pp. 12–15 and 629–31

(Man) has. . .everywhere conceived of himself as being formed of two radically heterogeneous beings: the body and the soul. Even when the soul is represented in a substantive form, it is not thought of as being of the same nature as that of the body. It is said that it is more ethereal, rarified and plastic, that it does not affect the senses as do the other objects to which they react, that it is not governed by the same laws as these objects, and so on. And not only are these two beings substantially different, they are to a large extent independent of each other, and are often even in conflict. For centuries it was believed that after this life the soul could escape from the body and lead an autonomous existence far from it. This independence was made manifest at the time of death when the body dissolved and disappeared, while the soul survived and continued to follow, under new conditions and for varying lengths of time, the path of its own destiny. It can even be said that, although the body and the soul are closely connected they do not belong to the same world. The body is an integral part of the material universe, since we come to know it through sensory experience; the dwelling-place of the soul is elsewhere, and it tends ceaselessly to return to it. This is the world of the sacred. Therefore, the soul is invested with a dignity that has always been denied to the body, which is considered essentially profane, and the soul inspires those feelings that are everywhere reserved for that which is divine. It is made of the same substance as are sacred beings: it differs from them only in degree.

A belief that is as universal and permanent as this cannot be purely illusory. There must be something in man that gives rise to this feeling that he possesses a dual nature, a feeling that man in all known civilisations has experienced. Psychological analysis has, in fact, confirmed the existence of this duality, showing it to be at the very heart of our inner life.

Our thought, like our actions, takes two very different forms: on the one hand, there are sensations and sensory tendencies; on the other, conceptual thought and moral activity. Each of these two parts of ourselves represents a separate pole of our existence, and these two poles are not only distinct from one-another but are opposed to one-another. Our sensory appetites are necessarily egoistic: they relate solely to our individuality. When we satisfy our hunger, our thirst, and so on, without involving any other tendency, it is ourselves, and ourselves alone, that we satisfy. The distinctive features of moral activity on the other hand are to be traced to the fact that the rules of conduct to which it conforms can be universalised. Thus by definition, they relate to impersonal ends. Morality begins with disinterest, with attachment to something other than ourselves. A sensation of colour or sound is closely dependent on my individual organism, and cannot be detached from the organism. In addition, it is impossible for me to make my awareness pass over into someone else. I can, of course, invite another person to face the same object and expose himself to its effect, but the perception that he will have of it will be his own, and specific to him, as mine is specific to me. Concepts, on the contrary, are always common to a plurality of men. They are formed by means of words, and neither the vocabulary nor the grammar of a language is the product of one particular person. They are rather the result of a collective elaboration, and they express the anonymous collectivity that employs them. The ideas of 'man' or 'animal' are not personal and restricted to me; I share them, to a large degree, with all the men who belong to the same social group. Because they are held in common, concepts are the supreme instrument of all intellectual exchange. Men communicate by means of them. No doubt, when an individual utilises the concepts that he receives from the community, he individualises them and marks them with his personal imprint; but there is nothing impersonal that is not open to this type of individualisation.

These two aspects of our psychic life are, therefore, as opposed to each other as the personal and the impersonal. There is in us a being that represents everything in relation to itself and from its own point of view; in everything that it does, this being has no other object but itself. There is another being in us, however, which knows things *sub specie aeternitatis*, as if it were sharing in some thought other than its own, and which tends through its actions to accomplish ends that surpass its own. The old formula *homo duplex* is therefore verified by the facts. Far from being simple, our inner life has something that is like a double centre of gravity. On the one hand there is our individuality and, more particularly, our body in which it is based; on the other there is everything in us that expresses something other than ourselves. . .

As we have said, the soul has everywhere been considered a sacred thing; it has been seen as a divine element which lives only a brief terrestrial life and tends, by itself, as it were to return to its place of origin. Thus the soul is opposed to the body, which is regarded as profane; and everything in our mental life that is related to the body – the sensations and the sensory appetites – has this same character. For this reason, we consider that sensations are inferior forms of activity, and we accord a higher respect to reason and moral activity, which are the faculties by which, so it is said, we communicate with god. Even the man who is freest from professed convictions makes this sort of differentiation, valuing our various psychic processes differently, and ranging them in a hierarchy, in which those that are most closely related to the body are placed at the bottom. Moreover, as we have shown, there is no morality that is not infused with religiosity. Even to the secular mind, duty, the moral imperative, is something dignified and sacred; and reason, the essential ally of moral activity, naturally inspires similar feelings. The duality of our nature is thus only a particular instance of that division of things into the sacred and the profane that is the foundation of all religions, and it must be explained on the basis of the same principles.

Sci., 1914, pp. 207–9 and 216–17

Index

Alpert, H., 38
altruism, 113–14
anomie, 173–88
  class conflict a symptom of, 14
  division of labour, 42
  obstacle to freedom, 27
  occupational associations and, 183–8
  pessimistic view, 44
  theory of, 15
Aristotle, 57, 147, 264
art, 110–11
authority, 98–9

Belot, A., 119
Bentham, J., 146, 147
Block, M., 56
Bluntschli, 190
Bourciez, J.-P., 212
Bücher, W., 85

Campanella, T., 166, 167
causal analysis, 35, 36
Christianity
  development of, 239–43
  education and, 206–7
  compared with Ancient and Oriental
    religion, 21–2
  moral regulation, 16, 240–1
church, 223–4
clan
  crime and, 131
  mechanical solidarity and, 142–3
  totemism and, 25, 70, 224–8, 255–9
  phratries, 259–60, 263
class
  anomic division of labour, 11
  origins of, 144
  working class, 164, 5
class conflict
  not a vehicle of social reorganisation,
    48
  socialism and, 164

collective representations
  state and, 18, 132
  primitive religion and, 26
communism
  response to egoism, 13
  socialism and, 13, 46, 166–72
comparative method, empirical verifi-
    cation, 36
Comte, A., 1, 29, 30, 56, 63, 244
  positive stage of society, 4
  Spencer, 53–4
  statics and dynamics, 54–5
conceptual thought
  sensation and, 267–8
  social nature of, 26
  religious origin of, 26
Condorcet, M. J., 30
conflict, 47–8
conscience collective, 5–8, 54
  crime and, 123
  despotism and, 46–7
  dynamic density and, 8
  freedom and, 27–8, 45
  mechanical solidarity and, 6, 144–5
  organic solidarity and, 7, 42
  Parsons' interpretation of Durkheim's
    conception of, 39
  punishment and, 124–8
  religion and, 222, 241
  religious element of, 5–6
  restitutive law, 136–7, 145–6
  symbolic content of, 24–5
constraint, 43, 64–5
  social facts, 73
Coser, L.,
  on Durkheim as a conservative
    thinker, 44
  on Durkheim's analysis of education,
    44
  compares Durkheim and Freud, 44
  his interpretation of Durkheim criti-
    cised, 45, 46, 48

crime, 106, 123–35
  social change and, 131–2

Darwin, C., 153
democracy, 19, 20
  nature of, 196–202
  rationality and, 21
  religion and, 20
Division of Labour, 3–12, 13, 14, 15, 32,
  39, 40, 43, 116
  background to writing of, 1–3
  basis of later work, 12
  central theme of, 36–7
  Elementary Forms and, 24
  Parsons' interpretation of, 41
  political power discussed in, 46
  Preface to 2nd Edition, 17
division of Labour
  anomic, 10
  elimination of anomic, 11, 16
  anomie and, 42, 178–9
  development of, 8, 150–4
  incomplete development of, 11
  forced, 41, 179–83
  moral particularism, 9
  restitutive law and, 137
  social differentiation, 141–54
  social inequality and, 12
  state and, 17
Durkheim, E.,
  supposed authoritarian doctrine of, 16
  interpreted as conservative, 38, 44
  compared with Freud, 45
  criticism of Hobbes, 42
  concern with institutional change, 41
  two interpretations of his work, 39
  criticism of liberal economists, 67
  criticism of naturalist thesis, 62
  social and political context of work,
    41–2
  criticism of state of social sciences,
    84–5
  criticism of speculative philosophy, 60
dynamic density, 8, 151

education, 45
  Christianity and, 206–8
  custom and, 204–5
  definition of, 204
  function of, 203
  Erasmus and, 212
  Rabelais and, 212
  Rationalists and, 215–18
  social bases of, 203–18
  systems of, 205–15
egoism, 113–14

Elementary Forms of Religious Life,
  13, 20–8, 32, 247, 259
  relationship to *Division of Labour*, 24
equality, class system and, 11
Erasmus, 212
ethics, 89–90, 93, 94, 115–19, 121
L'évolution pedagogique en France, 45

Fouillée, A. J. E., 117, 119
Fourier, C., 166, 167
Frazer, Sir J. G., 12, 262
freedom, 27–8, 150
  discipline and, 111
  social development, 45
Freud, S., compared with Durkheim,
  44–5
function
  cause and, 82
  role in sociological explanation, 81
functional interpretation
  causal analysis and, 35
  basic to sociology, 35

geography
  demography, 83
  Ratzel's treatment of, 86–7
Gemeinschaft and *Gesellschaft*, 146–7
Guyau, M., 219, 220

Hegel, G. W. F., 17
history
  nature of, 36, 78
  sociology and, 78–9
Hobbes, T., 42, 99, 100
Horton, J., 44

Idealists, Durkheim's criticism of, 1–2,
  10, 17
individual
  collectivity and, 27
  morality and, 102
  social and biological capacities of,
    26, 267–8
  social facts, 71
  social nature of, 27
  social sentiments, 228, 229–32
  state and, 193, 195–6, 201
individualism, 42
  Christian ideals and, 21–2
  education and, 45
  egoism and, 22–3
  freedom and, 28
  growth of, 9
  ideals of, 16–17
  individuation and, 6, 43
  Kant and Rousseau and, 148
  mechanical solidarity and, 145–50

as moral phenomenon, 5
organic solidarity and, 7
rationalism and, 217
religious character of, 23–4
state and, 18
theme in social thought, 2
individuation, 42
division of labour and, 18–19
egoism and, 22
individualism and, 6, 9
inequality
private property and, 11
forced division of labour and, 182
inheritance
abolition of, 11
as primitive survival, 8
institutions, 71
Introduction à la morale, 44

Jankélévitch, S., 60–3

Kant, I., 3, 90, 91, 96, 108, 134, 148; 246
Kantian philosophy, 21, 29, 95
knowledge
religious origins of, 255–9
sociology of, 250–68
systems of classification of, 259–64

Labriola, A., 160
Landry, A., 116
law
repressive, 6, 9, 123–4, 131–2, 138
restitutive, 9, 124, 131, 132, 135–40
types of, 129–30
Leçons de sociolgie, 40, 41
Lévy-Bruhl, L., 117, 246–9

Machiavelli, N., 101
Marx, K., 10, 14, 156, 163
Marxism, 159–62
materialism, 160
Mill, J. S., 90
de Molinari, G., 147
Montesquieu, C., 29, 30, 47
on social classification, 52
moral authority, 12, 28, 33
moral regulation, 11, 16
relation to freedom, 28
morality
authority and, 98–9
obligatory element in, 3, 29, 33, 93, 100
properties of, 3, 86–8
religion, 108–10
satisfaction from adherence to, 3, 29
science of, 3, 102–22, 216
social change and, 112–13

More (Sir Thomas), 13, 166, 167, 168

Normality
social pathology and, 36–8, 102–7
generality and, 105

Objectivity, 65–6, 117–18
occupational associations, 17
anomie and, 183–8
democracy and, 20
the state and, 19, 47
Owen, R., 166, 167

Pathology, social, social normality and, 36–8, 102–7
Plato, 58, 166, 251
positivism, 40
pragmatism, 251
sociology and, 252–3
property, private, inequality and, 11
psychology
development of, 75
in Durkheim's times, 34–5
positivism, 35
sociology and, 33–4, 70
critique of Tarde's conception of, 76–7

Rabelais, F., 212
rationalism
individualism and, 217
pragmatism and, 251
Ratzel, F., 84, 86, 87, 88
religion, 20–6, 219–38
anomie and, 177
categories of thought and, 259–64
Catholic and Protestant compared, 241–3
church and, 223
collective activity and, 161
conscience collective, 241
definition of, 24–5, 224
magic and, 223–4
persistence of, 243–6
reality and, 250
science and, 221, 248
social origins of, 219, 224–8
symbols and practice of, 25
remoralisation, 16
Reybaud, M. R. L., 166
ritual
functions of, 232–8
totemic emblems and, 256–8
Robertson-Smith, W., 12
Rousseau, J.-J., 29, 30, 42, 56, 67, 99, 101, 148, 190

Rules of Sociological Method, 29, 31, 33, 40, 42, 106

Sacred, profane and, 25, 232–8
Saint-Simon, H. de, 15, 166, 167, 176, 177
Schäffle, A., 1
Schmoller, G., 1, 85, 86, 91
school, 208
science
  attributes of, 57
  development of, 55
  education and, 216
  ethics and, 120–1
  religion and, 221, 248
sentiments, 219–20, 228
social evolution, 81–2, 150–4
social facts
  collective nature of, 71
  explanation of, 66, 74
  externality of, 32–4, 64, 72–3
  normal, 103–4
  obligatory character of, 33, 64, 73
  psychological facts and, 33, 70, 74
  'treated as things', 31–2, 58–9
social morphology, 82–6
social order
  conscience collective and, 7
  organic solidarity and, 10
  in traditional and modern societies, 4
social philosophy, 30
socialism, 12–14, 15
  communism and, 13, 46
  defined, 162–6
  deregulation of industry and, 13–14
  not scientific, 156–7, 160
  state and, 15, 17
  study of, 155–9
  utilitarianism, political economy and, 15
sociological method, 29–38, 69–88
  preliminary definitions and, 32, 65
  functional interpretation and, 35
sociology
  basic conceptions of, 30–1
  definition of, 71
  development of, 29–30, 51–7
  geography and, 88
  history and, 78–9
  philosophy and, 54
  policy and, 37–8
  pragmatism and, 252–3
  psychology and, 33–4, 70, 73–7
  reductive explanations and, 35

as a science, 57
social sciences and, 30, 53
  subject matter of, 64–7
solidarity, mechanical
  the clan and, 141–2
  decline of, 144–50
  moral individualism and, 144–7
  repressive sanctions and, 123–8, 139, 141
  structure of simple organisms and, 6
  symbolic content of, 24–5
solidarity, organic, 7–8, 141
  incomplete development of, 10
  moral character of, 9
  restitutive law and, 9, 135–40
  structure of advanced organisms and, 8
soul, body and, 266–8
Spencer, H., 29, 30, 90, 91, 147, 185
  Comte and, 53–4
  notion of constraint, 100
state, 17–18, 47, 189–96
  defined, 192
  democratic society and, 19, 20, 196–9
  division of labour, 17
  individual freedom and, 18, 192–6, 201–2
  law and, 129–30
  occupational associations and, 147
  religion and, 194
  social solidarity and, 56
  socialism and, 46
  traditional societies and, 18, 194
'struggle for existence', 153–4
Suicide, 113
  definition of, 32

Tarde, G., 76, 106
Tönnies, F., 4, 146–7
totemism, 161, 255–9, 260, 262
  religion and, 224–8
  sacred objects and, 25
truth, 25, 252–3, 254–5
Tylor, E. B., 12

Unions, trade, 186–7
utilitarians, 1, 2, 7, 10, 14, 17, 29, 147

Wagner, A., 91
Weber, M., 40
Wundt, W., 91, 92, 93

Zeitlin, I., 44